Instructor's Manual

for

PASCALGORITHMS

Edwin D. Reilly, Jr.
State University of New York at Albany

Francis D. Federighi
Union College

HOUGHTON MIFFLIN COMPANY BOSTON

Dallas Geneva, Illinois
Princeton, New Jersey Palo Alto

Printed in the U.S.A.

IBSN: 0-395-45300-3

BCDEFGHIJ-A-93210/89

CONTENTS

PREFACE

This Instructor's Manual is organized into chapters whose numbers correspond to those of the main text. For each chapter, we present some of the philosophy that we had in mind when the chapter was written, and make certain recommendations as to how its material might be presented.

For the chapters that correspond to textbook Parts I and II, solutions are given for the programming problems whose answers were not given in Appendix A. A few additional solutions are given for the problems of Parts III and IV, but we did not strive for completeness lest this Manual approach the thickness of the text itself. Whenever possible, the problem solutions given were designed to work when used with a Standard Pascal compiler on a computer that uses the ASCII character set. However, some compromises were necessary. In a few cases, the absence of a variable length string type in Standard Pascal proved to be a cumbersome restriction, and in these cases we have used the string type *string*[..] used by several Pascal compilers. Also, most compilers require the opening and closing of files in addition to invoking the *reset* and *rewrite* commands. We adopted the form used by UCSD and most Macintosh Pascals: *reset(FileVar, FileName)* and *rewrite(FileVar, FileName)*. In addition to performing the usual functions of the Standard Pascal's *reset(FileVar)* and *rewrite(FileVar)*, these procedures also associate the external file named *FileName* (a string) with the file variable *FileVar*.

We have attempted to give complete, executable programs (except when only a procedure or function was asked for) and so there is some duplication of routines such as the random number generator and the uppercase converter. In the interest of saving space, abbreviated and uncommented versions of the functions have been used. You can find complete versions in the text or elsewhere in this manual. A diskette containing all programs appearing in the text or this manual is available from the publisher.

We recognize that problem statements, like programs, can have bugs too. If you think you have spotted one, or if you believe you have found an error of any kind in the text or in this Manual, please write to us. Note however, that the solutions shown are not always the most efficient ones that we know. We frequently give students a contest assignment chosen from one of the latter chapters (e.g. The Sum is 100, Fusaro Pairs, Strolling Players). All students must do the assignment, and any that are interested may enter a contest that awards a prize (usually a CS related publication) to the programmer of the entry that computes correct results in the least amount of running time. All rules about structured programming are abandoned and sometimes the winning program is a rather baroque one, but one which is substantially faster that any previously known solution.

We have included proposed test questions, but again, only for the chapters that correspond to textbook Parts I and II and also Chapter 13. We certainly don't expect or recommend that you give an exam after every chapter, but wherever you pause for an exam, you might want to collect and use relevant questions from the set of chapters to be covered. Your philosophy may differ, but we give open-book exams because we choose not to place any emphasis on memorization. Our exams are a blend of theory and programming. A typical hour-long exam might contain 16 3-point multiple-choice questions and a 50-point programming question that is often divided into two 25-point parts. (If it bothers you that this adds up to only 98 points, give 1 point for the student's name and 1 for his or her TA's name.) For a two-hour midterm or final, you might try 25 two-point multiple-choice questions and 50 points of programming exercises. Grading programs is laborious, but we think that a blend of programs and theory is much more fair than a test that includes only theory or only programming.

So you have a text with extensive glossary, index, and appended material, this Manual, and, upon request from the Publisher, diskettes containing all of the programs and important data files in the book. If there is anything more that we can help you with, please let us know. Happy Pascalgorithms!

Ed Reilly
Fran Federighi

CHAPTER 1 — COMPUTERS

Much of this chapter can be assigned as background reading, but we do have a few recommendations as to what you might say in your first lecture or two. To supplement what we say about the early history of computing, present some personal anecdotes that relate your own experience to more recent history. Even though we have no more to say about analog computers beyond this chapter, make sure that your students grasp the difference between analog and digital devices. Start a class discussion as to whether certain common items are analog or digital or hybrid. We always find the automobile odometer and any kind of clock to be controversial, especially those called "digital".

Point out to your students that the text has many appendices and that there is an easy way to remember what each contains: A is for Answers, B is for Binary, C is for Codes, and so forth, as can be seen from the Table of Contents. Be aware, and tell your students, that a boldface problem number indicates that an answer to at least part of that problem is given in Appendix A. When you give your first reading assignment, include the Preface (especially the part headed To the Student), Chapter 1, and Appendix M (for Milestones) which relates to history.

You have an important decision to make right away: to what extent do you want to cover internal number representations and when do you wish to do it. In the original draft of this text, what is now Appendix B (for Binary) was Chapter 2, and we have very mixed feelings about relegating that material to an appendix. If you have limited time and learning to write Pascal programs is paramount, then we concede that much can be done without stressing internal number representations. But if you are teaching potential computer science majors, we strongly recommend that your first substantive lecture material be taken from Appendix B, which covers integers and simple fractions. As an added incentive, we point out that the text contains several programming exercises that assume a knowledge of binary arithmetic, and that one of the more novel examples of recursion in Chapter 9 also assumes such knowledge. Without the foundation that Appendix B provides, you will have to skip that example and refrain from assigning some of the more challenging and interesting exercises.

We feel less strongly about the timing of your coverage of Appendix F, which describes several floating-point representations, but your students should be given some appreciation for the vastly different ways that 1 and 1.0 are stored in memory. If the floating-point representation for your computer is not among those given, prepare a handout that explains it.

We find that there is usually a significant start-up time in getting students on the computer; they may need to apply for an account, they must learn to use terminals and editors, and they will need at least a lecture or two based on Chapter 3 before they can be given a programming assignment. We use that time to cover number systems and to assign problems that can be done with pencil and paper rather than the computer. These include conversions among decimal, binary, hexadecimal, and ASCII, and some of the problems at the end of Chapters 1 and 2.

CHAPTER 2 — ALGORITHMS AND PROGRAMMING

The student will have to learn much of the material of this chapter if only in self-defense: he or she will have to learn how to log on to the computer and to use simple operating system commands. Learning to use the editor is important, of course, so we recommend that you assign the chapter exercise that makes them practice. In anticipation of Pascal, you should give formal instruction regarding syntax diagrams. Ability to read them is more important than the ability to create them, but we believe computer majors should be able to do both, so assign exercises that pertain to such tasks. Since the ones at the end of the chapter are answered in Appendix A, we suggest a few more here.

Even though Pascal syntax is not discussed in depth until Chapter 3, it is time for you to consider the mechanics of just how students should run programs and submit answers to you. The early chapters are written on the (possibly wrong) assumption that you will be able to give the students written directions for using a particular runstream that will allow correspondence between an arbitrarily named system file and standard file *input*, and between a system file named by either you or the student and standard file *output*. For the VAX, for example, we have a system macro that, when executed with respect to a named file that contains Pascal source code, will ask the student what is the (true) name of the input file, and what is the name of the output file. (Responding with carriage returns will cause use of keyboard and screen by default.) If you can do this, then all Pascal details that pertain to using external files — the need to *reset* or *rewrite*, among other things — can be left until later. If your op system is bankrupt in this regard, you'll have to reach into Chapter 11 and teach those aspects of external file handling that are needed to accomplish the same effect.

Suggested Test Questions

1. Given

<funsound>

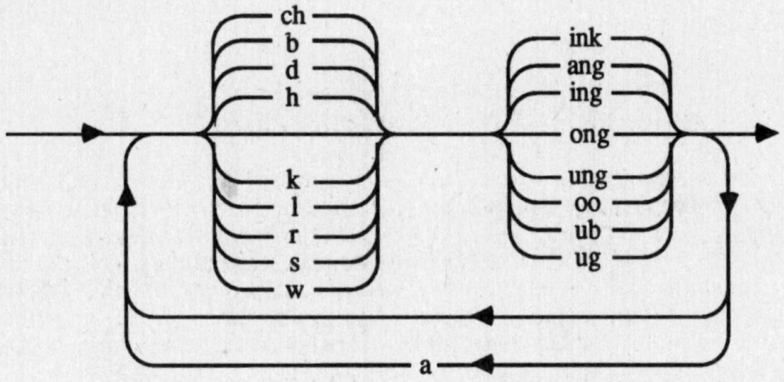

Mark all of the following that are not legal <funsound>s:

dingaling	• dingbat	inkadinkadoo
dingdong	bugaboo	• oolala
ringadingding	kangaroo	boohoohoo
rubadubdub	choochoo	inkling
• along	chugalug	wingding
singalong	singsing	• klink
singsong	• achoo	sinksub
hubbub	bangbangbang	kangaroodung
ringling	kingkong	booboo
hubahuba	• aching	lunging
chungking	choosing	linking

b) Note that *boolaboola* is an illegal <funsound>. Too bad. Sketch in the minor change to <funsound> that would make it legal, then list five other new <funsound>s.

Answer: Putting a wire that short-circuits the second group of options would allow, among many other things, *oolala*, *achoo*, and *aching*.

2. Write a syntax chart that defines <a's and b's> as being a string of an odd number of a's (but at least one) followed by an even number of b's (but at least one pair). Some legal <a's and b's> are:

abb   aaabb   aaabbbb   aaaaabbbbbbb

3. Given that all of the following are legal <display number>s:

7 29 136 4,305 12,498 139,562 ... 3,976,433,084,972 ...

and so on to any length. Given also that <d> is already defined as a digit from 0 to 9, write a syntax chart for <display number>.

CHAPTER 3 — A PASCAL PRIMER

Chapter 3 covers the rudiments of Pascal "once over, lightly." The view taken is that Pascal is such a simple language that a knowledge of 10-statement Pascal will let us solve virtually any computational problem. We conceded, and do again here, that a "Seven Statement Pascal" would be feasible; **const**, **for**, and **repeat–until** are luxuries, but 10 seemed like a nicer number and we hated to delay saying at least a little bit about those constructs. But almost everything said in Chapter 3 is repeated later in more depth, the idea being that it will be to later chapters that students return late in the course for reference to nuances such as, for example, the dangling else problem.

When we say that Pascal is simple, we mean of course that its syntax is simple, not that programming is simple. We suspect that most of your students will have programmed in some other language, Basic probably. But some will be raw beginners, and they are certain to have their difficulties. Try to steer some middle course between boring the experienced students and destroying the neophytes. Encourage experimentation, but not, of course, the "monkey at the typewriter" kind. Users have always complained about strangely-worded diagnostics, but our experience is that some students profess bewilderment over something as straightforward as "BEGIN expected." Be patient with them; it's not that they can't read, it's that they have panicked. The almighty infallible computer scolded them and they froze in terror rather than remaining calm enough to assimilate what their compiler was trying to tell them.

This is the time to make sure that your students know of the existence of several appendices that will be helpful even at such at early stage. ASCII, EBCDIC, and CDC codes are given in Appendix C (for Codes, naturally). Tell your students which of these (if any) your computer uses. If, as we recommended in these notes for Chapter 1, you covered number systems, call to their attention that the codes are given in both decimal and hexadecimal.

Appendix D is a very important Appendix. Given that you taught syntax charts in Chapter 2, show how to follow the charts for some of the simple constructs covered in this chapter. The one for <unsigned integer> is an instructive example, because it shows that certain numbers like 0.75 must have a leading zero and that others such as "seven" must be written as either 7.0 or just 7, not 7. alone. Cover that diagram and a couple of others of your choice.

Appendix E gives some examples of Pascal constructs in (a semimeaningful) context. Students will probably refer to these more often than they try to follow syntax charts, but you should never concede that they are a replacement for syntax charts.

Appendix G is a glossary that should prove useful for definitions. We confess to trying to have a little fun with some of them, usually only through an occasional spurious second meaning that we hope students will know not to take seriously. (It helps to be a baseball fan.)

Finally, there is Appendix I (for Implementations). Though hardly essential, we deem it useful to keep a running record of the various ways in which the Pascal we are using is either limited or enhanced. Take a look at it to see the kind of information that we believe is useful to accumulate. If you agree, encourage, or perhaps even require, that your students build this database as they progress. You might give them some entries right away, such as whether your computer uses one's or two's complement and the value of *maxint*. Give other items when the time is ripe or, rather than handing students something on a silver platter (or a disk platter), make them earn the information through experimentation.

SUGGESTED TEST QUESTIONS

Multiple-Choice Questions (Correct answers are indicated by •)

1.Which of the following could not be the name of a Pascal program?

a Pascal
b print
•c label
d run
e link

2. Which of the following characters may be used to help form part of an identifier?

a $
b _ (underscore)
c   (blank)
d - (hyphen)
•e None of the above

3. Which of the following is not a valid <constant>?

a *false*
•b *–maxint – 1*
c 'p'
d *7E–6*
e all are valid constants

4. How many times will *something* in the following statement be executed?

```
for ch := '?' to '!' do something
```

•a 0
b 1
c 30
d 31
e none of the above

5. Given

```
for outer := -4 to 7 do
   for inner := 8 downto -2 do
      writeln(outer, inner);
```

How many times is the *writeln* statement executed?

a 18
•b 132
c 110
d 11
e none of the above

6. Which of the following is the least essential member of 10-statement Pascal?

•a **const**
b **var**
c **if**
d **while**
e assignment

7. Which of the three looping constructs of 10-statement Pascal is most general?

   a **for – do**
   •b **while – do**
   c **repeat – until**
   d the **while** and **repeat** loops are equally general
   e the **for** and **repeat** loops are equally general

8. With regard to the structure of a Pascal program, which of the following is true?

   a A Pascal program may contain only one **begin–end** pair.
   b A constant may be given the same name as a variable.
   c A *read* or *readln* statement must be used to read a value for every variable
   d Blanks have no significance no matter where they are used
   •e None of the above are true

9. In which of the given situations does the case of a letter (capital vs. lowercase letter) have the least significance?

   a input data
   b output data
   •c identifiers (*ThEtA* = *tHeTa*)
   d within comments such as { Unless we lie, case is important here }
   e quoted literals such as 'Beware the Ides of March!'

Programming Questions

1. Write a complete Pascal program that reads characters, one at a time, and prints any letter read that is followed by a digit.

2. Write a complete Pascal program that reads a series of single-digit integers until it reads a zero (0). Each time it reads an integer *n* that is not 0, it should print a line of output with that integer repeated *n* times. Your output should look like the following when the integers 4 8 5 0 are read:

```
4444
88888888
55555
```

3. Write a complete Pascal program that prints powers of two from 2^0 through 2^{12}. Your table should look like the following:

```
         N
N       2
--------
0       1
1       2
2       4
3       8
...     ...
```

4. Write a complete Pascal program that reads positive integers until a zero is found and prints the largest integer found.

5. Write a program that uses a single **for** loop to print all of the integers from –10 to +10 except 0.

6. Write a program that prints the lowercase alphabet backward.

7. Write a program that reads two real numbers into variables *a* and *b* and that prints their sum, difference, product, and quotient (provided *b* is not 0) all on one line. When *b* is 0, print '***' in place of the quotient.

8. Write a program that uses loops to read input digits, one digit per line, looking first for a 0, then for a 1, then for a 2, ... , then for an 8 and finally for a 9. Your program should prompt for input and announce each success.

SOLUTIONS TO PROGRAMMING EXERCISES

3.12 SQUEEZE

```
program squeeze(input, output);
  {
   Reads a line of text and prints it with blanks and adjacent duplicate characters removed.
  }
  var
   newch, oldch : char;
  begin
   write('Enter a line ending with a period (.): ');
   read(oldch);                                          { Read first character }
   write('The squeezed line is: ');                      { and write label }
   if oldch <> ' ' then write(oldch);                    { and write and save as oldch }
   repeat
     read(newch);                                        { Read a new character }
     if newch <> oldch then if newch <> ' ' then
       begin
         write(newch);                  { Print and save if not blank and not same }
         oldch := newch                 { as prior nonblank character }
       end
   until oldch = '.';           { and keep doing so until a period has been printed }
   writeln
  end { squeeze } .
```

3.14 TWO DIGITS

```
program TwoDigits(input, output);
  {
   Reads integers until a negative number is found. A count of the two-digit integers read
   is then printed.
  }
  var
   n, count : integer;
  begin
   count := 0;                                           { Initialize count }
   writeln('Count Double-Digit Numbers');
   writeln;
   writeln('Enter a sequence of integers.');
   writeln('End data with a negative integer.');
   writeln;
   repeat
     read(n);                                            { Read an integer }
     if n > 9 then if n < 100 then count := count + 1  { Add to count if two-digits }
   until n < 0;
   readln;
   writeln;
   writeln('There were ', count : 1, ' two-digit numbers found.')
  end { TwoDigits } .
```

3.15 DOLLARS

```
program dollars(input, output);
  {
   Reads a series of monetary values and prints their sum.
  }
  var
    amount, total : real;
    dollarsign : char;
  begin
    total := 0;
    writeln('Dollar Total');
    writeln;
    writeln('Enter amounts to total, one per line.');
    writeln('Enter 0 when finished.');
    writeln;
    write('Amount: ');
    readln(amount);
    dollarsign := '$';                              { To print with first amount only }
    while amount <> 0 do
      begin
        writeln(' ' : 20, dollarsign, amount : 6 : 2);
        dollarsign := ' ';                  { Blanks will be printed for remaining input }
        total := total + amount;
        write('Amount: ');
        readln(amount)
      end;
    writeln(' ' : 21, '------');
    writeln(' ' : 20, '$', total : 6 : 2)
  end { dollars } .
```

CHAPTER 4 — PROGRAMMING PROCEDURES

By now you have noticed that we have opted not only for a certain style in the way we arrange Pascal programs but also for a particular typography for the way they are presented in the text. We are fussy. Since there are so many Pascal books, we reject immediately any whose programs shout (through use of unrelieved upper case), or any that are so inelegant as to use semicolons after (rather than between) statements. (If you find an unnecessary semicolon in *Pascalgorithms*, we'll be embarrassed; tell us quickly so we can expunge it in the next printing.)

More seriously, we do not expect that you agree with us on all style counts; the important thing is to develop a coherent style and follow it. Some take the view that since the students can't highlight through boldface and italic, then we should use upper case at least for reserved words. Fine; that's what Modula-2 will force us to do anyway. But if students typically send output to a laser printer or to a good dot-matrix printer, you might want to consider development of a program that uses the right mixture of bold, italic, and roman automatically. (And we are aware that MacPascal can not only print programs that way, it can display them just as nicely on the screen. Development of Pascal programs that can do these things is not trivial; either would make a challenging student exercise, but only very late in the course.)

Now that we are into program development, the instructor has a decision to make with regard to the language or notation to be used for describing algorithms. The text is written as though you will use pseudocode: a mixture of English, Pascal, and (occasionally) mathematical statements. But there is a competitive alternative based on structured flowcharts called, after their inventors, Nassi-Shneiderman diagrams. If you know about them or would like to see what they are like, look ahead to Chapter 15, a chapter that we would not expect that you will be covering formally in a first course. We gave some consideration to introducing them early and then using them instead of pseudocode, and you might want to do exactly that in your lectures. The critics of this approach think that such diagrams give away the ball game, that is, once a good structured flowchart is drawn, about the only things missing are a few keywords and the declarations needed to make an executable Pascal program. The compromise we made is to use pseudocode early on but to suggest that it is up to you when, if at all, you teach the Nassi-Shneiderman method. (We have a stronger suggestion as to what *not* to do: for heaven's sake, don't use old-fashioned spaghetti-like flowcharts made of boxes and wires. Ugh!)

Finally, you have undoubtedly noticed that the chapter title is a *double entendre*. The chapter provides coequal emphasis on the procedures (style) that should be followed to write readable programs and on the subdivision of programs into user-defined Pascal procedures. As its title suggests, procedures and (library) functions will be "revisited" in Chapter 9, but the early introduction of procedures here is in keeping with prevailing pedagogical wisdom.

SUGGESTED TEST QUESTIONS

Multiple-Choice Questions (Correct answers are indicated by •)

1. Which of the following cannot be claimed as an advantage for a procedure as compared to writing out the equivalent logic in the main program?

   a Procedure variables may be given the same names as main program names
   b Use of procedures makes a program more readable
   c Use of procedures that are called more than once leads to shorter programs
   •d The object code generated by a procedure runs faster
   e All of the above are genuine advantages

2. Given that *r* is *real*, *s* is *integer* and *t* is of type *char*, which of the following is a valid call to

   procedure *test*(**var** *a* : *integer*; *b* : *real*; **var** *c* : *char*); ?

   a *test*(7, 9.2, 'c');
   b *s*:= *test*(*s*, 4.5, *t*);
   •c *test*(*s*, 7.2 + *r*, *t*);
   d *test*(*s*, *test*(*s*, *r*, *t*), *t*);
   e All of the above

3. A main program contains the statement *crackle*(*a* – 1, *b*, 3 * *c*) where all of *a*, *b*, and *c* are real. Which of the following headers is consistent with the stated invocation of *crackle*?

   •a **procedure** *crackle*(*c*, *b*, *a* : *real*);
   b **procedure** *crackle*(**var** *a*, *b*, *c* : real);
   c **procedure** *crackle*(**var** *a* : *real*; *b* : *real*; *var c* : *real*);
   d **procedure** *crackle*(*a*, *b*, *c* : *integer*);
   e not enough information to tell

The next five questions refer to the following procedure

```
procedure X(a : integer; var b : integer);
  var
    c : integer;
  begin
    a := 3;
    b := a + 1;
    c := b + 1;
    d := c + 1
  end;
```

4. In **procedure** *X*, variable *a* is

   a a local variable
   b a global variable
   •c a value parameter
   d a var parameter
   e Use of this variable must be an error

5. In **procedure** *X*, variable *b* is

   a a local variable
   b a global variable
   c a value parameter
   •d a var parameter
   e Use of this variable must be an error

6. In **procedure** *X*, variable *c* is

- •a a local variable
- b a global variable
- c a value parameter
- d a var parameter
- e Use of this variable must be an error

7. In **procedure** *X*, variable *d* is

- a a local variable
- •b a global variable
- c a value parameter
- d a var parameter
- e Use of this variable must be an error

8. What output is printed when the following program segment calls **procedure** *X* given above?

```
a := 4; b := 8; c := 12; d := 16;
X(a, b);
writeln(a : 3, b : 3, c : 3, d : 3);
```

```
 a 4  8 12 16
 b 3  4  5  6
•c 4  4 12  6
 d 3  8  5 16
 e Nothing
```

Programming Questions

1. Write **procedure** *PowersOf(x : integer)*; that prints all the powers of *x* from the zero[th] to the largest power of *x* that is less than *maxint*.

2. Write a program that repeatedly calls **procedure** *print(n : integer)* so as to print a symmetric tree, centered with respect to the output screen, whose branch height and base height are specified as input. For example, for inputs of 15 and 5 for the branch height and base height, output should be

3. Complete the definition of this procedure:

procedure *print(sp, n1, n2, fw : integer)*;
{
Prints *sp* spaces followed on the same line by the numbers *n1* to *n2* inclusive, each printed with a field width of *fw*.
}

Then write a main program that makes the successive calls to *print* that will print this number pattern:

```
    1
  2   3
4   5   6
  7   8
    9
```

4. Complete the definition of this procedure:

procedure *alphasequence(L1, L2 : char)*;
{
Prints a line of characters from *L1* to *L2* if *L1* <= *L2* or the characters from *L2* to *L1* if *L2* < *L1*
}

Then write a main program that calls *alphasequence* five times to produce

```
ABCDE
JIHGF
KLMNO
TSRQP
UVWXY
```

5. Complete the definition of the following procedure:

procedure *RootsAndSquares(a, b : integer)*;
{
Prints a 3-column labeled table of the integers from *a* to *b* inclusive and their corresponding squares and square roots.
}

6. Complete the definition of the following procedure:

procedure *PrintAlpha(letter : char)*;
{
Prints a cyclic alphabet that starts with *letter*.
Example: if *letter* is 'P', the output would be the line:
`PQRSTUVWXYZABCDEFGHIJKLMNO`
}

Then write a main program that uses a for loop to call *PrintAlpha* 26 times so as to produce the printer test pattern:

```
ABCDEFGHIJKLMNOPQRSTUVWXYZ
BCDEFGHIJKLMNOPQRSTUVWXYZA
CDEFGHIJKLMNOPQRSTUVWYXZAB
...
...
```

7. Write a program that reads in four integers *a*, *b*, *c*, and *d*, orders their values, and prints the results. You should order the integers by using repeated calls to predefined procedure *order(a, b, c)* that orders its 3 arguments *a*, *b*, and *c*.

8. Write **procedure** *print(n : integer; c : char)*; that writes a line of output consisting of *n* spaces followed by the single character *c*. Then write a main program that reads two integers *height* and *waves* and then uses loops to issue repeated calls to *print* so that a picture of *waves* waves each of height *height* is printed. Example: If the input is 4 for *height* and 3 for *waves* your program should produce the output shown below.

```
\
 \
  \
   \
   /
  /
 /
/
\
 \
  \
   \
   /
  /
 /
/
\
 \
  \
   \
   /
  /
 /
/
```

SOLUTIONS TO PROGRAMMING EXERCISES

4.5 BLOCK LETTERS

```
program BlockLetters(output);
  {
    Prints banner-size letters.
  }
  procedure left;
    begin writeln('*  *'); writeln('*  *') end;
  procedure right;
    begin writeln('            * *'); writeln('            * *') end;
  procedure both;
    begin writeln('* *         * *'); writeln('* *         * *') end;
  procedure center;
    begin writeln('      * *'); writeln('      * *') end;
  procedure bar;
    begin writeln('* * * * * * * *'); writeln('* * * * * * * *') end;
  procedure A;
    begin bar; both; bar; both; both; writeln; writeln end;
  procedure C;
    begin bar; left; left; left; bar; writeln; writeln end;
  procedure E;
    begin bar; left; bar; left; bar; writeln; writeln end;
  procedure F;
    begin bar; left; bar; left; left; writeln; writeln end;
  procedure H;
    begin both; both; bar; both; both; writeln; writeln end;
  procedure I;
    begin center; center; center; center; center; writeln; writeln end;
  procedure J;
    begin right; right; right; right; bar; writeln; writeln end;
  procedure L;
    begin left; left; left; left; bar; writeln; writeln end;
  procedure O;
    begin bar; both; both; both; bar; writeln; writeln end;
  procedure P;
    begin bar; both; bar; left; left; writeln; writeln end;
  procedure S;
    begin bar; left; bar; right; bar; writeln; writeln end;
  procedure T;
    begin bar; center; center; center; center; writeln; writeln end;
  procedure U;
    begin both; both; both; both; bar; writeln; writeln end;
  procedure Y;
    begin both; both; center; center; center; writeln; writeln end;
  begin { main }
    A; C; E; F; H; I; J; L; O; P; S; T; U; Y;
    P; A; S; C; A; L
  end { BlockLetters } .
```

4.6 RANK3 REVISITED

```
program rank3(input, output);
  {
    Test of rank3 rewritten as a procedure.
  }
  var
    a, b, c : integer;                          { The three numbers to be ordered }

  procedure order(var a, b, c : integer);
    {
      Procedure to sort the three arguments so that a <= b <= c
    }
    var
      t : integer;                      { A temporary variable needed for swapping }
    begin { order }
      if a > b then { swap } begin t := a; a := b; b := t end;
      if b > c then { swap } begin t := b; b := c; c := t end;
      if a > b then { swap } begin t := a; a := b; b := t end
    end { order } ;

  begin { main }
    writeln('Three-Integer Sort');
    writeln;
    write('Enter 3 integers: ');
    readln(a, b, c);
    order(a, b, c);
    writeln;
    write('Sorted integers:   ');
    writeln(a : 1, ' ', b : 1, ' ', c : 1)
  end { rank3 } .
```

4.8 CALENDAR MONTH

```
program calendar(input, output);
  {
    Generates a calendar year.
  }
  var
    firstday, month : integer;
    leapyear : Boolean;
    ly : char;

  procedure calendarmonth(firstday, numdays : integer);
  {
    Generates a calendar month.
  }

    procedure labels;
      {
        Prints day labels.
      }
      begin { labels }
        writeln;
        writeln('  Sun  Mon  Tue  Wed  Thu  Fri  Sat');
        writeln
      end { labels } ;
```

```
procedure firstrow(n : integer);
  {
    Prints the first row of a month's dates with blanks for the days before the first.
  }
  var
    i : integer;
  begin { firstrow }
    for i := 1 to n - 1 do write('  ' : 5);
    for i := 1 to 8 - n do write( i : 5);
    writeln
  end { firstrow } ;

procedure middlerows(n : integer);
  {
    Prints a 3 x 7 arrangement of 21 consecutive integers starting with n.
  }
  var
    i, j : integer;
  begin { middlerows }
    for i := 1 to 3 do
      begin
        for j := 1 to 7 do
          begin
            write(n : 5);
            n := n + 1
          end;
        writeln
      end
  end { middlerows } ;

procedure nextrow(first, last : integer);
  {
    Prints nothing if last < first (through natural behavior of the for loop), otherwise
    prints integers from first to last, but at most 7.
  }
  var
    i, limit : integer;
  begin { nextrow }
    if (last - first in [0..6]) or (last < first)
          then limit := last else limit := first + 6;
    for i := first to limit do write(i : 5);
    writeln
  end { nextrow } ;

begin { calendarmonth }
  labels;
  firstrow(firstday);
  middlerows(9 - firstday);
  nextrow(30 - firstday, numdays);
  nextrow(37 - firstday, numdays)
end { calendarmonth } ;

begin { main }
  writeln('Calendar Generator');
  writeln;
  writeln('Enter the day number of January 1st - S M T W T F S');
  writeln('                                      1 2 3 4 5 6 7');
  readln(firstday);
  writeln;
  write('Is the year a leap year? (Y/N): ');
  readln(ly);
  leapyear := (ly = 'Y') or (ly = 'y');
  writeln;
```

```
writeln('                    January');
calendarmonth(firstday, 31);
firstday := ((firstday + 30) mod 7) + 1;        { To get first day of next month }
writeln;
writeln('                    February');
if leapyear then
  begin
    calendarmonth(firstday, 29);
    firstday := ((firstday + 28) mod 7) + 1
  end else
  begin
    calendarmonth(firstday, 28);
    firstday := ((firstday + 27) mod 7) + 1
  end;
writeln;
writeln('                    March');
calendarmonth(firstday, 31);
firstday := ((firstday + 30) mod 7) + 1;
writeln;
writeln('                    April');
calendarmonth(firstday, 30);
firstday := ((firstday + 29) mod 7) + 1;
writeln;
writeln('                    May');
calendarmonth(firstday, 31);
firstday := ((firstday + 30) mod 7) + 1;
writeln;
writeln('                    June');
calendarmonth(firstday, 30);
firstday := ((firstday + 29) mod 7) + 1;
writeln;
writeln('                    July');
calendarmonth(firstday, 31);
firstday := ((firstday + 30) mod 7) + 1;
writeln;
writeln('                    August');
calendarmonth(firstday, 31);
firstday := ((firstday + 30) mod 7) + 1;
writeln;
writeln('                    September');
calendarmonth(firstday, 30);
firstday := ((firstday + 29) mod 7) + 1;
writeln;
writeln('                    October');
calendarmonth(firstday, 31);
firstday := ((firstday + 30) mod 7) + 1;
writeln;
writeln('                    November');
calendarmonth(firstday, 30);
firstday := ((firstday + 29) mod 7) + 1;
writeln;
writeln('                    December');
calendarmonth(firstday, 31);
writeln
end { calendar } .
```

CHAPTER 5 — SIMPLE DATA TYPES

This chapter is quite straightforward and we have little more to say here. Of the four simple data types, students seem to recognize the utility of *integer*, *real*, and *char* pretty quickly, but they underuse *Boolean*. Time after time, we see programs that use a flag that takes on the values 1 or 0 and then say something like **if** *flag = 1* **then** *proc1* rather than declaring a Boolean flag and writing something like **if** *guilty* **then** *confess*. You should point out the opportunity for self-documenting code that they are missing.

The emphasis on inverse functions is just a pedagogical ploy. We find that it is easier to retain a large body of factual material if it can be systematized or categorized in some way. By remembering inverse pairs of functions, there are then, in some sense, only half as many things to remember. Should the functions *exp* and *ln* be old friends to the students by now? Of course. Will they be? Of course not. We spend a bit of time with them because the concept of both logarithmic and exponential behavior will be encountered in later chapters that discuss the analysis of algorithms.

Find out in advance of your lectures on enumerated data types whether your Pascal is able to read and write enumerated elements, or at least write them. If your Pascal adheres to the Standard, which does not support input-output of enumerated elements, emphasize that their utility is pretty much confined to self-documentation. If they can be, you will have to decide whether to let your students do so, or, for that matter, whether you allow them to use any nonstandard feature. We see no harm in letting them use the full power of their translator, so long as you remind them from time to time that using nonstandard features ruins portability (which is seldom of concern for student exercises anyway).

SUGGESTED TEST QUESTIONS

Multiple-Choice Questions (Correct answers are indicated by •)

1. Which of these is (or is equivalent to) *succ*(*Saturday*)?

   a *Sunday*
   b *pred*(*Monday*)
   c *succ*(*pred*(*Sunday*))
   •d no way to tell
   e none, the expression is illegal

2. If *ch* is of type *char*, then *succ*(*pred*(*ch*)) = *ch* unless *ch* is

   a ' ' (blank)
   b '0'
   c 'a'
   d 'A'
   •e *chr*(0)

3. An expression that will round real number *n* to 3 places after the decimal point is

   •a *round*(1000 * *n*) / 1000
   b *round*(1000 * *n*) **div** 1000
   c *trunc*(1000 * *n*) **div** 1000
   d *round*(*n*, 3)
   e none of the above

4. The expression *chr*((*ord*('A') + *ord*('Z')) **div** 2) evaluates to

   a 'A'
   b 'L'
   •c 'M'
   d 'N'
   e 'Z'

5. The largest integer *n* that can safely be squared via *sqr*(*n*) is

   a *round*(*sqrt*(*maxint*))
   •b *trunc*(*sqrt*(*maxint*))
   c *abs*(*sqrt*(*maxint*))
   d *maxint* **div** 2
   e *round*(*ln*(*maxint*))

6. If *letter* is of type *char* and known to be in ['A'..'Z'], which of the following expressions will yield the next higher letter in a cyclic sense: 'A' → 'B'; 'B' → 'C'; ...; 'Y' → 'Z'; 'Z' → 'A'?

   a *succ*(*letter*)
   b *succ*((*letter* + 1) **mod** 26)
   c *chr*((*ord*(*letter*) + 1) **mod** 26)
   •d *chr*(*ord*('A') + (*ord*(*letter*) – *ord*('A') + 1) **mod** 26)
   e none of the above

7. Which of the following Standard Pascal data types has values that may be written to the output file but not read from the input file?

   •a Boolean
   b real
   c char
   d integer
   e enumerated

8. The expression $0 = ord(3 > round(2.8))$ evaluates to

   a 0
   b 1
   •c true
   d false
   e maybe

9. Consider the fragment

```
x := -1;
repeat
   x := -2 * x
until x > 32;
```

   How many times does the loop run?

   a 1
   b 5
   c 6
   •d 7
   e an infinite number of times

10. The expression *pred*('A') evaluates to

   •a '@'
   b 'z'
   c '}'
   d undefined
   e None of the above

Programming Questions

1. Write a program that, **while not** *eof*, reads positive integers and echoes them followed by the words "is (or is not) a perfect square." The perfect squares are the squares of the integers, i.e. 0, 1, 4, 9, 16, 25, 36, ...

2. Write a program that reads positive integers *n* and computes and prints the alternating sum $1 - 2 + 3 - 4 + \ldots \pm n$. Examples of your output:

```
n = 3 :  1 - 2 + 3  = 2
n = 4 :  1 - 2 + 3 - 4 = -2
n = 6 :  1 - 2 + 3 - 4 + 5 - 6 = -3
```

3. Read characters one by one **while not** *eof* and encipher them according to this simple scheme: If the character is not a letter (of either case), print it unchanged. If the character is in ['a'..'z', 'A'..'Z'], output the successor to the letter if its ordinal value is odd, otherwise output its predecessor.

   Example: The input `Strike three, you're out!`
   is output as `Tsqjlf sgqff, zpv'tf pvs!`

4. Complete the definition of this procedure:

```
procedure pow(a, b : real; var c : real; var err : Boolean);
   {
      Sets c to 0 and err to true if a <= 0, otherwise sets c to a to the
      bth power and err to false.
   }
```

   (Instructor: You may want to tell students that $a^b = e^{b \ln a}$.)

5. Given

type
month = (*Jan, Feb, Mar, Apr, May, Jun, Jul, Aug, Sep, Oct, Nov, Dec*);

Complete the definition of this procedure:

procedure *PrintInterval*(*m1, m2 : month*);
{
Prints the number of months between *m1* and *m2*.
Examples:
PrintInterval(*Jan, Feb*) => 1
PrintInterval(*Jan, Dec*) => 11
PrintInterval(*May, Dec*) => 7
PrintInterval(*Dec, May*) => –7
PrintInterval(*Jun, Jun*) => 0
}

6. Given

type
month = (*Jan, Feb, Mar, Apr, May, Jun, Jul, Aug, Sep, Oct, Nov, Dec*);

Define *YourType* and then complete the definition of this procedure:

procedure *Days*(*m : month*; **var** *D31, D30, D28 : YourType*);
{
If *m* is a month with 31 days, *D31* is set to *true*; *D30* and *D28* are set to *false*.
If *m* is a month with 30 days, *D30* is set to *true*; *D31* and *D28* are set to *false*.
If *m* is *Feb*, *D28* is set to *maybe*; *D30* and *D31* are set to *false*.
}

7. Although we are used to dealing in dollars and cents when dealing with money, it is conventional for the stock market to quote stock prices in dollars and eighths of dollars. Write the following procedures to help us convert back and forth between these two ways of stating an amount of money:

procedure *ToEighths*(*dollars : real*; **var** *WholeDollars, eighths : integer*);

Converts the amount *dollars* (a real number where the cents are the fractional part) to the number of *WholeDollars* and the number of *eighths* (integers). Round the result to the nearest number of *eighths*.

procedure *FromEighths*(*WholeDollars, eighths : integer*; **var** *dollars : real*);

Converts the amount of *WholeDollars* plus *eighths* to *dollars*. Round the result to the nearest cent (0.01 *dollars*).

8. Write a program that tests the trig identity $sin(2x) = 2\ sin(x)cos(x)$. Do so by printing a four-column table for values of x from 0 to π in steps of 0.2 radians. Label the columns `x`, `sin(2x)`, `2sin(x)cos(x)`, and `delta`. Print the appropriate values under each heading. Print *delta*, the difference between values in columns 2 and 3, using field width : 12 : 9.

SOLUTIONS TO PROGRAMMING EXERCISES

5.11 PI AND SUCH

```
program piandsuch(output);
  {
    Prints certain familiar real numbers to test precision of your computer.
  }
  begin
    writeln('    Real Number Precision Test');
    writeln;
    writeln('4 * arctan(1)      ', 4.0 * arctan(1.0) : 16 : 12);
    writeln('exp(1)             ', exp(1.0) : 16 : 12);
    writeln('sqrt(2)            ', sqrt(2.0) : 16 : 12)
  end { piandsuch } .
```

5.14 HAL AGAIN

```
program HalAgain(input, output);
  {
    Raises all capital letters of a text line up one letter except for Z's which become A's.
    Other characters are unchanged.
  }
  var
    ch : char;
  begin
    writeln('HAL Letter Conversion');
    writeln;
    write('Enter a line of text: ');
    while not eof do
      begin
        while not eoln do
          begin
            read(ch);
            if ch in ['A'..'Y'] then write(succ(ch)) else
            if ch = 'Z' then write('A') else write(ch)
          end;
        readln;
        writeln;
        writeln;
        write('Enter a line of text: ')
      end
  end { HalAgain } .
```

5.16 PAYDAY

```
program payday(input, output);
  {
    Computes weekly wages based on time-and-a-half for overtime (over 40 hours on
    Monday-Friday) and Saturday and double time for Sunday.
  }
  var
    count : integer;
    rate, MFhours, Overtime, pay : real;
    Sunday, Monday, Tuesday, Wednesday, Thursday, Friday, Saturday : real;
  begin
    count := 1;
    write('Enter data for worker #1: ');
    while not eof do
      begin
        read(rate);
        readln(Sunday,Monday,Tuesday,Wednesday,Thursday,Friday,Saturday);
        MFhours := Monday + Tuesday + Wednesday + Thursday + Friday;
        If MFhours > 40 then Overtime := MFhours - 40 else Overtime := 0;
        pay := rate * (2 * Sunday + MFhours + 0.5 * Overtime + 1.5 * Saturday);
        writeln;
        writeln('Total pay for worker #', count : 1, ' is $', pay : 1 : 2);
        writeln;
        count := count + 1;
        write('Enter data for worker #', count : 1, ': ')
      end
  end.
```

CHAPTER 6 — READING AND WRITING DATA OF SIMPLE TYPE

Students invariably have a hard time mastering the intricacies of whether to use *read* or *readln*, especially when they are trying to use them in conjunction with *eof* and *eoln*. We confess to similar difficulties when we first began to use Pascal, even though it was our umpteenth high-level language. What finally worked for us was to envision "movies" in our heads just like the chapter diagrams that try to show where the moving file-buffer pointer is at all times. We try to teach this method to students through such diagrams and the attendant narrative. Until they do catch on, make them follow the template for nested *eof* and *eoln* loops that is given both in this chapter and in an earlier one. By the end of the course, you hope and expect that the good students know why what they are doing works, but at least the poorer ones can attain some success in getting their programs to run.

You may have noticed that our text makes much earlier use of *eof* and *eoln* than most other Pascal books. Without them, one is forced to use ugly homemade data sentinels. We consider such practice inelegant and an unnecessary imposition on program users, so, except for one brief exercise and some exam questions in this volume, we began to emphasize proper use of *eof* and *eoln* quite early. As just mentioned in the preceding paragraph, you can tell students to "do it this way" until you come to this Chapter, where, we hope, the beauty and coherence of Wirth's I/O handling is painstakingly explained.

Watch out if you are using Turbo Pascal[1]. While there is much we like about this translator, its I/O is notoriously nonstandard. But Turbo can be made to obey *eof* and *eoln*. To make it do so, you must place {$B–} before every program that relies on those functions. (For other reasons, we recommend that all student Turbo programs be preceded by {$B–,U+,R+}.) The chapter program called *numlist2* works for both Turbo and VAX Pascal, among many other translators. Test yours to see if it does so that you can relate what you say in lecture to what we show in the text.

[1] We are refering here to Turbo Pascal Version 3.0. Version 4.0 was announced while this manual was in preparation and may treat I/O in ways closer to the standard.

SUGGESTED TEST QUESTIONS

Multiple-Choice Questions (Correct answers are indicated by •)

1. Consider

```
s := 2;
for s := 1 to 5 do write(s : s);
writeln;
```

Which of the following best describes the appearance of the output produced by the above?

```
a 1 2 3 4 5
b 1   1   1   2   2   3   3   4   4   5   5
c 1   4   9  16  25
•d 1 2  3   4    5
e s ss sss ssss sssss
```

2. If we could freeze execution of a running Pascal program at an arbitrary instant, which combination of the status of *eoln* and *eof* is impossible?

	eoln	eof
•a	*true*	*true*
b	*true*	*false*
c	*false*	*true*
d	*false*	*false*
e	All of the above combinations are possible	

3. Consider:

```
c := 0;
while not eof do
  begin
    if eoln then c := c + 1;
    readln
  end;
```

Which of the following best describes what the fragment does?

a Counts the number of times *readln* is executed
b Counts the number of lines in the input file
•c Counts the number of empty lines in the input file
d The loop does nothing but waste time
e None of the above

4. Which of the following lines of data cannot be read by Pascal?

a `I #$' dare you &^@" ' to read this.`
b `5.`
c `2/29/1989`
•d All can be read
e None of a through c can be read

5. Assuming that any variable referred to has a reasonable type, which input statement will read all of an input line that contains –37.e0.75 ? { The ? is part of the question, not part of the input. }

a *read(r, n);*
•b *read(n, c, c, r);*
c *read(r, c, n);*
d *read(n, c, r)*
e none of the above

6. Given the three lines of data

```
1 2 3
4 5 6
7 8 9
```

What is the output of the fragment

```
sum := 0;
while not eof do
  begin
    readln(n);
    sum := n
  end;
writeln(sum);
```

•a 7
b 8
c 9
d 36
e 45

7. With respect to reading data from standard file input, which of the following is true?

a *eoln* can be true only once
•b *eof* can be true only once
c we may not read the end-of-line character
d input may be reread provided we first issue *reset*(*input*)
e none of the above are true

8. Which of the following is true?

a *eoln* cannot be true until we have read at least one item
b *eof* cannot be true until we have read at least one item
c If a line of data contains only one item, *read* and *readln* are equivalent
d An integer data value cannot be read into a real variable
•e None of the above are true

Programming Questions

1. Write a program that, **while not** *eof*, reads lines of text character by character. As lines are read, accumulate a count of how many lines start and end with the same nonblank character. When all lines are processed, print the count in properly labeled form. Consider that lines of exactly one character meet the test (and hence contribute to the count), but that empty lines (that contain only an end-of-line sentinel) do not.

2. Write a program that reads lines of text character by character **while not** *eof* and, for each nonblank line read, prints the character corresponding to the average ordinal value of all characters on that line. For example, if a line contains just DAZ, its average ordinal value would be (68 + 65 + 90) **div** 3 = 73 which corresponds to the character J.

3. Write a program that reads an arbitrary number of integers and prints a count of how many are odd numbers that immediately follow an even number.

4. Each of several lines of data consists of characters in ['I','V','X'] that represent Roman numerals from 1 to 10. For each line of characters **while not** *eof*, echo the characters and print the equivalent decimal value. Sample output:

```
III   =  3
X     = 10
IV    =  4
VII   =  7
IX    =  9
```

5. Suppose that input consists of an arbitrarily long character sequence like

```
B!a#37N264q91c282r
```

Write a program that prints all 2-character subsequences that sum to 10. Output using the sample data shown should be

```
37
64
91
28
82
```

6. Suppose that input consists of an arbitrarily long character sequence like

```
B!a#37N264q91c2825r
```

Write **procedure** *GetInteger*(**var** *n* : *integer*); that reads this input until it finds a complete integer and assigns the value of that integer to *n*. No integer will be split across lines. Example: Successive calls to *GetInteger* with the above input would return the values:

```
37
264
91
2825
```

7. Write a program that reads lines of text, one character at a time. Each of these lines will be no longer than 50 characters, but may be shorter. If the line is empty, ignore it. Echo the input for all other lines, and beginning at column 55 of that line, print a labelled count of the number of nonblank characters on that line. After the last line of input (when *eof* is reached) print the average number of nonblank characters per nonempty line.

8. Given that input consists of several lines of text such as

```
Can the cat catch the mouse?  Our cat▨
can but our dog cannot.  Can your dog do▨
good things like that?▨
```

Write a program that prints a count of all occurrences of 'cat' and 'dog' (all lower case) in the text, regardless of surrounding context. (The 'cat' of 'catch' counts, but neither 'Cat' nor 'CAT' is a 'cat'.) Consider that a blank breaks the sequence (there is no 'dog' in 'Fido growled') but that end-of-line characters do not (there is a 'dog' in 'do▨good'). Thus the sample text has 3 'cat's and 3 'dog's.

{ Note to the instructor: ▨ is our symbol for end of line character. The rules force the student to detect end-of-line sentinels rather than just letting them turn into blanks. }

SOLUTIONS TO PROGRAMMING EXERCISES

6.8 ALPHABET

```
program alphabet(input, output);
  {
    Read a line of characters and for each capital letter found, print the part of the alphabet
    from that letter through Z.
  }
  var
    ch, c : char;
  begin
    writeln('Alphabetic Capitals');
    writeln;
    write('Enter a line of text: ');
    while not eoln do
      begin
        read(ch);
        if ch in ['A'..'Z'] then                          { If a letter, then }
          begin
            for c := ch to 'Z' do write(c);             { print rest of alphabet }
            writeln
          end { if }
      end { while };
    writeln;
    writeln('Done')
  end { alphabet } .
```

6.10 STARS

```
program stars(input, output);
  {
    Read lines of text and print them with *'s between each pair of characters.
  }
  var
    ch : char;
  begin
    writeln('Add Stars');
    writeln;
    write('Enter a line of text: ');
    while not eof do
      begin
        if not eoln then
          begin
            read(ch);                              { Read and write first character }
            write(ch)
          end;
        while not eoln do
          begin
            read(ch);                              { and rest of line with *s added }
            write('*', ch)
          end { eoln loop };
        readln;
        writeln;
        writeln;
        write('Enter a line of text: ')
      end { eof loop }
  end { stars } .
```

6.11 CUBES

```
program cubes(output);
  {
    Prints a table of n vs n cubed.
  }
  var
    i : integer;
  begin
    writeln(' n   n cubed');
    writeln(' -   -------');
    for i := 1 to 20 do writeln(i : 2, i * i * i : 9)
  end { cubes } .
```

6.13 COUNT WORDS

```
program CountWords(input, output);
  {
    Counts words in a selection of text.
  }
  var
    ch : char;
    count : integer;
    LastIsLetter, ThisIsLetter : Boolean;
  begin
    writeln('Count Words');
    writeln;
    writeln('Enter the text for the word count: ');
    writeln;
    count := 0;
    while not eof do
      begin
        LastIsLetter := false;                    { To remember what last character was }
        ThisIsLetter := false;                        { To hold info about this character }
        while not eoln do
          begin
            read(ch);
            LastIsLetter := ThisIsLetter;
            ThisIsLetter := ch in ['A'..'Z', 'a'..'z', '0'..'9'];
                        { Increment word count if a non-letter is followed by a letter }
            if (not LastIsLetter) and ThisIsLetter then count := count + 1
          end;
        readln
      end;
    writeln;
    writeln('There are ', count : 1, ' words in the input text.')
  end { CountWords } .
```

CHAPTER 7 — OPERATORS, EXPRESSIONS, AND ASSIGNMENT STATEMENTS

The novel feature of this chapter is our insistence that [ ] be treated as an operator. To teach just Pascal programming, it certainly isn't necessary to do so, and most texts don't mention subscripting until their chapter on arrays. But we consider the classification of [ ] as an operator in good standing to be good computer science, and that, not Pascal, is our subject — Pascal is just the medium of discourse. Accordingly, we have given [ ] its proper place in the hierarchy of operator precedence. (You should remind students that, for review purposes, it is easier to look up precedence in Appendix H, for Hierarchy, than to pore through the chapter narrative when they need to check.)

We said this in the chapter, but it bears repeating: of all of Pascal's operators, **mod** is both the most useful and the most neglected. We keep seeing student programs that involve code that is equivalent to **mod**, sometimes because students forget both **mod** and the existence of the *odd* function. Unfortunately, otherwise good Pascal translators such as Turbo Pascal do not have a **mod** operator, they have a remainder operator. For positive left operands, there is no difference, but many a neat expression based on **mod** goes down the tubes in Turbo because it does the wrong thing for negative left operands. The behavior is clearly "wrong" because both the original Jensen and Wirth Standard and the current ISO Standard specify that **mod** be the mathematical mod. (The C language errs, too, but less drastically. What it calls **mod** is also a remainder operator, but the language specifications describe a remaindering operation and then misname it.) Try (–13) **mod** 5 on your Pascal. (Because of the low precedence of minus, you must use those parentheses.) You should get +2, but Turbo and many other translators give –3. Tell your students to enter the result of the experiment in their Appendix I.

SUGGESTED TEST QUESTIONS

Multiple-Choice Questions (Correct answers are indicated by •)

1. Given that $a = 4$, $b = 5$, $c = 6$, the Boolean expression

   not (**not** $(a = b)$ **or not** $(c < a)$)

   has the value:

   a 0
   •b false
   c 1
   d true
   e can't tell; there is a syntax error

2. Which of the following is not a valid <factor>? [Check syntax diagram]

   a $(a * b - c)$
   b abs$(x - y)$
   c ['a'..'z']
   •d $a + b$
   e *ace*[3].score

3. The expression 10 / 4 evaluates to

   a 2
   b 2.0
   •c 2.5
   d 3
   e None of the above, the expression is illegal

4. If *r* is real and *j* is integer, which assignment is legal?

   a *r* := *j*
   b *r* := *round*(*r*)
   c *r* := *trunc*(*r*)
   d *r* := *j* **div** 7
   •e All of the above are legal

5. Consider the statement **if** *a* = *b* **or** *c* **then** *write*('OK'). Which of the following is true?

   a The statement is definitely legal
   b The statement is definitely illegal
   c The statement is legal if *a* and *b* are integers and *c* is Boolean
   •d The statement is legal if all of *a*, *b*, and *c* are Boolean
   e None of the above

6. Which of the following is not a valid <term>?

   a *r* **div** *s*
   •b $r + s$
   c $(r + s) * (t - u)$
   d *r* and *s*
   e all of the above are terms

7. Which of the following is not a Pascal operator

   a **mod**
   b [ ]
   •c **
   d **not**
   e /

8. Integer operands of the division operator / are automatically changed to type real prior to the division. This is an example of the process called

   a intimidation
   b realization
   c flotation
   d strong typing
   • e none of the above

Programming Questions

1. You are working on a program that grades the special forms used for answers to multiple choice questions. Each question has 5 possible answers (*a* through *e*) and the only correct response to each question is to match the key. This key will have one or more of *a* through *e* checked. If several answers are checked in the key, then all of those answers must be checked in the student's response. You have defined the following:

   type
   responses = (*a*, *b*, *c*, *d*, *e*);
   answers = **array**[*responses*] **of** *Boolean*;

   Write **procedure** *MultiChoice*(*student*, *correct* : *answers*; **var** *right* : *Boolean*); that compares each element of the array *student* with each element of the array *correct* and sets *right* to *true* if all elements match and to *false* if there are any differences.

2. You are working on a program that grades the special forms used for answers to multiple choice questions. Each question has 5 possible answers (*a* through *e*) and the only correct response to each question is to match the key. This key will have one or more of *a* through *e* checked. If several answers are checked in the key, then any one of those answers (but only one) must be checked in the student's response if it is to be considered correct. You have defined the following:

   type
   responses = (*a*, *b*, *c*, *d*, *e*);
   answers = **array**[*responses*] **of** *Boolean*;

   Write **procedure** *OneChoice*(*student*, *correct* : *answers*; **var** *right* : *Boolean*); that sets *right* to *true* if exactly one element of the array *student* is *true* and that element corresponds to one of the *true* elements in the array *correct*.

3. Write **procedure** *EveryNth*(*n* : *integer*); that displays every *n*th minute starting at 12:00 am and ending 11:59 pm. Example: A call to *EveryNth*(17) should display the output shown in part below:

```
12:00 am
12:17 am
12:34 am
12:51 am
 1:08 am
 ...
```

4. Write **procedure** *NthDay*(*n* : *integer*; *LeapYear* : *Boolean*); that displays every *n*th day starting at January 1 and ending December 31 of a year that is a leap year if *LeapYear* is *true* or of a year that is not a leap year if *LeapYear* is *false*. Example: A call to *NthDay*(17, *false*) should display the output shown in part below:

```
January 1
January 18
February 4
February 21
March 10
...
```

5. Write **procedure** *roundoff(r : real;* **var** *i : integer;* **var** *c : char)*; that rounds its real argument *r* to the nearest integer and stores that integer at *i*. If *r* is rounded up set *c* to '−'; if *r* is rounded down set; *c* to '+'; if no rounding is done (i.e. the real *r* and the integer *i* represent the same number) set *c* to '='. Use this procedure in a main program that computes the square root of all whole numbers from 100 to 200, and prints the number, its real square root, and its *roundoffed* square root followed by '−', '+', or '=' depending on the rounding done. Part of your output should look like:

```
x          sqrt(x)       rounded
...          ...            ...
142        11.916375       12-
143        11.958260       12-
144        12.000000       12=
145        12.041594       12+
146        12.083045       12+
...          ...            ...
```

6. If **mod** and **div** followed the distributive law of algebra, then these operators would obey

the **mod** rule	a **mod** $b = (a + b)$ **mod** b
and the **div** rule	$(a$ **div** $b) + 1 = (a + b)$ **div** b

Write **procedure** *TestModAndDiv(a, b : integer;* **var** *Tmod, Tdiv : Boolean)*; that for input values *a* and *b* tests these equalities and sets *Tmod* to *true* or *false* depending on whether the **mod** function on your Pascal satisfies the **mod** rule and *Tdiv* to *true* or *false* depending on whether the **div** function on your Pascal satisfies the **div** rule. What do you expect the results to be when you test your procedure?

7. The true mathematical **mod** operator obeys the distributive law of algebra and hence, since b **mod** $b = 0$, **mod** obeys

the **mod** rule	a **mod** $b = (a + b)$ **mod** b

However, this may not be true for some Pascal **mod** operators when *a* is negative. Write **procedure** *NewMod(a, b : integer;* **var** *c : integer)*; that for input values *a* and *b* sets *c* to the value that would be returned by a new **mod** operator that does obey the **mod** rule. Assume that your **mod** operator does satisfy the **mod** rule for positive *a*.

8. The / division operator is distributive i.e. $(a + b) / b = a/b + b/b = a/b + 1$. If **div** were distributive it would obey the similar rule

the **div** rule	$(a + b)$ **div** $b = (a$ **div** $b) + 1$

However, this may not be true when *a* and/or *b* are negative. Write the Pascal **procedure** *NewDiv(a, b : integer;* **var** *c : integer)*; that for input values *a* and *b* sets *c* to the value that would have been returned by a hypothetical **div** operator that does obey the **div** rule. (The actual **div** operator satisfies the **div** rule for positive *a* and *b*.)

SOLUTIONS TO PROGRAMMING EXERCISES

7.8 DeMORGAN

```
program DeMorgan(output);
  {
    Verifies validity of two laws of logical operations.
  }
  var
    a, b, c : Boolean;
    check : Boolean;
  begin
    check := true;
    for a := false to true do                { Checking not (a and b) = not a or not b }
        for b := false to true do
            if not (a and b) <> (not a) or (not b) then check := false;
    writeln('not (a and b) = not a or not b is ', check);
    check := true;
    for a := false to true do             { Checking (a or b) and (a or c) = a or (b and c) }
        for b := false to true do
            for c := false to true do
            if (a or b) and (a or c) <> a or (b and c) then check := false;
    writeln('(a or b) and (a or c) = a or (b and c) is ', check)
  end { DeMorgan } .
```

7.9 PASCALINE

```
program Pascaline(input, output);
  {
    Program to retrieve data about the sales of the Pascaline Corporation.
  }
  type years = 1645..1650;
  var
    year : years;
    sales : array[years] of integer;
    T1, T2 : integer;
  begin
    sales[1645] := 5417;                       { Enter data into the sales table }
    sales[1646] := 7809;
    sales[1647] := 12891;
    sales[1648] := 23047;
    sales[1649] := 20113;
    sales[1650] := 3462;
    write('Enter a year in the range 1645 to 1650: ');
    while not eof do
      begin
        readln(year);                          { Retrieve requested data }
        if year < 1645 then
          begin
            write('The Pascaline Corporation was not yet ');
            writeln('in business in ', year : 4, '.')
          end else
        if year > 1650 then
          begin
            write('The Pascaline Corporation was no longer ');
            writeln('in business in ', year : 4, '.')
          end else
          begin
            write('Sales of the Pascaline Corporation for ');
            write(year : 4, ' totalled ');
            T1 := sales[year] div 1000;
            T2 := sales[year] mod 1000;
            if T1 > 0 then
              begin
                write(sales[year] div 1000 : 1, ',');
                if T2 < 100 then write(0 : 1);
                if T2 < 10 then write(0 : 1)
              end;
            writeln(T2 : 1, ' francs.')
          end;
        writeln;
        write('Enter a year in the range 1645 to 1650: ')
      end
  end { Pascaline } .
```

CHAPTER 8 — CONTROL STRUCTURES

Much of this chapter is for review and reference because of earlier coverage. But the **case** statement is new and deserves illustration in lecture. Check to see if your Pascal allows use of either an **else** or **otherwise** clause with **case** and tell your students to enter the answer in Appendix I. Application of **case** to the simulation of a calculator is standard fare, but the application to finite-state machines is somewhat novel. In a strictly language course, you might skip the latter, but if you are teaching embryonic computer scientists, we hope you won't. The chapter exercise that suggests an extension of the calculator to unary operators makes a good assignment, or, since it is less difficult to modify an existing program than to make a new one from scratch, you might want to save it for an exam.

We admit in the chapter that, yes Virginia, there is a **goto**. We risk offending both those of you who think we should have banned its reference and those who think that avoiding its use under all circumstances is an affectation that is overdone. Whatever your view, students should be shown that use of an auxiliary Boolean variable can avoid most temptations to use **goto**.

Again, we note that it is time for an instructor decision. When, if at all, do you want to discuss loop invariants? To even suggest that you might not is heresy. The syllabus for the Advanced Placement test in Computer Science includes the topic, so its formulators must believe that all or most college instructors teach loop invariance in a first course. We think you should too, but couldn't quite bring ourselves to do so in the early chapters. We have much to say about proving programs correct in Chapter 15, so those who want to get into this earlier should tell their students to read that chapter out of (our) order, show loop invariants as a matter of course when programs are discussed in lecture, and perhaps and most ambitiously, require students to embed comments in their programs that state the invariant for every loop that they write. They'll love you for it. (And if you believe that, we've got some land in Florida ...)

SUGGESTED TEST QUESTIONS

Multiple-Choice Questions (Correct answers are indicated by •)

1. Which of the following keywords exerts influence over more than one of the statements that follow it without use of a compound statement?

   a **else**
   b **for**
   •c **repeat**
   d **while**
   e **with**

2. Which of the following could cannot be used as a case statement label?

   a 17
   b 's'
   c *true*
   d *Saturday*
   •e 'October'

3. The action taken at a given case statement label cannot be

   a a compound statement
   b another case statement
   c null { just a semicolon }
   d an I/O statement
   •e none of the above is prohibited

4. Which of the following is true with respect to the case constants used to label case actions?

   a such constants must be unique within the same case statement
   b all case constants must have the same type as their case selector
   c case constants must be ordinal
   •d all of the above are true
   e none of a through c is true

5. Given **type** *numbers* = (*four*, *three*, *two*, *one*), then *ord*(*four*) evaluates to

   •a 0
   b 1
   c 2
   d 3
   e 4

6. A programmer has started to write a recursive function called *zip*. So far, she has written

```
function zip(x : real) : real;
  begin
    if x <= 5
      then zip := x                    { The bootstrap condition }
      else ...{ The inductive step goes here }
  end { zip };
```

   Which of the following is a plausible inductive step, that is, one that could replace the second comment so as to create a meaningful definition of *zip*?

   a *zip* := *zip*(2 * *x*)
   b *zip* := *zip*(*sqr*(*x*))
   •c *zip* := *zip*(*sqrt*(*x*))
   d *zip* := *zip*(*exp*(*x*))
   e any of the above could be used; we need more information

7. Consider this program fragment, where *ch* is of type *char*:

```
123 : read(ch);
      if ch < ' ' then goto 123;
```

This loop could be replaced by a single statement that is

a a **for** loop
b a **while** loop
•c a **repeat** loop
d either a **for** or a **while** loop
e either a **while** or a **repeat** loop

8. Which of the following is true about the **if** statement:

a There should never be a semicolon following **else**.
b The keyword **if** must never follow the word **else**.
•c There should never be a semicolon before **else**.
d The keyword **then** is optional.
e None of the above are true.

Programming Questions

1. For each integer read **while not** *eof*, print any number that is in [1..20] and its equivalent Roman numeral representation. A 10% bonus will be awarded if you use a case statement that has significantly fewer than 20 lines.

2. Write a program that, for each of several data cases **while not** *eof*, computes and prints the perimeter of a polygon according to the formula to be given. A polygon is a possibly irregular figure that consists of nonintersecting straight sides that form a closed path, for example:

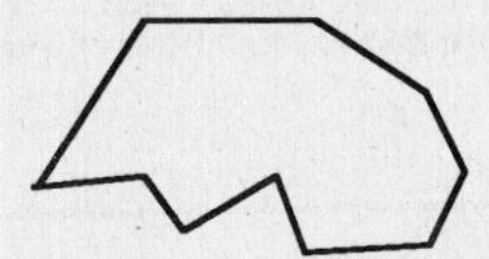

The polygon shown happens to have ten sides; your program must deal with any number. Input for one case consists of pairs of real coordinates such that the last pair is the same as the first (indicating closure of the path that defines the polygon). For example, for a four-sided polygon, input would consist of 5 pairs of coordinates, perhaps

```
3.7  4.2
4.9  5.1
5.3  7.4
4.1  9.6
3.7  4.2
```

You may assume that all input figures have at least 3 sides (4 coordinate pairs).

For n sides, the perimeter is

$$\sum_{i=1}^{n} \sqrt{(x_{i+1} - x_i)^2 + (y_{i+1} - y_i)^2}$$

3. Write a program that reads integers in the range 2..12 each of which represents one roll of a pair of dice. Your program is to read at least one number, possibly more. Call the first value read *n*. Use a case statement that takes one of these actions according to the value of *n*:

   if *n* is 2 or 3, write "You lose"

   if *n* is 7 or 11, write "You win"

   if *n* is one of the other possible values, call procedure *roll* which you have defined so that it reads more integers until either

   a) a 7 is read, in which case it prints "You lose", or
   b) a value equal to *n* is read, in which case it prints "You win."

4. Given **type** *figure* = (*circle*, *square*, *triangle*);

   Write a program that, **while not** *eof*, read pairs of numbers such as

```
1  0.89
0  4.97
2  12.71
```

   The first number in each pair is a key to a particular regular figure: 0 ⇒ circle, 1 ⇒ square, 2 ⇒ equilateral triangle. The second number is either the length of a side of a square or rectangle or the radius of a circle. Your program must use a case statement whose case labels are elements of type *figure*. Each case action should write the area of the corresponding figure.

5. Assume that you know that the integers less than 20 that are prime are 2, 3, 5, 7, 11, 13, 17, and 19. All others other than 1 are called "composite". The integer 1 is considered neither prime nor composite. Write a program that, for each integer read until end-of-file, echoes the number and prints one or another of these messages next to it, whichever is sensible:

```
'is not in the range 1..20'
'is neither prime nor composite'
'is an odd prime'
'is an even prime'
'is even and composite'
'is odd and composite'
```

   Use a case statement.

6. Write a program that, **while not** *eof*, reads 2-character sequences each of which is one of the nine Roman numerals II, IV, IX, VI, VV, VX, XI, XV, XX. If you detect a letter that is not in ['I','V','X'], print an error message. If you detect VV, write 'should have been written as X'. If you detect VX, write 'should have been written as just V'. For any of the seven valid 2-character combinations, print the corresponding decimal value. Use nested case statements.

7. Write a program that reads and echos lines of text until it finds two successive lines that contain all the lower case vowels ('a', 'e', 'i', 'o' and 'u') or until it reaches the end-of-file. If it finds the two lines, it should re-write them. If it does not find them it should write "Not found."

8. One way (but far from the best way) to generate all the permutations of the digits 1, 2, 3, 4, and 5 would be to set up a 5-deep nested loop for indices *i*, *j*, *k*, *l*, and *m* each running from 1 to 5 and then print out only those for which *i*, *j*, *k*, *l*, and *m* were all different. Write a program that implements this algorithm to print all the permutations. The program should also keep track of how many comparisons are made and print the result after all the permutations are printed. Be as efficient as you can within the confines of this rather poor algorithm

SOLUTIONS TO PROGRAMMING EXERCISES

8.7 FOOTBALL SCORES

```
program FootballScores(input, output);
  {
    Computes all the ways input football scores can be produced
  }
  var
    points,   { Points to be scored }
    tdep,     { Number of touchdowns with extra points }
    td,       { Number of touchdowns without extra points }
    fg,       { Number of field goals }
    sf,       { Number of safeties }
    count     { Count of the different ways found }
        : integer;
  begin
    write('Enter a football score: ');
    while not eof do
      begin
        count := 0;
        readln(points);
        writeln;
        writeln('The following will total ',points:0,' points: ');
        writeln;
        writeln('  TD''s   PAT''s    FG''s  Safeties');
        for tdep := 0 to points div 7 do
        for td := 0 to (points - 7 * tdep) div 6 do
        for fg := 0 to (points - 7 * tdep - 6 * td) div 3 do
        for sf := 0 to (points - 7 * tdep - 6 * td - 3 * fg) div 2 do
          if 7 * tdep + 6 * td + 3 * fg + 2 * sf = points then
            begin
              count := count + 1;
              writeln(tdep + td : 4, tdep : 7, fg : 9, sf : 9)
            end { if (and all for loops) };
        writeln;
        writeln('There are ', count : 0, ' combinations.');
        writeln;
        writeln;
        write('Enter a football score: ')
      end
  end { FootballScores } .
```

8.8 HEX TABLE

```
program HexTable(output);
  {
    Computes and displays the hexadecimal multiplication table
  }
  var
    i, j, k, m : integer;
  begin
    writeln('The Hexadecimal Multiplication Table' : 52);
    writeln;
    write('x   |');
    for i := 0 to 9 do write(i : 4);                        { Label columns of table }
    for i := 10 to 15 do write(chr(i - 10 + ord('A')) : 4);
    writeln;
    write('---+');
    for i := 0 to 15 do write('----');
    writeln;
    for i := 0 to 15 do
      begin
        if i < 10                                            { Label row i }
          then write(i : 1)
          else write(chr(i - 10 + ord('A')) : 1);
        write('  |');
        for j := 0 to 15 do
          begin
            k := i * j;                                      { Generate product }
            m := k div 16;                            { m is high order hex digit }
            if m = 0 then write('    ') else
              if m < 10 then write(m : 3) else write(chr(m - 10 + ord('A')) : 3);
            m := k mod 16;                          { m is now low order hex digit }
            if m < 10 then write(m : 1) else write(chr(m - 10 + ord('A')) : 1)
          end;
        writeln
      end;
    writeln
  end { HexTable } .
```

8.9 QPA

```
program QPA(input, output);
  {
    Computes quality point average as defined in problem statement.
  }
  var
    qp, ch, num, denom, totalnum, totaldenom, counter, flag : integer;
    letter, LetGrade : char;
  begin
    writeln('QPA Calculator');
    writeln;
    writeln('Enter data for each student in the form: ');
    writeln;
    writeln('NAME  G1 CH1  G2  CH2  ...  #');
    writeln;
    writeln('NAME may contain single blanks.');
    writeln('Leave at least 2 blanks after NAME.');
    writeln;
    totalnum := 0;                          { Initialize cumulative numerator }
    totaldenom := 0;                       { and denominator of overall QPA }
    counter := 1;                                       { and student counter }
```

```
write('Enter data for student #', counter : 1, ': ');
while not eof do
  begin
    write('Student #', counter : 1, ': ');
    flag := 0;
    while flag < 2 do                    { Read and print name of this student }
      begin
        read(letter);
        if letter = ' ' then flag := flag + 1 else flag := 0;
        write(letter)
      end;
    num := 0;                                          { Initialize numerator }
    denom := 0;                            { and denominator for this student }
    repeat                                               { Read first grade }
      read(LetGrade)
    until LetGrade <> ' ';
    while LetGrade <> '#' do
      begin
        read(ch);                                        { Get credit hours }
        case LetGrade of                    { Converts letter grade to QP's }
      'A', 'B', 'C', 'D' : qp := 4 + ord('A') - ord(LetGrade);
                     'F' : qp := 0;
                'I', 'W' : begin
                             qp := 0;
                             ch := 0
                           end
        end {case};
        num := num + ch * qp;             { Add current grades to fraction parts }
        denom := denom + ch;
        repeat                                      { Find next letter grade }
          read(LetGrade)
        until LetGrade <> ' '
      end;
    readln;
    write('QPA = ');
    if denom = 0
      then writeln('----')
      else writeln(num / denom : 4 : 2);
    writeln;
    totalnum := totalnum + num;                        { Accumulate totals }
    totaldenom := totaldenom + denom;
    counter := counter + 1;
    write('Enter data for student #', counter : 1, ': ')
  end { while not eof loop } ;
  writeln;
  writeln;
  write('Overall Class QPA = ');
  if totaldenom = 0
    then writeln('----')
    else writeln(totalnum / totaldenom : 4 : 2)
end { QPA } .
```

8.10 NUMERIC NAMES

```
program NumericNames(input, output);
  {
    Reads integers in 0..99 and prints them as words.
  }
  var
    n, first, second : integer;
  begin
    write('Enter a number in [0..99]: ');
    while not eof do
      begin
        readln(n);
        if (n < 0) or (n > 99) then write('Input is out of range') else
          begin
            write(n : 1, ' in words is ');
            first := n div 10;
            second := n mod 10;
            case first of                                    { For first digit }
              0 : ;
              1 :   case second of         { If first digit is 1, must see second digit }
                        0 : write('ten');
                        1 : write('eleven');
                        2 : write('twelve');
                        3 : write('thirteen');
                        4 : write('fourteen');
                        5 : write('fifteen');
                        6 : write('sixteen');
                        7 : write('seventeen');
                        8 : write('eighteen');
                        9 : write('nineteen')
                    end { case };
              2 :   write('twenty');
              3 :   write('thirty');
              4 :   write('forty');
              5 :   write('fifty');
              6 :   write('sixty');
              7 :   write('seventy');
              8 :   write('eighty');
              9 :   write('ninety')
            end { case };
            if first <> 1 then                               { For second digit }
              begin
                if first * second > 0 then write('-');
                case second of
                      0 : if first = 0 then write('zero');
                      1 : write('one');
                      2 : write('two');
                      3 : write('three');
                      4 : write('four');
                      5 : write('five');
                      6 : write('six');
                      7 : write('seven');
                      8 : write('eight');
                      9 : write('nine')
                end { case }
              end
          end;
        writeln('.'); writeln; write('Enter a number in [0..99]: ')
      end
  end { NumericNames } .
```

8.15 MONTHLY CASELOAD

```
program MonthlyCaseload(input, output);
  {
    Print the month and day of an input day number. The user may input day numbers
    indefinitely until the end-of-file sentinel is typed.
  }
  type
    month = ( January, February, March, April, May, June, July, August,
              September, October, November, December);
    var
    daynum : integer;                          { The day number received as input }
    m : month;                { The name of the month that contains the day number }
    day : integer;                                       { The day within that month. }
   procedure printmonth(m : month);
    {
      Prints the name corresponding to month m. You do not need this procedure if your
      Pascal is willing to output enumerated type elements.
    }
    begin { printmonth }
      case m of
     January : write('January');
    February : write('February');
       March : write('March');
       April : write('April');
         May : write('May');
        June : write('June');
        July : write('July');
      August : write('August');
   September : write('September');
     October : write('October');
    November : write('November');
    December : write('December')
      end { case }
    end { printmonth } ;

  begin { main }
    write('Enter a day number in the range 1 to 365: ');
    while not eof do
      begin
        readln(daynum);
        write('Day number ', daynum : 1, ' is ');
        if (daynum < 1) or (daynum > 365) then writeln('out of range') else
         begin
          if daynum < 32   then begin m := January;   day := daynum         end else
          if daynum <  60  then begin m := February;  day := daynum -  31   end else
          if daynum <  91  then begin m := March;     day := daynum -  59   end else
          if daynum < 121  then begin m := April;     day := daynum -  90   end else
          if daynum < 152  then begin m := May;       day := daynum - 120   end else
          if daynum < 182  then begin m := June;      day := daynum - 151   end else
          if daynum < 213  then begin m := July;      day := daynum - 181   end else
          if daynum < 244  then begin m := August;    day := daynum - 212   end else
          if daynum < 274  then begin m := September; day := daynum - 243   end else
          if daynum < 305  then begin m := October;   day := daynum - 273   end else
          if daynum < 335  then begin m := November;  day := daynum - 304   end else
                                begin m := December;  day := daynum - 334   end;
          printmonth(m);
          writeln(' ', day : 1)
         end;
        writeln; write('Enter a day number in the range 1 to 365: ')
      end
  end { MonthlyCaseload } .
```

8.16 WHAT'S NEXT

```
program WhatsNext(output);
  {
    Prints all the series starting with a two-digit integer when each term in a given series is
    the product of the two decimal digits of the previous term.
  }
  var
    i, n : integer;
  begin
    writeln('The What''s Next sequences');
    writeln;
    for i := 10 to 99 do
      begin
        n := i;                                       { First term in a sequence }
        while n <> 0 do
          begin
            write(n : 4);                                     { Write the term }
            n := (n mod 10) * (n div 10)                    { Compute next term }
          end;
        writeln
      end { for loop }
  end { WhatsNext } .
```

8.17 WHO GOES THERE?

```
program WhoGoesThere(input, output);
  {
    Finite State Machine <identifier> tester.
  }
  type
    statetype = (S0, S1);
    characterkind = (letter, digit, blank, other, endst, done);
  var
    S : statetype;
    chkind : characterkind;

procedure getkind(var kind : characterkind);
  {
    Reads and writes a character and assigns its characterkind to the argument.
  }
  var
    ch : char;
  begin { getkind }
    if eof then kind := done else                     { No more strings to test }
    if eoln then kind := endst else                    { This string has ended }
      begin                                           { To find next character }
        read(ch);                                                  { Read it }
        write(ch);                                                { Write it }
        if ch in ['A'..'Z', 'a'..'z'] then kind := letter else       { If letter, }
        if ch in ['0'..'9'] then kind := digit else                     { digit, }
        if ch = ' ' then kind := blank else kind := other             { or other }
      end
  end { getkind } ;

procedure finish;
  {
    Mop up when this string is not an <identifier>.
  }
  var
    ch : char;
```

```
  begin { finish }
    while not eoln do
      begin
        read(ch);
        write(ch)
      end;
    readln
  end { finish } ;

procedure accept;
  {
    Indicates a legal <identifier>, ends read line, and resets S to initial state.
  }
  begin { accept }
    S := S0;
    finish;
    writeln(' is a legal identifier.');
    writeln;
    write('Enter a string to test: ')
  end { accept } ;

procedure reject;
  {
    Indicates an illegal <identifier>, ends read line, and resets S to initial state.
  }
  begin { reject }
    S := S0;
    finish;
    writeln(' is not a legal identifier.');
    writeln;
    write('Enter a string to test: ')
  end { reject } ;

begin { main }
  S := S0;                                              { Initially in state S0 }
  writeln('Identifier Tester');
  writeln;
  write('Enter a string to test: ');
  getkind(chkind);                                      { Get first character }
  while chkind <> done do
    begin                                               { Input  |   S0   |  S1 }
      case chkind of                                    { -------+--------+---- }
            letter : S := S1;                           { letter |   S1   |  S1 }
            digit : if S = S0 then reject;              { digit  |  (R)   |  S1 }
            blank : if S = S1 then reject;              { blank  |   S0   | (R) }
            other : reject;                             { other  |  (R)   | (R) }
            endst : case S of                           { endst  |  (R)   | (A) }
                      S0 : reject;
                      S1 : accept
                    end { case S }
      end { case chkind } ;
      getkind(chkind)                                   { Get next character }
    end { while }
end { WhoGoesThere } .
```

8.18 FSM BASEBALL

```
program FSMbaseball(input, output);
  {
    Simulates baseball as a finite state machine.
  }
  const
    gamelength = 9;                                              { Innings }
  type
    atbat = (out, single, double, triple, HR, K, W, SB, doublesteal, CS,
    groundout, longsingle, longdouble, FC2, FC3, FC4, DP2, DP3, DP4, sac,
    flyout, shortsingle, SF, error);          { Only plays allowed in this version }
    string7 = packed array[1..7] of char;
    string11 = packed array[1..11] of char;
  var
    play : atbat;
    st : record                                              { State indicator }
          outs : 0..3;
          rnrs : 0..7
        end;
    runs, hits, errors, PlayNo, inning, i : integer;
    HomeTeam, GameEnd, Team, B : Boolean;
    BoxScore : array[Boolean, atbat] of integer;
    innings : array[Boolean, 1..30] of integer;
    score : array[Boolean] of integer;
    TeamName : array[Boolean] of string7;
    up : array[atbat] of string11;
    list : array[Boolean, atbat] of integer;
    ab : atbat;

  function InverseOrd(n : integer) : atbat;
    {
      InverseOrd returns a value of type atbat such that ord(InverseOrd(n)) = n.  Thus
      InverseOrd is the inverse function to ord.
    }
    var
      i : integer;
      ab : atbat;
    begin { InverseOrd }
      ab := out;
      if n < 24 then
        for i := 1 to n do ab := succ(ab);
      InverseOrd := ab
    end { InverseOrd } ;

  procedure Illegal;
    {
      Handles illegal plays.
    }
    begin { Illegal }
      writeln('Illegal Play.')
    end { Illegal } ;

  procedure NewHalfInning(var B : Boolean);
    {
      Starts a new half inning
    }
    var
      x : char;
    begin { NewHalfInning }
      innings[HomeTeam, inning] := runs;        { Record runs scored in line score }
      writeln; writeln;                                        { Summarize inning }
      writeln(runs : 1, ' runs, ', hits : 1, ' hits, ', errors : 1, ' errors.');
```

```
    GameEnd := (Inning >= gamelength) and ((score[true] > score[false]) or
        (HomeTeam and (score[true] <> score[false])));          { Is game over? }
    if not GameEnd then
      begin
        if HomeTeam then
          begin
            inning := inning + 1;
            writeln; writeln('Inning #', inning : 1)
          end;
        writeln;
        runs := 0; hits := 0; errors := 0;
        st.rnrs := 0; st.outs := 0;
        HomeTeam := not HomeTeam;
        writeln(TeamName[HomeTeam], ' now batting.'); writeln;
        B := false
      end
  end { NewHalfInning } ;

procedure addruns(i : integer);
  {
    Adds i to run totals and checks to see if winning run just scored.
  }
  begin { addruns }
    score[HomeTeam] := score[HomeTeam] + i;
    runs := runs + i;
    GameEnd := (Inning >= gamelength)
            and HomeTeam and (score[true] > score[false]);
    if GameEnd then
      begin                                           { Winning run just scored }
        innings[HomeTeam, inning] := runs;
        writeln; writeln;
        writeln(runs : 1,' runs, ', hits : 1,' hits, ',errors : 1, ' errors.')
      end
  end { addruns } ;

procedure batting(play : atbat; var B : Boolean);
  {
    This is the FSM machine.
  }
  begin { batting }
    B := true;
    case play of
            out,                                      { Baserunners unchanged. }
             K : case st.outs of
                         0, 1 : st.outs := st.outs + 1;
                            2 : begin
                                  st.outs := 0;
                                  NewHalfInning(B)
                                end
                 end;
            sac,                                      { Baserunners move 1 base. }
    groundout : case st.outs of
                         0, 1 : begin
                                  st.outs := st.outs + 1;
                                  case st.rnrs of
                                                0 : illegal;
                            1, 2, 3, 4, 5, 6, 7 : begin
                                                    addruns(st.rnrs div 4);
                                                    st.rnrs := (2 * st.rnrs) mod 8
                                                  end
                                  end
                                end;
                            2 : illegal
                 end;
```

```
flyout : case st.outs of              { Baserunners on 2 and 3 move up. }
              0, 1 : begin
                       st.outs := st.outs + 1;
                       addruns(st.rnrs div 4);
                       case st.rnrs of
                              0, 1 : illegal;
                              2, 6 : st.rnrs := 4;
                              3, 7 : st.rnrs := 5;
                                 4 : st.rnrs := 0;
                                 5 : st.rnrs := 1
                       end
                     end;
                 2 : illegal
         end;
    SF : case st.outs of              { Like flyout, but must be runner on 3 }
              0, 1 : begin
                       st.outs := st.outs + 1;
                       addruns(st.rnrs div 4);
                       case st.rnrs of
                         0, 1, 2, 3 : illegal;
                                  6 : st.rnrs := 4;
                                  7 : st.rnrs := 5;
                                  4 : st.rnrs := 0;
                                  5 : st.rnrs := 1
                       end
                     end;
                 2 : illegal
         end;
single : begin      { Runners on 2 and 3 score, runner on 1 goes to 2. }
           case st.rnrs of
                   0, 1 : ;
             2, 3, 4, 5 : addruns(1);
                   6, 7 : addruns(2)
           end;
           case st.rnrs of
             0, 2, 4, 6 : st.rnrs := 1;
             1, 3, 5, 7 : st.rnrs := 3
           end
         end;
shortsingle,                                   { All runners advance 1 base. }
   error : begin
           case st.rnrs of
             0, 1, 2, 3 : ;
             4, 5, 6, 7 : addruns(1)
           end;
           case st.rnrs of
                   0, 4 : st.rnrs := 1;
                   1, 5 : st.rnrs := 3;
                   2, 6 : st.rnrs := 5;
                   3, 7 : st.rnrs := 7
           end
         end;
longsingle : begin                             { All runners advance 2 bases. }
           case st.rnrs of
                   0, 1 : ;
             2, 3, 4, 5 : addruns(1);
                   6, 7 : addruns(2)
           end;
           case st.rnrs of
             0, 2, 4, 6 : st.rnrs := 1;
             1, 3, 5, 7 : st.rnrs := 5
           end
         end;
```

```
       double : begin                          { All runners advance 2 bases }
                   case st.rnrs of
                           0, 1 : ;
                     2, 3, 4, 5 : addruns(1);
                           6, 7 : addruns(2)
                   end;
                   case st.rnrs of
                     0, 2, 4, 6 : st.rnrs := 2;
                     1, 3, 5, 7 : st.rnrs := 6
                   end
                 end;
   longdouble : begin                                   { All runners score }
                   case st.rnrs of
                              0 : ;
                          1, 2, 4 : addruns(1);
                          3, 5, 6 : addruns(2);
                              7 : addruns(3)
                   end;
                   st.rnrs := 2
                 end;
       triple : begin                                   { All runners score }
                   case st.rnrs of
                              0 : ;
                          1, 2, 4 : addruns(1);
                          3, 5, 6 : addruns(2);
                              7 : addruns(3)
                   end;
                   st.rnrs := 4
                 end;
           HR : begin                                   { All runners score }
                   case st.rnrs of
                              0 : addruns(1);
                          1, 2, 4 : addruns(2);
                          3, 5, 6 : addruns(3);
                              7 : addruns(4)
                   end;
                   st.rnrs := 0
                 end;
            W : begin                          { Forced runners advance 1 base }
                   case st.rnrs of
          0, 1, 2, 3, 4, 5, 6 : ;
                              7 : addruns(1)
                   end;
                   case st.rnrs of
                              0 : st.rnrs := 1;
                           1, 2 : st.rnrs := 3;
                     3, 5, 6, 7 : st.rnrs := 7;
                              4 : st.rnrs := 5
                   end
                 end;
           SB :                          { Stolen base. Steal of home not allowed }
                 case st.rnrs of
                     0, 4, 6, 7 : illegal;
                           1, 2 : st.rnrs := 2 * st.rnrs;
                              3 : st.rnrs := 5;
                              5 : st.rnrs := 6
                 end;
           CS :                                         { Caught stealing }
                 case st.outs of
                           0, 1 : begin
                                     st.outs := st.outs + 1;
                                     case st.rnrs of
                                       0, 4, 6, 7 : illegal;
                                             1, 2 : st.rnrs := 0;
```

```
                        3 : st.rnrs := 1;
                        5 : st.rnrs := 4
                  end
                end;
              2 : case st.rnrs of
                    0, 4, 6, 7 : illegal;
                    1, 2, 3, 5 : NewHalfInning(B)

                end
        end;
doublesteal : case st.rnrs of                  { Steal of home not allowed }
      0, 1, 2, 4, 5, 6, 7 : illegal;
                        3 : st.rnrs := 6
        end;
    DP2 :                                      { Double play with extra out at 2 }
        case st.outs of
              0 : begin
                    st.outs := 2;
                    if st.rnrs in [6, 7] then addruns(1);
                    case st.rnrs of
                      0, 2, 4, 5 : illegal;
                               1 : st.rnrs := 0;
                            3, 6 : st.rnrs := 4;
                               7 : st.rnrs := 6
                    end
                  end;
              1 : case st.rnrs of
                    0, 2, 4, 5 : illegal;
                    1, 3, 6, 7 : NewHalfInning(B)
                  end;
              2 : illegal
        end;
    DP3 :                                      { Double play with extra out at 3 }
        case st.outs of
              0 : begin
                    st.outs := 2;
                    if st.rnrs > 5 then addruns(1);
                    case st.rnrs of
                            0, 1 : illegal;
                         2, 4, 6 : st.rnrs := 0;
                               5 : st.rnrs := 1;
                            3, 7 : st.rnrs := 2
                    end
                  end;
              1 : case st.rnrs of
                    0, 2, 4, 5 : illegal;
                    1, 3, 6, 7 : NewHalfInning(B)
                  end;
              2 : illegal
        end;
    DP4 :                                      { Double play with extra out at 4 }
        case st.outs of
              0 : begin
                    st.outs := 2;
                    case st.rnrs of
                      0, 1, 2, 3 : illegal;
                               4 : st.rnrs := 0;
                               5 : st.rnrs := 2;
                               6 : st.rnrs := 4;
                               7 : st.rnrs := 6
                    end
                  end;
```

```
                         1 : case st.rnrs of
                               0, 2, 4, 5 : illegal;
                               1, 3, 6, 7 : NewHalfInning(B)
                             end;
                         2 : illegal
          end;
      FC2 :                                  { Fielder's choice with out at 2 }
          case st.outs of
                      0, 1 : begin
                               st.outs := st.outs + 1;
                               if st.rnrs in [5, 7] then addruns(1);
                               case st.rnrs of
                                 0, 2, 4, 6 : illegal;
                                       1, 5 : st.rnrs := 1;
                                       3, 7 : st.rnrs := 5
                               end
                             end;
                         2 : case st.rnrs of
                               0, 2, 4, 6 : illegal;
                               1, 3, 5, 7 : NewHalfInning(B)
                             end
          end;
      FC3 :                                  { Fielder's choice with out at 3 }
          case st.outs of
                      0, 1 : begin
                               st.outs := st.outs + 1;
                               if st.rnrs > 5 then addruns(1);
                               case st.rnrs of
                                       0, 1 : illegal;
                                    2, 4, 6 : st.rnrs := 1;
                                          3 : ;
                                       5, 7 : st.rnrs := 3
                               end
                             end;
                         2 : case st.rnrs of
                                       0, 1 : illegal;
                           2, 3, 4, 5, 6, 7 : NewHalfInning(B)
                             end
          end;
      FC4 :                                  { Fielder's choice with out at 4 }
          case st.outs of
                      0, 1 : begin
                               st.outs := st.outs + 1;
                               case st.rnrs of
                                 0, 1, 2, 3 : illegal;
                                          4 : st.rnrs := 1;
                                          5 : st.rnrs := 3;
                                          6 : st.rnrs := 5;
                                          7 :
                               end
                             end;
                         2 : case st.rnrs of
                               0, 1, 2, 3 : illegal;
                               4, 5, 6, 7 : NewHalfInning(B)
                             end
          end
  end { case play }
end;
```

```
begin { main }
  TeamName[false] := 'Dodgers';                                { Initialization }
  TeamName[true] := 'Yankees';
  up[out] := 'out          ';
  up[single] := 'single       ';
  up[double] := 'double       ';
  up[triple] := 'triple       ';
  up[HR] := 'HR           ';
  up[K] := 'K            ';
  up[W] := 'W            ';
  up[SB] := 'SB           ';
  up[doublesteal] := 'doublesteal';
  up[CS] := 'CS           ';
  up[groundout] := 'groundout  ';
  up[longsingle] := 'longsingle ';
  up[longdouble] := 'longdouble ';
  up[FC2] := 'FC2         ';
  up[FC3] := 'FC3         ';
  up[FC4] := 'FC4         ';
  up[DP2] := 'DP          ';
  up[DP3] := 'DP3         ';
  up[DP4] := 'DP4         ';
  up[sac] := 'sac         ';
  up[flyout] := 'flyout      ';
  up[shortsingle] := 'shortsingle';
  up[SF] := 'SF          ';
  up[error] := 'error       ';
  inning := 1;
  runs := 0;
  hits := 0;
  errors := 0;
  st.rnrs := 0;
  st.outs := 0;
  score[false] := 0;
  for Team := false to true do
    begin
      score[Team] := 0;
      for ab := out to error do list[Team, ab] := 0;
      for i := 1 to 30 do innings[Team, i] := -1
    end;
  HomeTeam := false;
  i := 0;
  writeln('Finite State Baseball' : 49);
  writeln;
  writeln('Enter plays under the following code:');
  writeln;
  write(' | ');
  for play := out to error do
    begin
      write(i : 3, '   ', up[play] , '   | ');
      i := i + 1;
      if i in [4, 8, 12, 16, 20] then
        begin
          writeln;
          write(' | ')
        end
    end;
  writeln;
  writeln;
  writeln;
```

```
writeln('Inning #1');
writeln;
writeln(TeamName[false], ' now batting.');
writeln;
GameEnd := false;
while not GameEnd do
  begin
    writeln;
    write('Enter a play: ');                                    { Get a play }
    readln(PlayNo);
    writeln;
    ab := InverseOrd(PlayNo);                                     { Do play }
    if ab in [single..HR, longsingle, shortsingle, longdouble]    { Keep stats }
      then hits := hits + 1;
    if ab = error then errors := errors + 1;
    list[HomeTeam, ab] := list[HomeTeam, ab] + 1;
    writeln(up[ab]);                                          { Describe play }
    writeln;
    batting(ab, B);
    if B then if not GameEnd then                   { Show runners and outs }
      begin
        if odd(st.rnrs div 2) then writeln('    *') else writeln('    -');
        if odd(st.rnrs div 4) then write('*') else write('-');
        if odd(st.rnrs) then write('      *') else write('      -');
        writeln(st.outs : 4, ' outs');
        writeln('    -')
      end
  end { while not GameEnd } ;
writeln;                                                        { Game over }
write('Team     ');
for i := 1 to inning do write(i : 3);               { Show line score and stats }
writeln('      R  H  E');
for Team := false to true do
  begin
    hits :=  list[Team, single] + list[Team, longsingle] +
             list[Team, shortsingle] + list[Team, double] +
             list[Team, longdouble] + list[Team, triple] +
             list[Team, HR];
    errors := list[not Team, error];
    write(TeamName[Team]);
    for i := 1 to inning do
      if innings[Team, i] = -1
        then write('  x')
        else write(innings[Team, i] : 3);
    writeln(' - ', score[Team] : 2, hits : 3, errors : 3)
  end
end { FSMbaseball } .
```

8.19 BINARY FRACTIONS

```
program binfrac(input, output);
  {
     Converts positive decimal fractions to their binary equivalent
  }
  const
    places = 24;                    { Number of bits in mantissa on your computer }
  var
    df : real;
  { The decimal fraction received as input }
    k : 0..places;                            { Running index for repeat loop }
  begin
    writeln('Decimal to Binary Fraction Converter');
    writeln;
    write('Enter a decimal fraction: ');
    while not eof do
      begin
        readln(df);
        df := abs(df);                                  { Make sure df is positive }
        if df >= 1 then writeln(df, ' is not a fraction') else
          begin
            write('   decimal ', df : 10 : 8, ' is binary 0.');
            k := 0;
            repeat                                    { Compute bits of fraction }
              k := k + 1;
              df := 2 * df;                                 { by multiplication }
              write(trunc(df) : 1);                        { Integer part is a bit }
              df := df - trunc(df)             { Fraction is next number to multiply }
            until (df = 0) or (k = places);
            writeln
          end;
        write('Enter a decimal fraction: ')
      end
  end { binfrac }.
```

8.20 SUPERCALC

```
program supercalc(input, output);
  {
    Like program calculator, this program will evaluate expressions of the form

      number op number op number ... op number =

    consisting of numeric constants separated by the operators +, –, *, and / and terminated
    by an = sign followed by an end-of-line. But this version will also allow use of certain
    unary operators that operate on the result developed up to that point of the left to right
    scan. A unary op is followed immediately by another op (or = ).
  }
  var
    result   : real;                                        { Result so far }
    operator : char;                            { Next operation to perform }
    number   : real;                     { Second operand for that operation }

  begin
    write('Calc: ');
    while not eof do
      begin
        result := 0;                         { Pretend operation starts with 0 + }
        operator := '+';
        repeat                          { Evaluate operations from left to right }
          if operator in ['+', '-', '*', '/'] then
            begin
              read(number);                                { Read a numeric operand }
              case operator of
                '+' : result := result + number;
                '-' : result := result – number;
                '*' : result := result * number;
                '/' : result := result / number
              end { dyadic cases }
            end else                                     { Operator must be unary }
              case operator of
                's', 'S' : result := sin(result);
                'c', 'C' : result := cos(result);
                't', 'T' : result := sin(result) / cos(result);
                'e', 'E' : result := exp(result);
                'l', 'L' : result := ln(result);
                'i', 'I' : result := 1 / result;
                'r', 'R' : result := round(result);
                     '2' : result := result * result;
                     '3' : result := result * result * result
              end { unary cases };
          repeat read(operator) until operator <> ' '  { Skip blanks until next op }
        until operator = '=';
        writeln(result : 12 : 5);
        readln;                                  { To advance to next problem }
        write('Calc: ')
      end { while not eof }
  end { calculator } .
```

CHAPTER 9 — PROCEDURES AND FUNCTIONS REVISITED

The principal objective of this chapter is that students learn to define functions of their own. To supplement your lecture examples, we recommend that you assign several of the chapter exercises that require the creation and testing of such functions. Much is made of problems and functions relating to random numbers, partly because we believe that students find such exercises enjoyable, but mostly because use of random numbers is so important to real world problems involving some kind of simulation. If your Pascal has a library random number function, teach your students to use it instead of the one given in the text. But you might still want to cover our *ran* and *ranfrac* to satisfy student curiosity as to how a computer can generate "random" sequences. Also, if your Pascal's random number generator returns random integers, relate it to *ran*; if it returns random fractions, relate it to *ranfrac*.

The chapter material on procedures is partly a review of some things said about procedures in Chapter 4 and partly a recitation of some fine points that serve as much for later reference as for assimilation here. Though Pascal has but two parameter passing mechanisms, call-by-value and call-by-reference, we chose to present them in a somewhat broader context that also allowed us to mention call-by-name. The discussion on this point and the relation to the concept of "binding time" is of importance to you and your class in proportion to the extent that you are teaching an introduction to computer science rather than an introduction to Pascal programming.

You will note that as soon as we discuss user-defined functions, we admit that such function can be recursive. In bringing in recursion so early, we ask you to identify with our premise that teaching how to use recursion is not as hard as understanding how recursion works. The latter concept we defer until the chapter on data structures, the plan being that we try to make students comfortable with the creation and use of stacks first, then apply them to the implementation of recursion. It is important that use of recursion be tackled here, in this chapter, because several of the examples given in the next two chapters on arrays and records use recursion, and because recursion is essential to the effective use of pointers in Chapter 12.

Two of the chapter subsections are marked optional, one that describes how to pass function and procedure names as parameters, and one that describes why at least one of two mutually recursive subprograms must be declared to be *forward*. Not all Pascals allow the first capability, and the need for the second is somewhat rare.

SUGGESTED TEST QUESTIONS

Multiple-Choice Questions (Correct answers are indicated by •)

1. Which of the following is true with regard to procedures and functions?

  a A function must have at least one argument
•b A function must return exactly one answer
  c A procedure must have at least one argument
  d A procedure must return exactly one answer
  e None of the above is true

2. Pascal is fussy about the order of most parts of the declaration section but not about the relative order of parts that start with

  a **const** and **type**
  b **type** and **var**
  c **var** and **function**
•d **function** and **procedure**
  e None of the above; all have a prescribed order

3. When a function changes a global variable or one of its parameters, the change is said to be a

  a disaster
  b byproduct
•c side effect
  d miscalculation
  e none of the above

4. Which of the following is true?

  a The name of every procedure has a particular type
  b A function cannot call a procedure
  c All of a procedure's arguments must have the same type
•d Functions and procedures may have their own declaration section
  e None of the above

5. Any pseudo-random number generator must eventually cycle because of

  a the necessary use of a global variable as a seed
•b the pigeonhole principle
  c coercion
  d binding
  e none of the above

6. How many calls to a random number function are needed in order to produce a random permutation of the integers from 1 to 10?

  a 0
  b 1
•c 9
  d 10
  e 11

7. If the expression *three* * *five* evaluates to 15, then we can conclude that the identifiers *three* and *five* must be

  a constants equated to 3 and 5 respectively
  b variables that have current values of 3 and 5 respectively
  c functions of no argument that return 3 and 5 respectively
•d any of the above might be true
  e none of a through c; you can't do arithmetic with literal names

8. What is printed by the following program?

```
program zephyr(output);
  var
    a, b, c : integer;

  procedure ace(var j : integer; k, m : integer);
    var
      a, c : integer;
    begin
      a := 6;
      c := a - m;
      j := a + c;
      k := 7;
      b := 13
    end { ace };

  begin { main }
    a := 1;
    b := 2;
    c := 3;
    ace(c, b, a);
    writeln(a : 3, b : 3, c : 3)
  end { zephyr }.
```

```
 a 1  2  3
•b 1 13 11
 c 1 13  3
 d 6  2  3
 e 6  2 11
```

9. A certain procedure has the heading

procedure *sputter(a : real;* **var** *b : integer;* c : *integer);*

If *d* is real and *e* and *f* are integers, which of the following is a correct invocation of *sputter*?

a *sputter(7, f, e – f);*
b *sputter(–6.4, e, round(d));*
c *sputter(2.4, f, ord(d > e));*
•d all of the above
e none of a through c

10. A certain function has the header **function** *lucky(n : integer) : Boolean.* Someone tests it and finds that *lucky*(7) returns *true*, *lucky*(2) returns *false*, and *lucky*(5) returns *maybe*. What is your reaction?

a *lucky* must necessarily call a random number function
b *lucky* must necessarily be recursive
c The Pascal translator being used is definitely nonStandard
d There can be no such function; type *Boolean's* only values are *true* and *false*
•e The main program must include declaration of an enumerated type named *Boolean* that supersedes default type *Boolean*

Programming Questions

1. Write a Pascal function *sign* of two arguments *x* and *y* that are both real. This function should return as its value a real result that is the magnitude of *x* with the sign of *y*. If *x* is 0, return 0. If *y* is 0 return the absolute value of *x*. Include your function in a main program that tests it.

2. Write a Pascal function *partner* of one argument *a* that must be an uppercase letter. The function should return as its value the uppercase letter that is as far from the end of the alphabet as *a* is from the beginning. Thus *partner*('A') returns 'Z', *partner*('B') returns 'Y', *partner*('Z') returns 'A', etc. Return a blank ' ' if *a* is not an uppercase letter. Include your function in a main program that tests it.

3. Write a Pascal function $f(x)$ that incorporates the logic

   $f(x) = 0$ for $x < \pi$ or $x > \pi$

   $f(x) = e^{x} \cos^{2} x + e^{-x} \sin^{2} x$ for $\pi \leq x \leq \pi$

   Your function should make as few library function calls as possible. Include your function in a main program that tests it.

4. Write a recursive Pascal procedure *decrev* that has one argument *k* that must be an integer. This procedure should print the decimal reverse of *k*. For example, *decrev(783)* prints 387. Include your procedure in a main program that tests it.

5. Write a recursive Pascal function *digitsum* that has one argument *a* that must be an integer. This function returns the sum of the decimal digits of *a*. For example, *digitsum(732)* returns 12. Include your function in a main program that tests it.

6. Write a recursive Pascal function *dignum* that has two arguments *k* and *d* that must both be integers. This function returns the *d*-th digit from the right of *k*. For example, *dignum(30295, 3)* returns 2 and *dignum(29483, 7)* returns 0. Include your function in a main program that tests it.

7. Write a Pascal function *timediff* with integer arguments *hr1*, *min1*, *sec1*, *hr2*, *min2*, and *sec2* that returns the number of seconds in the time interval between two time readings taken on the same day. Use a 24-hour clock. (The difference will be negative if the second time is earlier than the first. So be it.) Include your function in a main program that tests it.

8. Write a Pascal function *GtrLtr* of two arguments *A1* and *A2* both of which are characters. The function should return *true* if the character *A1* follows the character *A2* in the alphabet and *false* otherwise. This function should work whether *A1* and/or *A2* are upper or lower case. Thus *GtrLtr*('s','E') is *true* and *GtrLtr*('b','g') is *false*. Include your function in a main program that tests it.

SOLUTIONS TO PROGRAMMING EXERCISES

9.7 POW WOW

```
function pow(a : real; n : integer) : real;
  {
    Iterative version of function pow.
  }
  var
    p : real;
  begin { pow }
    p := 1;
    while n > 0 do
      begin
        while not odd(n) do
          begin
            a := sqr(a);
            n := n div 2
          end;
        n := n - 1;
        p := p * a
      end;
    pow := p
  end { pow } ;
```

9.10 FLOORS AND CEILINGS

```
function floor(x : real) : real;
  {
    floor(x) is the largest integer <= x
  }
  begin { floor }
    if x > 0
      then floor := trunc(x)
      else if trunc(x) = x then floor := x else floor := trunc(x) - 1
  end { floor } ;

function ceil(x : real) : real;
  {
    ceil(x) is the smallest integer >= x
  }
  begin { ceil }
    if x < 0
      then ceil := trunc(x)
      else if trunc(x) = x then ceil := x else ceil := trunc(x) + 1
  end { ceil } ;
```

9.12 COMMON LOGS

```
function log10(x : real) : real;
  {
    log to base 10.
  }
  begin { log10 }
    log10 := ln(x) / 2.3025850930                { 2.3025850930 = ln(10) }
  end { log10 } ;

function log2(x : real) : real;
  {
    log to base 2.
  }
  begin { log2 }
    log2 := ln(x) / 0.69314718056                { 0.69314718056 = ln(2) }
  end { log2 } ;
```

9.14 RAISED LETTERS

```
function upper(ch : char) : char;
  {
    Returns the upper case version of the argument if it is a letter, otherwise the unchanged
    argument is returned.
  }
  begin { upper }
    if ch in ['a'..'z']
      then upper := chr(ord(ch) – ord('a') + ord('A'))
      else upper := ch
  end { upper } ;
```

9.15 REAL HEROES

```
function Hero(a, b, c : real) : real;
  {
    Computes the area of a triangle given its three sides.  Returns 0 if the three sides given
    do not make a triangle.
  }
  var
    s, Ay : real;
  begin { Hero }
    s := (a + b + c) / 2.0;                                  { s is semi-perimeter }
    Ay := s * (s – a) * (s – b) * (s – c);                       { Hero's formula }
    if Ay <= 0.0 then Hero := 0.0 else Hero := sqrt(Ay)
  end { Hero } ;
```

9.18 SINE TEST

```
program SineTest(input, output);
  {
    Tests the recursive sine and cosine functions
  }
  var
    s, c, x : real;

  function cosine(x : real) : real; forward;          { Because of mutual recursion }

  function sine(x : real) : real;
    {
      Computes sine(x) recursively.
    }
    const
      epsilon = 0.02;
    begin { sine }
      if abs(x) < epsilon
        then sine := x * (1 – x * x / 6)
        else sine := 2 * sine(x / 2) * cosine(x / 2)
    end { sine } ;

  function cosine{ (x : real) : real } ;
    {
      Computes sine(x) recursively.
    }
    const
      epsilon = 0.02;
    begin { cosine }
      if abs(x) < epsilon
        then cosine := 1 – x * x / 2
        else cosine := sqr(cosine(x / 2)) – sqr(sine(x / 2))
    end { cosine } ;
```

```
begin { main }
  writeln('Test program for sine(x) and cosine(x) functions.');
  writeln;
  write('Enter a value for x: ');
  while not eof do
    begin
      readln(x);
      writeln;
      writeln('sine(',x:0:5,') = ',sine(x):15:13,
              '         cosine(',x:0:5,') = ',cosine(x):15:13);
      writeln(' sin(',x:0:5,') = ',sin(x):15:13,
              '            cos(',x:0:5,') = ', cos(x):15:13);
      writeln;
      write('Enter a value for x: ')
    end
end { SineTest } .
```

9.20 ACKERMANN'S FUNCTION

```
program AckermannsFunction(output);
  {
    Tests the Ackermann Function.
  }
  var
    i,j : integer;

  function A(m, n : integer) : integer;
    {
      Ackermann's function.
    }
    begin
      if m = 0 then A := n + 1 else
      if n = 0 then A := A(m - 1, 1) else
      A := A(m - 1, A(m, n - 1))
    end { A } ;

  begin { main }
    writeln;
    writeln('The Ackermann Function A(n,m)':50);
    writeln;
    write('n \ m    0');
    for j := 1 to 8 do write(j : 8);
    writeln;
    write('---\');
    for j := 0 to 7 do write('--------');
    writeln('-----');
    for i := 0 to 4 do
      begin
        write(i : 1,'   |');
        write(a(i, 0) : 5);                                { For neat spacing }
        if i < 4 then for j := 1 to 8 do write(A(i, j) : 8);
                                                   { Other entries take too long }
        writeln
      end;
    writeln
  end { AckermannsFunction } .
```

9.21 NEGATIVE POWERS

```
function pow(a : real; n : integer) : real;
  {
    Improved function pow which will take negative powers.
  }
  begin { pow }
    if n < 0 then pow := 1 / pow(a, -n) else { Take reciprocal for negative power }
      if n = 0 then pow := 1 else
        if odd(n)
          then pow := a * pow(a, n - 1)
          else pow := sqr(pow(a, n div 2))
  end { pow } ;
```

9.22 LEAP YEAR
9.23 DAY NUMBERS
9.24 DAY TO DAY OPERATIONS

```
function interval(day1, month1, year1, day2, month2, year2 : integer) : integer;
  {
    Returns the number of days between month1/day1/year1 and month2/day2/year2.
  }
  var
    c1, c2 : real;
    ym1 : integer;

  function daynum(day, month, year : integer) : integer;
    {
      Returns the integer corresponding to month/day/year 's position in the year.
    }
    var
      LeapYearCorrection : integer;

    function leap(year : integer) : Boolean;
      {
        Returns true of year is a leap year and false if not.
      }
      begin { leap }
        leap := (year mod 400 = 0) or ((year mod 4 = 0) and (year mod 100 <> 0))
      end { leap } ;

  begin { daynum }
    if leap(year) then LeapYearCorrection := 1 else LeapYearCorrection := 0;
    daynum := 0;
    case month of
       1 : if day <= 31   then daynum := day;
       2 : if day <= 28 + LeapYearCorrection then daynum := 31 + day;
       3 : if day <= 31   then daynum :=  59 + day + LeapYearCorrection;
       4 : if day <= 30   then daynum :=  90 + day + LeapYearCorrection;
       5 : if day <= 31   then daynum := 120 + day + LeapYearCorrection;
       6 : if day <= 30   then daynum := 151 + day + LeapYearCorrection;
       7 : if day <= 31   then daynum := 181 + day + LeapYearCorrection;
       8 : if day <= 31   then daynum := 212 + day + LeapYearCorrection;
       9 : if day <= 30   then daynum := 243 + day + LeapYearCorrection;
      10 : if day <= 31   then daynum := 273 + day + LeapYearCorrection;
      11 : if day <= 30   then daynum := 304 + day + LeapYearCorrection;
      12 : if day <= 31   then daynum := 334 + day + LeapYearCorrection
    end { case }
  end { daynum } ;
```

```
begin { interval }
  c1 := daynum(day1, month1, year1);
  ym1 := year1 - 1;
  c1 := c1 + 365.0 * ym1 + ym1 div 400 - ym1 div 100 + ym1 div 4;
                                    { Days from 0/0/0000 to day1/month1/year1 }
  c2 := daynum(day2, month2, year2);
  ym1 := year2 - 1;
  c2 := c2 + 365.0 * ym1 + ym1 div 400 - ym1 div 100 + ym1 div 4;
                                    { Days from 0/0/0000 to day2/month2/year2 }
  interval := round(c2 - c1)              { Difference is days between dates }
end { interval } ;
```

9.25 MONTHLY PAYMENTS

```
program MonthlyPayments(input, output);
  {
    Compares the various formulas for computing monthly payments due on a loan.
  }
  var
    P, i1, delta, i2, i, limit : real;
    n : integer;

  function pow(a : real; n : integer) : real;
    {
      Returns a to the nth power.
    }
    begin { pow }
      if n = 0 then pow := 1 else
        if odd(n)
          then pow := a * pow(a, n - 1)
          else pow := sqr(pow(a, n div 2))
    end { pow } ;

  function R(P, i : real; n : integer) : real;
    {
      Exact formula.
    }
    var
      t : real;
    begin { R }
      i := i / 100;
      t := pow(1.0 + i / 12.0, n * 12);
      R := P * i * t / (12 * (t - 1))
    end { R } ;

  function R1(P, i : real; n : integer) : real;
    {
      First approximate formula.
    }
    begin { R1 }
      i := i / 100;
      R1 := P * i / (12 * (1 - exp(-i * n)))
    end { R1 } ;

  function R2(P, i : real; n : integer) : real;
    {
      Second approximate formula.
    }
    begin { R2 }
      i := i / 100;
      R2 := P * i / (12 * (1 - exp(-i * n * (1 - i / 24))))
    end { R2 } ;
```

```
begin { main }
  write('Enter Principal: ');
  readln(P);
  writeln; write('Enter Repayment Time in Years: ');
  readln(n);
  writeln; write('Enter Lower Bound for Interest Rate %: ');
  readln(i1);
  writeln; write('Enter Upper Bound for Interest Rate %: ');
  readln(i2);
  writeln; write('Enter Delta for Interest Rate %: ');
  readln(delta);
  writeln; writeln('Monthly payment needed to amortize ',
          P:1:2,' dollars in ',n:1,' years: ');
  writeln;
  writeln('Interest    Exact          1st            2nd');
  writeln(' Rate %     Payment    Approxmiation Approximation');
  writeln('----------------------------------------------------');
  i := i1;
  limit := i2 + delta / 10;
  while i < limit do
    begin
      writeln(i : 5 : 2,R(P,i,n) : 12 : 2,R1(P,i,n) : 14 : 2,R2(P,i,n) : 14 : 2);
      i := i + delta
    end
end { MonthlyPayments } .
```

9.26 SHARPER DARTS

```
program SharperDarts(input, output);
  {
    Approximates pi by "throwing darts" and applying two formulas to the results.
  }
  var
    i, n, hits : integer;
    x, y, sum : real;
    seed : real;

  function ranfrac : real;            { Declare and initialize seed in main program }
    begin seed := 1011.0*seed; seed := seed-trunc(seed); ranfrac := seed end;

  begin { main }
    writeln('Sharper Darts');
    writeln;
    seed := 0.713907;                                      { Initialize seed }
    write('Enter number of trials: ');
    while not eof do
      begin
        readln(n);
        hits := 0;
        sum := 0;
        for i := 1 to n do
          begin
            x := ranfrac;                        { Get two random fractions }
            y := ranfrac;
            if x * x + y * y <= 1.0 then hits := hits + 1;          { Count hits }
            sum := sum + sqrt(1.0 - x * x)         { Accumulate sum using x only }
          end;
        writeln('For ',n:1,' trials, pi[a] = ',4.0 * hits / n:9:7,
                ', pi[b] = ',4.0 * sum / n:9:7);
        writeln; write('Enter number of trials: ')
      end { while not eof }
  end { SharperDarts } .
```

9.27 BUFFON'S NEEDLE

```
program BuffonsNeedle(input, output);
  {
    Approximates pi by simulating the throwing of needles onto a grid.
  }
  var
    i, C, N : integer;
    a, x, seed : real;

  function ranfrac : real;            { Declare and initialize seed in main program }
    begin seed := 1011.0*seed; seed := seed–trunc(seed); ranfrac := seed end;

  begin { main }
    writeln('Buffon''s Needle');
    writeln;
    seed := 0.822357;
    write('Enter number of trials: ');
    while not eof do
      begin
        readln(N);
        C := 0;
        for i := 1 to N do
          begin
            a := 1.5708 * ranfrac;                          { The angle in radians }
            x := ranfrac;                             { Position of the midpoint * 2 }
            if cos(a) > x then C := C + 1 { Increment count if needle crosses a line }
          end;
        writeln('For ',N:1,' trials',', pi = ',2 * N / C : 9 : 7);
        writeln;
        write('Enter number of trials: ')
      end
  end { BuffonsNeedle } .
```

9.28 RACE AGAINST TIME

```
program RaceAgainstTime(output);
  {
    Finds the shortest route from ship to shore.
  }
  const
    trials = 1000;
  var
    x, y, z, told, tnew, f1, f2, f3, factor, seed : real;
    count : integer;

  function ranfrac : real;            { Declare and initialize seed in main program }
    begin seed := 1011.0*seed; seed := seed–trunc(seed); ranfrac := seed end;

  begin { main }
    seed := 0.87654321;                                        { Initialize seed }
    told := 100;
    writeln('Race Against Time');
    writeln;
    writeln('Trial #     x          y         z       Hours');
    for count := 1 to trials do
      begin
        f1 := ranfrac; f2 := ranfrac; f3 := ranfrac;      { Get three random fractions }
        factor := 15 / (f1 + f2 + f3);                   { and corresponding distances }
        x := f1 * factor; y := f2 * factor; z := f3 * factor;
        tnew := sqrt(64.0 + x * x) / 3.0 + y / 5.0 + sqrt(36.0 + z * z) / 4.0;
        if tnew < told then                        { If new time better than old time }
          begin
            told := tnew;            { update old best time and print new best time }
```

```
        writeln(count : 4, x : 10 : 4, y : 8 : 4, z : 8 : 4, tnew : 8 : 4)
      end
    end;
  writeln;
  writeln('Best time in ', trials : 1, ' trials is ', told : 1 : 4, ' hours.');
  writeln;
  writeln('The calculus result (x=6, y=1, z=8) is 6.0333 hours.')
end { RaceAgainstTime } .
```

9.29 TRACK 29

```
program track29(input, output);
  {
  Does a Monte Carlo calculation of the average distance moved by the read head on a
  disk unit.
  }
  var
    i, m, n, trials : integer;
    sum, seed : real;

  function ranfrac : real;            { Declare and initialize seed in main program }
    begin seed := 1011.0*seed; seed := seed–trunc(seed); ranfrac := seed end;
  function ran(i:integer) : integer;  begin ran := trunc((i)*ranfrac) end;

  begin { main }
    seed := 0.986521; sum := 0.0;                                 { Initialization }
    write('Enter number of trials: ');
    readln(trials);
    for i := 1 to trials do
      begin
        m := ran(1000);   n := ran(1000);                        { Get 2 random tracks }
        sum := sum + abs(m – n)                                  { Add in new distance }
      end;
    writeln('After ', trials : 1, ' trials, the average distance moved is ',
            round(sum / trials) : 1, ' tracks.')
  end { track29 } .
```

9.30 AGE OF REASON

```
program AgeOfReason(output);
  {
  Prints seven cards each of which contains 64 numbers. Your age will be the sum of the
  upper left number on each card that contains your age.
  }
  var
    a, i, j, count : integer;
  begin
    a := 1;                                                          { Start with 2^0 }
    for i := 1 to 7 do
      begin
        writeln; writeln('Card-', i : 1); writeln;
        count := 0;
        for j := 1 to 127 do if (j div a) mod 2 = 1 then           { Test for bit of 2^i }
          begin
            write(j : 6);
            count := count + 1;
            if count mod 8 = 0 then writeln                        { For 8 numbers/line }
          end;
        writeln;
        a := a * 2                                               { Get next power of two }
      end
  end { AgeOfReason } .
```

9.31 MAX HEADROOM

```
function max(i, j : integer) : integer;
  {
    Computes the maximum of its two arguments without using a conditional statement.
  }
  begin { max }
    max := (i + j + abs(i - j) ) div 2
  end { max };
```

9.32 TOWER POWER

```
procedure Move(n : disk; a, b : peg);
  {
    Moves n disks from peg a to peg b for Tower of Hanoi problem.
  }
  begin { Move }
    if n > 0 then
      begin
        Move(n - 1, a, 6 - a - b);                          { 6 - a - b is other peg }
        writeln('Move a disk from', a : 2, ' to', b : 2);
        Move(n - 1, 6 - a - b, b)
      end
  end { Move } ;
```

9.33 HEXREP

```
program HexRep(input, output);
  {
    Reads integers and prints their hex representations.
  }
  var
    n : integer;

  procedure WriteHexRep(i : integer);
    {
      Writeln's the hex digits of i.
    }
    procedure MakeHexRep(i, prototype, carry : integer; neg : Boolean);
      {
        Writes i in its hex representation with the same number of hex digits as the hex
        representation of prototype. When i is negative, we will find the digits of its
        positive counterpart and then find its two's complement. We get the two's
        complement by adding one to the one's complement. We get the one's complement
        by subtracting each digit from hex F which is decimal 15.
      }
      var
        digit : integer;

      function hex(n : integer) : char;
        {
          Returns the character which represents the hex digit n.
        }
        begin { hex }
          if n < 10  then hex := chr(n + ord('0'))
                     else hex := chr(n - 10 + ord('A'))
        end { hex } ;

      begin { MakeHexRep }
        if neg then i := -i;                                  { Make i positive }
        digit := i mod 16;                               { Get low order hex digit }
        i := i div 16;                                 { i is now the rest of the number }
        prototype := prototype div 16;          { Shorten prototype by one hex digit }
```

```
    if neg then
      begin
        i := -i;                                      { Restore sign of i }
        digit := 15 - digit + carry;    { One's comp + carry = two's comp }
        carry := digit div 16;                        { In case the carry }
        digit := digit mod 16                   { propagates to other digits }
      end;
    if prototype > 0 then              { Recursive call to compute and write }
      MakeHexRep(i, prototype, carry, neg);     { all the leading digits of i }
      write(hex(digit))                         { then write this digit last }
  end { MakeHexRep } ;

begin { WriteHexRep }
  MakeHexRep(i, maxint, 1, i < 0); writeln
end { WriteHexRep } ;

begin { main }
  write('Enter an integer in range ',-maxint,'..',maxint:1,': ');
  while not eof do
    begin
      readln(n);
      write('The hex form of ',n:1,' is: ');
      WriteHexRep(n); writeln;
      write('Enter an integer in range ',-maxint,'..',maxint:1,': ')
    end
end { HexRep } .
```

CHAPTER 10 — ARRAYS

Students go through an interesting cycle with respect to arrays. First, they can't use them because they don't know about them. Next, they learn about them and use an array for everything, even when one is not needed. In the third stage, they begin to learn about more esoteric data structures and feel that they must use the new tools even in situations where the best choice of structure is the old familiar array. The mature stage, for those few who reach it, is to use exactly the best data structure for the problem at hand. If it's an array, fine, if not, so be it.

We once thought that the concept and use of an array was so simple that no student could possibly have trouble grasping the basic idea very quickly. Since we now know that that is not true, just what is the problem? Certainly it is not the idea of random access to an array component through use of a subscript. Students know what they are getting when they write *A*[*7*]. They may even know what they are getting when they write *A*[*j*]. But how about *A*[*j*,*n*–*j*]? It makes a difference as to whether you ask the student to tell you what is retrieved for given values of *n* and *j* (easy), or ask them to write their own array reference for use in a for loop that processes the components along the minor diagonal of a matrix (apparently hard). That is why we have two sections labeled "subscript management", one for one-dimensional arrays and one for multidimensional ones. Our best advice is to teach the student to use pencil and paper to list what particular subscripts should be for each of the first few values of some running index, and then to generalize to an expression that takes on exactly those values as the index changes.

Here is another of those times when the instructor must make a decision. What is to be your attitude toward variable-length strings? One possibility is to ignore them because Standard Pascal does not support them. If your Pascal is Standard (unlucky you), then you'll just have to show how much of a struggle it is to cope with the fixed-length "strings" that are really (packed) arrays of characters. (But learn the definition carefully; the type *packed* **array**[*1*..*1*] **of** *char* is neither a character nor a string, it's a degenerate one-dimensional array. We can assign a character to a variable of this type only if we append the subscript [*1*] to the variable.) But we sure hate to confess to our students who know some Basic (which is most of them) that Pascal can't even concatenate easily, i.e., there is no Standard operator or procedure for doing so. For this reason we do teach variable-length strings because so many of our favorite Pascal compilers support them. (All six of the "Popular Dialects" cited after the chapter summary do.) Throughout the book, there are many exercises that are fun to do with variable length strings but agony without them. But suit yourself.

In this day and age of excellent screen and printer resolution, we must apologize in some sense for the section of the chapter that shows how to make text-mode screen and printer plots. We do so because we believe that the concept of building a stored image in its entirety before trying to print or display it is an important tool that is quite comprehensible even to beginning students. But since we had no way of coping with the diverse resolution parameters that readers might have available, we show examples that use coarse resolution and expect that you will show how to change to the finer resolution that may be afforded by your particular equipment.

SUGGESTED TEST QUESTIONS

Multiple-Choice Questions (Correct answers are indicated by •)

1. Which of the following is true with regard to array subscripts (indexes)?

   a Subscripts must be integers
   b Subscripts may not be negative
   c Both subscripts used with a two-dimensional array must have the same type.
   •d Elements of an enumerated type may be used as subscripts
   e None of the above

2. Which of the following is not true with regard to arrays?

   a Array subscripts must have ordinal type
   b The upper and lower bound of each array dimension must have the same type
   c All array components must have the same type
   d Array bounds must be named constants or literal constants
   •e All of the above are true

3. Given **var** *A* : **array**[*char*] **of** *real*;

   on a computer that uses ASCII. What can we say about the above?

   a *A* is a two-dimensional array
   •b *A* is a one-dimensional array of size 128
   c *real* should be changed to *char*
   d *char* should be changed to *real*
   e the declaration is syntactically incorrect

4. A procedure parameter that is to be changeable must be declared as a var parameter. Another good reason to use a var parameter is

   a the corresponding actual parameter can then be an expression
   •b the parameter has structured type and we want to avoid copying components
   c all other parameters in the header are var parameters of the same type
   d the parameter is to be named *nish* and it's more polished to write **var** *nish*
   e none of the above is a good reason to use a var parameter

5. Given

```
var
   A : array[0..4, 0..4] of char;
   i, j,k : integer;
begin
   ...
   ...
   for k := 0 to 24 do
      begin
         i := k div 5;
         j := k mod 5;
         A[i, j] := chr(k + 1 + ord('A'))
      end;
```

The **for** loop will fill array *A* with

   a The letters from 'A' to 'X'
   b The letters from 'A' to 'Y'
   •c The letters from 'B' to 'Z'
   d 25 copies of 'A'
   e none of the above

6. Suppose we want to fill **var** *A* : **array**[1..5, 1..5] **of** 0..1 with an alternating pattern of 0's and 1's like this:

i \ j	1	2	3	4	5
1	0	1	0	1	0
2	1	0	1	0	1
3	0	1	0	1	0
4	1	0	1	0	1
5	0	1	0	1	0

The nested for loop structure that will do so can be outlined as

for *i* := 1 **to** 5 **do**
for *j* := 1 **to** 5 **do** *A*[*i*, *j*] := <*expression*>

Which of the following <*expression*>s can be used to do the job?

a *ord*(*odd*(*i* + *j*))
b *ord*(*odd*(*i*) <> *odd*(*j*))
c (*i* + *j*) **mod** 2
•d any of the above
e none of a through c

7. Given **var** *A* : **array**[*Boolean*,*char*] **of** 0..1; how many components does *A* have?

a 2
b 128
•c 256
d 128 if the first index is false, 256 if it is true
e Not enough information to tell

Programming Questions

1. Write a Pascal program that

   i) reads integers into an *n* x *n* array (where *n* is specified in the **const** section)

   ii) uses a procedure of your composition to print the array

   iii) rotates all numbers on the edges of the array clockwise by 1 cell and leaves all interior cells unchanged

   iv) uses the same procedure as written for ii) to print the revised array

```
e.g.    4 3 1 8           2 4 3 1
        2 9 0 3    =>     8 9 0 8
        8 7 2 6           5 7 2 3
        5 1 7 9           1 7 9 6
```

2. Declare a 5 x 5 **array of** *char* and fill it to look as follows:

```
ABCDE
FGHIJ
KLMNO
PQRST
UVWXY
```

You must fill the array component by component; no fair doing five 5-character string assignments.

3. You have defined **type** *SixDigits* = **array**[1 . . 6] **of** *integer*; so that variables of this type can contain up to 5 decimal digits of an unsigned number with the last digit being followed by a −1. Thus if the number were 1234, the elements of the array would be 1, 2, 3, 4, and −1, with the 6th element not used. Write a recursive Pascal **function** *makeint*(*A* : *SixDigits*) : *integer*; that converts the digits in the array *A* to an integer and returns this integer as its value.

4. Suppose that the consecutive integers from 1 to *n* are placed into an *n* x *n* array. For $n = 3$, we might have

```
4 9 2
3 5 7
8 1 6
```

This particular square is "magic" in the sense that every row, column, and diagonal sums to 15. Most *n* x *n* arrangements are not magic. When one is magic, its magic constant must necessarily be $n(n^2 + 1) / 2$.

Given

const *n* = { whatever };
type *square* = **array**[1..*n*, 1..*n*] **of** *integer*;

complete the definition of

function *ismagic*(**var** *s* : *square*) : *Boolean*;
{
Returns *true* iff *s* is magic.
}

Your program must check at most $2n + 2$ sums, but it should stop computing and return *false* if and as soon as it finds a sum that does not equal the magic constant.

5. Given **const** *n* = { whatever }
type *board* = **array**[1..*n*, 1..*n*] **of** *integer*;

Write **function** *checkeredsum*(**var** *B* : *board*) : *integer*; that returns the sum of just those cells of *B*, starting with *B*[1, 1], that form a checkerboard pattern:

sum := *B*[1, 1] + *B*[1, 3] + *B*[1, 5] + ...
+ *B*[2, 2] + *B*[2, 4] + *B*[2, 6] + ...
+ *B*[3, 1] + *B*[3, 3] + *B*[3, 5] + ...
+ ...

Since your function must work for any $n \geq 1$, use loops to do the summation. You may accumulate cell values in any order so long as you do not miss any or use one more than once.

6. You have entered an *n* by *n* table of distances between cities into *distances*, an *n* by *n* array of integers. As a way of checking your input you want to compare the distance from city *i* to city *j* for all pairs (*i*, *j*). The distance from city *i* to city *j* should, of course, be the same as that from city *j* to city *i*. Write procedure *Check*(*distances*) that writes all index pairs for which *distances*[*i*, *j*] <> *distances*[*j*, *i*]. Also include the diagonal elements that are not 0 (i.e. those indices for which *distances*[*i*, *i*] <> 0).

7. You wish to enter an *n* by *n* table of distances between cities into *distances*, an *n* by *n* array of integers. Since the distance from city *i* to city *j* should, of course, be the same as that from city *j* to city *i*, you want to enter only the distances below the diagonal of this array. Write procedure *Enter*(*distances*) that reads only the $n(n - 1) / 2$ entries for which $j < (i - 1)$. Your procedure should then copy the *distances*[*i*, *j*] to *distances*[*j*, *i*] and set *distances*[*i*, *i*] to 0.

8. Mathematical tables that are to be used with interpolation formulas are sometimes printed in the form shown below which is a table of x vs. x^3:

x	x^3	Δ	Δ^2	Δ^3
3.0	27.0			
		37.0		
4.0	64.0		24.0	
		61.0		6.0
5.0	125.0		30.0	
		91.0		6.0
6.0	216.0		36.0	
		127.0		6.0
7.0	343.0		42.0	
		169.0		
8.0	512.0			

The extra columns show what are known as the first (Δ), second (Δ^2), and third (Δ^3) differences. Each difference column is computed by subtracting two successive entries in the column to the left of it. Thus

$$\Delta_i = x_{i+1} - x_i \qquad \Delta^2{}_i = \Delta_{i+1} - \Delta_i \qquad \Delta^3{}_i = \Delta^2{}_{i+1} - \Delta^2{}_i$$

You have defined

type *list* = **array**[1..100] **of** *real*;

Write **procedure** *differences*(*A* : *list*; *n* : *integer*; **var** *diff* : *list*; **var** *m* : *integer*) that computes the $n - 1$ differences of the n entries in the array A and stores them as the $m = n - 1$ entries in the array *diff*. Use this procedure in a main program that prints the table shown above. Use two lines to form the heading (with exponents on the first) and use "del" in place of Δ.

SOLUTIONS TO PROGRAMMING EXERCISES

10.6 ROTATE

```
program rotation(input, output);
  {
    Test of the rotate procedure.
  }
  type
    str = array[0..9] of char;
  var
    s : str;
    pos, i : integer;

  procedure rotate(var a : str; n : integer);
    {
      Rotates the 10-character string a to the left n positions. The rotation will be to the
      right if n is negative.
    }
    var
      i : integer;
      b : str;
    begin { rotate }
      b := a;                                            { Copy a to b }
      while n < 0 do n := n + 10;          { A right shift of n is equivalent to }
                                                  { a left shift of n + 10 }
      for i := 0 to 9 do a[i] := b[(i + n) mod 10]    { Move b back to a rotated }
    end { rotate } ;

  begin { main }
    write('Enter a ten-character string to be rotated left: ');
    while not eof do
      begin
        for i := 0 to 9 do read(s[i]);
        readln;
        write('Enter the number of positions to rotate left:     ');
        readln(pos);
        writeln;
        write('The original string: ');
        for i := 0 to 9 do write(s[i]);
        writeln;
        rotate(s, pos);
        write('The rotated string:  ');
        for i := 0 to 9 do write(s[i]);
        writeln;
        writeln;
        write('Enter a ten-character string to be rotated left: ')
      end
  end { rotation } .
```

10.7 OPPOSITE NUMBERS

```
program OppositeNumbers(input, output);
  {
    Tests procedure opposites.
  }
  const
    n = 6;
  type
    Numbers = array[1..n] of integer;
  var
    A, B, C : Numbers;
    i : integer;
```

```
procedure opposites(a, b : Numbers; var c : Numbers);
  {
    Compares a with b and returns results in c. Therefore
              c[i] = -1 if a[i] < b[i]
              c[i] =  0 if a[i] = b[i]
          and c[i] = +1 if a[i] > b[i].
  }
  var
    i : integer;
  begin { opposites }
    for i := 1 to n do
      if a[i] < b[i] then c[i] := -1 else
      if a[i] > b[i] then c[i] := 1 else c[i] := 0
  end { opposites } ;

begin { main }
  writeln('Opposite Numbers');
  writeln;
  write('Enter the ',n:1,' elements of first array:  ');
  while not eof do
    begin
      write('Enter the ',n:1,' elements of second array: ');
      for i := 1 to n do read(A[i]);
      readln;
      for i := 1 to n do read(B[i]);
      readln;
      writeln;
      opposites(A, B, C);
      write('First array:        ');
      for i := 1 to n do write(A[i] : 6);
      writeln;
      write('Second array:       ');
      for i := 1 to n do write(B[i] : 6);
      writeln;
      write('Opposite numbers: ');
      for i := 1 to n do write(C[i] : 6);
      writeln; writeln;
      write('Enter the ',n:1,' elements of first array:  ')
    end
end { OppositeNumbers }.
```

10.8 BORDER PATROL

```
program border(output);
  {
    Tests procedure clearborder.
  }
  const
    n = 8;
  type
    grid = array[1..n, 1..n] of integer;
  var
    A : grid;

  procedure makearray(var A : grid);
    {
      Creates a nonsense array in A.
    }
    var
      i, j : integer;
    begin { makearray }
      for i := 1 to n do                                  { Create array }
        for j := 1 to n do A[i, j] := i + 2 * j
    end { makearray } ;
```

```
procedure clearborder(var B : grid);
  {
    Uses just one for loop to clear the border components of n x n array B.
  }
  var
    k : integer;
  begin { clearborder }
    for k := 1 to n - 1 do
      begin
        A[1, k]   := 0;
        A[k, n]   := 0;
        A[n, k + 1] := 0;
        A[k + 1, 1] := 0
      end
  end { clearborder } ;

procedure show(A : grid);
  {
    Prints the array A.
  }
  var
    i, j : integer;
  begin { show }
    for i := 1 to n do
      begin
        for j := 1 to n do
          begin
            write(A[i, j] : 4)
          end;
        writeln
      end
  end { show } ;

begin { main }
  makearray(A);
  writeln('Original Array'); writeln;
  show(A);
  clearborder(A);                                   { Clears borders of A }
  writeln; writeln('Cleared Border Array'); writeln;
  show(A)
end { Border } .
```

10.9 LOCAL PEAKS

```
program peaks(input, output);
  {
    Tests procedure LocalPeaks.
  }
  const
    N = 6;                                          { Size of array }
  type
    NxN = array[1..N, 1..N] of integer;
  var
    i, j : integer;
    X : NxN;

  procedure LocalPeaks(a : NxN);
    {
      Finds and prints each element of array a that is greater than the sum of its eight
      neighbors.
    }
    var
      i, j, k, l, sum : integer;
      none : Boolean;
```

```
  function value(a : NxN; i, j : integer) : integer;
    {
      Returns value of a[i, j] but 0 for values outside the borders of array.
    }
    begin { value }
      if (i < 1) or (j < 1) or (i > N) or (j > N)
        then value := 0
        else value := a[i, j]
    end { value } ;

  begin { LocalPeaks }
    writeln;
    none := true;
    for i := 1 to N do
    for j := 1 to N do
      begin                                   { Check each element for a local peak }
        sum := 0;
        for k := i - 1 to i + 1 do
          for l := j - 1 to j + 1 do
            sum := sum + value(a, k, l);
        if a[i, j] > sum - a[i, j] then
          begin
            writeln('Local Peak at A[', i : 1, ',', j : 1, '] = ', a[i, j] : 1);
            none := false
          end
      end;
    if none then writeln('No Local Peaks Found');
    writeln
  end { LocalPeaks } ;

begin { main }
  writeln('Test For Local Peaks');
  writeln;
  writeln('Enter the ', N*N : 1, ' elements of the array: ');
  writeln;
  for i := 1 to N do for j := 1 to N do read(X[i, j]);
  readln;
  writeln;
  writeln('The array: ');
  writeln;
  for i := 1 to N do
    begin
      for j := 1 to N do write(X[i, j] : 8);
      writeln
    end;
  LocalPeaks(X)
end { peaks } .
```

10.10 CORKSCREW

```
program corkscrew(output);
  {
    Produces an N x N corkscrew array.
  }
  const
    N = 20;                           { Set to size of desired square array but <= 20 }
  type
    NxN = array[1..N, 1..N] of integer;
    increment = integer;
  var
    X : NxN;
    i, j, k : integer;
    iinc, jinc : increment;
```

```
procedure Print(A : NxN);
  {
    Prints the array A.
  }
  var
    i, j : integer;
  begin { Print }
    for i := 1 to N do
      begin
        write(A[i, 1] : 3);
        for j := 2 to N do write(A[i, j] : 4);
        writeln
      end
  end { Print } ;

procedure RightTurn(var i, j : increment);
  {
    Adjusts the increments i and j so that they represent a right turn of direction in going
    from point to point in the array.
  }
  begin { RightTurn }
    if i = 0 then
      begin
        i := j;
        j := 0
      end else
      begin
        j := -i;
        i := 0
      end
  end { RightTurn } ;

begin { main }
  for i := 1 to N do                                        { Clear array }
    for j := 1 to N do
      X[i, j] := 0;
  i := 1;                                { Initialize starting point and increments }
  j := 1;
  iinc := 0;
  jinc := 1;
  for k := 1 to N*N do
    begin                              { Go from point to point entering values }
      X[i, j] := k;          { Make a right turn at a boundary or at a nonzero value }
      if (i + iinc > N) or (j + jinc > N) or (j + jinc < 1)
        then RightTurn(iinc, jinc)
        else if X[i + iinc, j + jinc] <> 0 then RightTurn(iinc, jinc);
      i := i + iinc;                    { Add increments to get next possible point }
      j := j + jinc
    end;
  writeln('The ', N : 1, ' by ', N : 1, ' corkscrew array: ');
  writeln;
  print(X)
end { corkscrew } .
```

10.11 LISSAJOUS FIGURES

```
program Lissajous(input, output);
  {
    Displays the Lissajous figure for parametric sine waves of frequency f and phase phi.
  }
  const
    pi = 3.14159265;                stepsize   = 0.01;
    ilim = 11;                      plotchar   = '*';
    jlim = 27;                      ScreenWdith = 80;
  type
    screenarray = array[-ilim..ilim, -jlim..jlim] of char;
  var
    f1,f2 : integer;                                      { Frequencies }
    w1, w2, phi1, phi2 : real;          { Circular frequencies and phases }
    screen : screenarray;

  procedure ClearScreen(var screen : screenarray);
    {
      Clears the screen
    }
    var
      i,j : integer;
    begin { ClearScreen }
      for i := -ilim to ilim do
        for j := -jlim to jlim do screen[i, j] := ' '
    end { ClearScreen } ;

  procedure FillScreen(f1 ,f2:integer; phi1, phi2 : real; var screen : screenarray);
    {
      Plots the figure by filling the screen array.
    }
    var
      w1, w2, t, x, y : real;
      i,j : integer;
    begin { FillScreen }
      w1 := 2 * pi * f1; w2 := 2 * pi * f2;
      phi1 := phi1 * pi / 180; phi2 := phi2 * pi / 180; { Convert angles to radians }
      t := 0;
      while t <= 1.0 do                                   { Plot points }
        begin
          x := sin(w1 * t + phi1); y := sin(w2 * t + phi2);
          i := round(y * ilim); j := round(x * jlim);
          screen[i, j] := plotchar;
          t := t + stepsize
        end
    end { FillScreen } ;

  procedure DisplayScreen(screen : screenarray);
    {
      Displays the screen.
    }
    var
      w1, w2, t : real;
      i,j : integer;
    begin { DisplayScreen }
      for i := -ilim to ilim do
        begin
          for j := 3 to ScreenWdith div 2 - jlim do write(' ');
          for j := -jlim to jlim do write(screen[i, j]); writeln
        end
    end { DisplayScreen } ;
begin { main }
```

```
begin { main }
  write('Enter two frequencies (integers): ');
  readln(f1,f2);
  write('Enter two phase angles (degrees): ');
  readln(phi1,phi2);
  ClearScreen(screen);
  FillScreen(f1,f2,phi1,phi2, screen);
  DisplayScreen(screen)
end { Lissajous }.
```

10.12 PALINDROMES

```
program palindrome(input, output);
  {
    Test sentences to see if they are palindromes when all spaces and punctuation are removed.
  }
  type
    sentence = packed array[1..80] of char;
  var
    m, n : integer;
    p : sentence;

  function pal(p : sentence; n : integer) : Boolean;
    var
      m : integer;

    function upper(c : char) : char;                              { ASCII version }
      begin if c in ['a'..'z'] then upper := chr(ord(c) - 32) else upper := c end;

    begin { pal }
      m := 1;                                                { m points at first character }
      while m < n do                                          { and n at last character }
        begin
          pal := true;
          while not (p[m] in ['A'..'Z', 'a'..'z']) do m := m + 1;         { Skip non- }
          while not (p[n] in ['A'..'Z', 'a'..'z']) do n := n - 1;            { letters }
          if upper(p[m]) = upper(p[n]) then                         { If m and n point to the }
            begin                                                 { same letter you may have }
              m := m + 1;                                         { a palindrome, so bump m }
              n := n - 1                                                          { and n }
            end else n := 0;                                              { If not, leave loop }
          pal := n <> 0                     { If we left loop because n = 0, not a palindrome }
        end
    end { pal } ;

  begin { main }
    writeln('Palindrome Tester'); writeln;
    write('Enter a sentence to test: ');
    while not eof do
      begin
        n := 0;
        while not eoln do                                               { Get an input line }
          begin
            n := n + 1;
            read(p[n])
          end;
        readln;
        write('"');
        for m := 1 to n do write(p[m]);                                    { Echo input line }
        write('" is '); if not pal(p, n) then write('not ');
        writeln('a Palindrome.'); writeln;
        write('Enter a sentence to test: ')
      end
  end { palindrome } .
```

10.13 SMARTER BUBBLES

```
procedure Bubblesort(var A : list; n : integer);
  {
    Sorts first n elements of A[1..lim], n <= lim. Quits as soon as it detects that there
    were no exchanges on the preceding pass, and begins comparisons at an index one less
    than wherever the first exchange occurred on prior pass.
  }
  var
    j, k, t : integer;
    firstk : integer;                { min(1, index of 1st exchange on prior pass – 1 }
    sorted : Boolean;
  begin
    firstk := 1;                     { Initialize to 1 since there hasn't yet been a pass }
    j := 1;                          { Counts passes. We will do at most n – 1 passes }
    repeat
      sorted := true;                { Will remain true only if there are no exchanges }
      if firstk = 0 then firstk := 1;
      for k := 1 to n – j do         { Each pass does 1 less comparison than prior one }
        if A[k] > A[k + 1] then                                          { Exchange }
          begin
            t := A[k];
            A[k] := A[k + 1];
            A[k + 1] := t;
            if sorted then                               { This is first exchange, so }
              begin
                firstk := k – 1;                     { save index of 1st exchange – 1 }
                sorted := false
              end
          end;
      j := j + 1
    until (j = n) or sorted
  end { Bubblesort };
```

10.14 SELECTION SORT

```
procedure SelectionSort(var A : list; n : integer);
  {
    Sorts the array A using the selection sort algorithm.
  }
  var
    i, j, min, mindex, temp : integer;
  begin { SelectionSort }
    for i := 1 to n – 1 do                                    { Do ith of n – 1 passes }
      begin
        min := A[i];                        { Initialize min as first number not yet sorted }
        mindex := i;                                           { and its index (mindex) }
        for j := i + 1 to n do                     { Search through array for a smaller one }
          if A[j] < min then                                    { Each time we find one, }
            begin
              min := A[j];                                             { keep its value }
              mindex := j                                                  { and index }
            end;
        temp := A[i];                                           { Switch it to its place }
        A[i] := A[mindex];
        A[mindex] := temp
      end
  end { SelectionSort } ;
```

10.16 TRANSPOSE

```
program TransposeTest(output);
  {
   Creates a square matrix and transposes it.
  }
  const
   n = 8;                                                  { Size of matrix }
  type
   matrix = array[1..n, 1..n] of real;
  var
   MAT : matrix;

  procedure make(var A : matrix; n : integer);
    {
     Creates an n x n nonsense matrix A.
    }
    var
     i, j, k : integer;
    begin { make }
     k := 0;
     for i := 1 to n do                                    { Create a matrix }
       for j := 1 to n do
         begin
           A[i, j] := k;
           k := k + 1
         end
    end { make } ;

  procedure show(A : matrix; n : integer);
    {
     Prints a matrix.
    }
    var
     i, j : integer;
    begin { show }
     for i := 1 to n do
       begin
         for j := 1 to n do write(A[i, j] : 7 : 1);
         writeln
       end;
     writeln
    end { show } ;

  procedure transpose(var A : matrix; n : integer);
    {
     Transposes a matrix.
    }
    var
     i, j : integer;
     temp : real;
    begin { transpose }
     for i := 2 to n do
       for j := 1 to i - 1 do
         begin                                             { Exchange A[i, j] with A[j, i] }
           temp := A[i, j];
           A[i, j] := A[j, i];
           A[j, i] := temp
         end
    end { transpose } ;
```

```
  begin { main }
    make(MAT, n);                                  { Make a matrix MAT }
    writeln('Original Matrix');                              { Print it }
    show(MAT, n);
    transpose(MAT, n);                                   { Transpose it }
    writeln('Transposed Matrix');                    { Print transpose }
    show(MAT, n)
  end { TransposeTest } .
```

10.17 SADDLE POINT

```
program SaddlePoint(input, output);
  {
    Finds saddle points in an array.
  }
  type
    arrray = array[1..20, 1..20] of integer;
  var
    r, c, k, minrow, maxrow, mincol, maxcol, nrows, ncols : integer;
    A : arrray;
    found1, found2, repeated : Boolean;

  procedure show(A : arrray; nrows, ncols : integer);
    {
      Prints an arrray.
    }
    var
      i, j : integer;
    begin { show }
      for i := 1 to nrows do
        begin
          for j := 1 to ncols do write(A[i, j] : 4);
          writeln
        end;
      writeln
    end { show } ;

  begin { main }
    writeln('Saddle Point Finder');
    writeln;
    write('Enter the number of rows in the array (maximum is 20): ');
    readln(nrows);
    writeln;
    write('Enter the number of cols in the array (maximum is 20): ');
    readln(ncols);
    writeln;
    writeln('Enter the ', nrows * ncols : 1, ' elements of the array');
    writeln;
    for r := 1 to nrows do                         { Read array elements }
      for c := 1 to ncols do read(A[r, c]);
    writeln;
    writeln('The array');
    writeln;
    show(A,nrows,ncols);
    found1 := false;
    r := 1;
    while (r <= nrows) and (not found1) do    { Search each row for minimum }
      begin
        mincol := 1;                  { which will occur at mincol initialized to 1 }
        repeated := false;   { For checking if minimum element is duplicated on row }
```

```
      for c := 2 to ncols do
        if A[r, c] = A[r, mincol]                            { Minimum is repeated }
          then repeated := true else
        if A[r, c] < A[r, mincol] then
          begin
            mincol := c;                                   { New minimum is found }
            repeated := false                                  { for the first time }
          end;
      if not repeated then              { If minimum is repeated then no saddle point }
        begin                    { Search column mincol for row of maximum element }
          maxrow := 1;                                   { which will occur at maxrow }
          for k := 2 to nrows do
            if A[k, mincol] = A[maxrow, mincol]                { Maximum is repeated }
              then repeated := true else
            if A[k, mincol] > A[maxrow, mincol] then
              begin
                maxrow := k;                               { New maximum is found }
                repeated := false                              { for the first time }
              end;
          if maxrow = r then found1 := not repeated                 { Saddle point if }
                                               { maximum is in row r and not repeated }
        end;
      r := r + 1
    end;
  if found1 then
    writeln('A[', maxrow :1, ',', mincol : 1, '] = ', A[maxrow, mincol] : 1,
          ' is a row-low, column-high saddle point.');
  found2 := false;
  r := 1;
  while (r <= nrows) and (not found2) do        { Search each row for maximum }
    begin
      maxcol := 1;                       { which will occur at maxcol initialized to 1 }
      repeated := false;  { For checking if maximum element is duplicated on row }
      for c := 2 to ncols do
        if A[r, c] = A[r, maxcol]
          then repeated := true else                         { Maximum is repeated }
        if A[r, c] > A[r, maxcol] then
          begin
            maxcol := c;                                   { New maximum is found }
            repeated := false                                  { for the first time }
          end;
      if not repeated then              { If maximum is repeated then no saddle point }
        begin                    { Search column maxcol for row of minimum element }
          minrow := 1;                                   { which will occur at minrow }
          for k := 2 to nrows do
            if A[k, maxcol] = A[minrow, maxcol]                { Minimum is repeated }
              then repeated := true else
            if A[k, maxcol] < A[minrow, maxcol] then
              begin
                minrow := k;                               { New minimum is found }
                repeated := false                              { for the first time }
              end;
          if minrow = r then found2 := not repeated                 { Saddle point if }
                                               { minimum is in row r and not repeated }
        end;
      r := r + 1
    end;
  if found2 then
  writeln('A[', minrow : 1, ',', maxcol : 1, '] = ', A[minrow, maxcol] : 1,
        ' is a row-high, column-low saddle point.');
  if (not found1) and (not found2) then writeln('No saddle point found.')
end { SaddlePoint } .
```

10.18 I-CHING

```
program IChing(output);
  {
    Creates an array holding the I-Ching tableau and displays it.
  }
  var
    i, j, k : integer;
    ich : array[0..7, 0..7] of array[0..5] of packed array[1..7] of char;

  function bit(j, i : integer) : char;
    {
      Returns the character '_' for 0 or ' ' for 1 corresponding to the jth bit of i (counting
      from the right).
    }
    var
      k: integer;
    begin { bit }
      for k := 1 to j do i := i div 2;
      if odd(i) then bit := ' ' else bit := '_'
    end { bit } ;

  begin { main }
    for i := 0 to 7 do                          { Create the array where i is the block row }
    for j := 0 to 7 do                                         { j is the block column }
    for k := 0 to 5 do                                    { k is the row within the block }
      begin
        ich[i, j][k] := '_______';
        ich[i, j][k][4] := bit(k, i * 8 + j)              { Fill in bit that depends on i and j }
      end;
    writeln('The I-Ching Tableau');
    writeln;
    for i := 0 to 7 do                                                  { Print the tableau }
      begin
        for k := 5 downto 0 do
          begin
            for j := 0 to 7 do write(ich[i, j][k], '   ');
            writeln
          end;
        writeln;
        writeln
      end
  end { IChing } .
```

10.20 TOURING MACHINE

```
program TouringMachine(input, output);
  {
    Simulates the Touring Machine.
  }
  type
    grid = array[0..21, 0..16] of integer;
  var
    i, j, max, m, n, r, c, count, mov : integer;
    g : grid;
    seed : real;
```

```
procedure move(var i, j : integer; g : grid);
  {
    Does one move of the Touring Machine by moving one step in a random direction
    and updating the input coordinates i and j to new values.
  }
  var
    iinc, jinc : integer;

  function ranfrac : real;                { Declare and initialize seed in main program }
    begin seed := 1011.0*seed; seed := seed–trunc(seed); ranfrac := seed end;
  function ran(i:integer) : integer;  begin ran := trunc((i)*ranfrac) end;

  begin { move }
    iinc := 0; jinc := 0;
    while (iinc = 0) and (jinc = 0) do
      begin
        case ran(8) of
          0 : begin iinc := –1;    jinc := –1 end;
          1 : begin iinc := –1;    jinc :=  0 end;
          2 : begin iinc := –1;    jinc :=  1 end;
          3 : begin iinc :=  0;    jinc := –1 end;
          4 : begin iinc :=  0;    jinc :=  1 end;
          5 : begin iinc :=  1;    jinc := –1 end;
          6 : begin iinc :=  1;    jinc :=  0 end;
          7 : begin iinc :=  1;    jinc :=  1 end
        end { case } ;
        if g[i + iinc, j + jinc] = –1 then
          begin                              { Generated move is illegal, so try again }
            iinc := 0;
            jinc := 0
          end
      end;
    i := i + iinc;
    j := j + jinc
  end { move } ;

begin { main }
  writeln('Touring Machine');
  writeln;
  writeln('Maximum grid size is 20 rows by 15 columns');
  writeln;
  write('Enter grid size -> rows  columns: ');
  readln(m, n);
  writeln;
  write('Enter starting point -> row  column: ');
  readln(i, j);
  writeln;
  write('Enter number of moves: ');
  readln(max);
  writeln;
  seed := 0.87654321;
  for r := 0 to m + 1 do                     { Put a border of –1's around the grid }
    begin
      g[r, 0] := –1;
      g[r, n + 1] := –1
    end;
  for c := 1 to n do
    begin
      g[0, c] := –1;
      g[m + 1, c] := –1
    end;
  for r := 1 to m do                               { and initialize all grid points to 0 }
    for c := 1 to n do g[r, c] := 0;
```

```
  mov := 0;
  count := 0;
  while (count < m * n) and (mov < max) do
    begin                        { Move until all points visited or for max moves }
      move(i, j, g);
      if g[i, j] = 0 then count := count + 1;           { Update point counter, }
      g[i, j] := g[i, j] + 1;                            { and visits to each point, }
      mov := mov + 1                                                 { and moves }
    end;
  writeln('Record of Visits');                                    { Show results }
  writeln;
  for r := 1 to m do
    begin
      for c := 1 to n do write(g[r, c] : 5);
      writeln
    end;
  writeln; writeln(mov : 1, ' moves were made.');
  if count = m * n then write('All ');
  write(count : 1, ' points');
  if count <> m * n then write(' out of ', m * n : 1);
  writeln(' were visited.')
end { TouringMachine } .
```

10.21 CLOSE ENCOUNTERS

```
program CloseEncounters(input, output);
  {
    Simulates two robots and computes close encounters of the nth kind.
  }
  type
    grid = array[0..21, 0..16] of integer;
  var
    k, m, n, r, c, count, mov, robot, sign, trace, idif, jdif : integer;
    i, j, sightings, evidence, contacts : array[1..2] of integer;
    g : grid;
    seed : real;

  procedure move(var i1, j1 : integer; i2, j2 : integer; g : grid);
    {
      Does one move of a robot at i1 and j1 by updating these input coordinates to new
      output values.  It will not move to the location i2, j2.
    }
    var
      iinc, jinc : integer;

    function ranfrac : real;          { Declare and initialize seed in main program }
      begin seed := 1011.0*seed; seed := seed-trunc(seed); ranfrac := seed end;
    function ran(i:integer) : integer;  begin ran := trunc((i)*ranfrac) end;

    begin { move }
      iinc := 0; jinc := 0;
      while (iinc = 0) and (jinc = 0) do
        begin
          case ran(8) of
            0 : begin iinc := -1;    jinc := -1 end;
            1 : begin iinc := -1;    jinc :=  0 end;
            2 : begin iinc := -1;    jinc :=  1 end;
            3 : begin iinc :=  0;    jinc := -1 end;
            4 : begin iinc :=  0;    jinc :=  1 end;
            5 : begin iinc :=  1;    jinc := -1 end;
            6 : begin iinc :=  1;    jinc :=  0 end;
            7 : begin iinc :=  1;    jinc :=  1 end
          end { case } ;
```

```
      if (g[i1 + iinc, j1 + jinc] = -1) or ((i1 + iinc = i2) and (j1 + jinc = j2)) then
        begin                                    { Generated move is illegal, so try again }
          iinc := 0;
          jinc := 0
        end
    end;
   i1 := i1 + iinc;
   j1 := j1 + jinc
  end { move } ;

begin { main }
  writeln('Close Encounters'); writeln;
  writeln('Maximum grid size is 20 rows by 15 columns');
  writeln;
  write('Enter grid size -> rows  columns: ');
  readln(m, n);
  writeln;
  write('Enter starting point for robot #1 -> row  column: ');
  readln(i[1], j[1]);
  write('Enter starting point for robot #2 -> row  column: ');
  readln(i[2], j[2]);
  writeln;
  write('Enter number of moves for each robot: ');
  readln(k);
  writeln;
  write('Enter number of moves that trace lasts: ');
  readln(trace);
  writeln;
  seed := 0.87654321;
  for r := 0 to m + 1 do                        { Put a border of -1's around the grid }
    begin
      g[r, 0] := -1;
      g[r, n + 1] := -1
    end;
  for c := 1 to n do
    begin
      g[0, c] := -1;
      g[m + 1, c] := -1
    end;
  for r := 1 to m do for c := 1 to n do g[r, c] := 0;          { Initialize grid to 0 }
  for robot := 1 to 2 do                                      { Initialize counters }
    begin
      sightings[robot] := 0;
      evidence[robot] := 0;
      contacts[robot] := 0
    end;
  mov := 0; count := 0; sign := 1;
  for mov := 1 to k do
    for robot := 1 to 2 do
      begin
        idif := abs(i[1] - i[2]);                             { Test for sightings }
        jdif := abs(j[1] - j[2]);
        if (idif = 0) or (jdif = 0) or (idif = jdif)  then
          sightings[robot] := sightings[robot] + 1;
        if (idif < 2) and (jdif < 2) then                          { and contacts }
          contacts[robot] := contacts[robot] + 1;
        move(i[robot], j[robot], i[3 - robot], j[3 - robot], g);         { Move robot }
        if (sign * g[i[robot], j[robot]] + robot > mov - trace + 1) and
              (sign * g[i[robot], j[robot]] > 0) then            { Test for evidence }
            evidence[robot] := evidence[robot] + 1;
        sign := -sign;                   { Evidence is + for robot 1 and - for robot 2 }
        g[i[robot], j[robot]] := mov * sign          { Store evidence for other robot }
      end;
```

```
  writeln('Record of Encounters                    Robot #1    Robot #2');
  writeln('---------------------------------------------------------');
  writeln('Close encounters of the first kind:  ',
          sightings[1] : 5, sightings[2] : 11);
  writeln('Close encounters of the second kind: ',
          evidence[1] : 5, evidence[2] : 11);
  writeln('Close encounters of the third kind:  ',
          contacts[1] : 5, contacts[2] : 11)
end { CloseEncounters } .
```

10.22 CALENDAR

```
program Calendar(input, output);
  {
    Generates a calendar for any year given the first day of the year.
  }
  type
    yeartype = array[1..4] of array[1..3] of array[1..6, 1..7] of integer;
    daysin = array[1..4] of array[1..3] of integer;
    dayname = packed array[1..3] of char;
  var
    YR : yeartype;
    days : daysin;
    year : integer;
    weekday : dayname;

  procedure makedaytable(year : integer; var days : daysin);
    {
      Sets up the table of days for year.
    }
    function leap(year : integer) : Boolean;
      {
        Return true for leap years and false otherwise.
      }
      begin { leap }
        leap := (year mod 400 = 0) or ((year mod 4 = 0) and (year mod 100 <> 0))
      end { leap } ;

    begin { makedaytable }
      days[1][1] := 31;
      if leap(year) then days[1][2] := 29 else days[1][2] := 28;
      days[1][3] := 31;
      days[2][1] := 30;
      days[2][2] := 31;
      days[2][3] := 30;
      days[3][1] := 31;
      days[3][2] := 31;
      days[3][3] := 30;
      days[4][1] := 31;
      days[4][2] := 30;
      days[4][3] := 31
    end { makedaytable } ;

  procedure makeyear(day : dayname; var YR : yeartype);
    {
      Creates the year in the YR array.
    }
    var
      i, j, k, date, date1, row, first : integer;
```

```
function daycode(day : dayname) : integer;
  {
    Returns the daycode for the day of the week i.e. Sun = 1, Mon = 2 etc.
  }
  function upper(c : char) : char;                              { ASCII version }
    begin if c in ['a'..'z'] then upper := chr(ord(c) - 32) else upper := c end;

  begin { daycode }
    case upper(day[1]) of
      'S' : case upper(day[2]) of
              'U' : daycode := 1;
              'A' : daycode := 7
            end { case day[2] } ;
      'M' : daycode := 2;
      'T' : case upper(day[2]) of
              'U' : daycode := 3;
              'H' : daycode := 5
            end { case day[2] } ;
      'W' : daycode := 4;
      'F' : daycode := 6
    end { case day[1] }
  end { daycode } ;

begin { makeyear }
  first := daycode(day);
  k := 1;
  for i := 1 to 4 do
    for j := 1 to 3 do
      begin
        while k < first do                          { Fill in 0's for leading days }
          begin
            YR[i][j][1][k] := 0;
            k := k + 1
          end;
        date := 1; row := 1;
        while row < 7 do    { Maximum of 6 rows will be done for all months }
          begin
            if date <= days[i][j]
              then date1 := date else date1 := 0;          { 0's for trailing days }
            YR[i][j][row][k] := date1;
            k := k + 1;
            if k > 7 then
              begin
                k := 1;
                row := row + 1
              end;
            date := date + 1
          end;
        first := ((first - 1 + days[i][j]) mod 7) + 1              { For next month }
      end
end { makeyear };

procedure printyear(year : integer; YR : yeartype);
  {
    Prints the array YR with heading year in a 4 x 3 grid of months.
  }
  var
    i, j, k, row : integer;
```

```
procedure print(day : integer);
  {
    Writes day, or blanks when day = 0.
  }
  begin { print }
    if day = 0 then write('      ') else write(day : 3)
  end { print } ;

begin { printyear }
  writeln(year : 37); writeln;
  for i := 1 to 4 do
    begin
      case i of
        1 : writeln('         January                    February',
                    '                  March');
        2 : writeln('          April                        May',
                    '                   June');
        3 : writeln('           July                      August',
                    '                September');
        4 : writeln('         October                    November',
                    '                December')
      end { case } ;
      writeln;
      for j := 1 to 3 do write('  S  M  T  W  T  F  S   ');
      writeln;
      for row := 1 to 6 do
        begin
          for j := 1 to 3 do
            begin
              for k := 1 to 7 do print(YR[i][j][row][k]);
              write('   ')
            end;
          writeln
        end;
      writeln
    end
end { printyear } ;

begin
  write('Calendar for what year? ');
  readln(year);
  makedaytable(year, days); writeln;
  writeln('January 1 of ',year:4,' is on what day of the week? ');
  write('Enter Sun, Mon, Tue, Wed, Thu, Fri, Sat: ');
  readln(weekday[1], weekday[2], weekday[3]); writeln;
  makeyear(weekday, YR);
  printyear(year, YR)
end { Calendar } .
```

10.23 POKER HANDS

```
program PokerHands(input, output);
  {
    Generates random poker hands and evaluates them.
  }
  type
    suit = (Club, Diamond, Heart, Spade);
    value = (two, three, four, five, six, seven, eight, nine, ten, Jack, Queen,
             King, Ace);
    deck = array[0..51] of integer;
    suitcards = array[suit] of integer;
    valuecards = array[value] of integer;
```

```
var
  d : deck;
  sc : suitcards;
  vc : valuecards;
  i, hands, count : integer;
  seed : real;
  flush, straight : Boolean;

function ranfrac : real;              { Declare and initialize seed in main program }
  begin seed := 1011.0*seed; seed := seed-trunc(seed); ranfrac := seed end;
function ran(i:integer) : integer;  begin ran := trunc((i)*ranfrac) end;

function InverseSuitOrd(n : integer) : suit;
  {
    InverseSuitOrd returns a value of type suit such that ord(InverseSuitOrd(n)) = n.
    Thus InverseSuitOrd is the inverse function to ord applied to variables of type suit.
  }
  var
    i : integer;
    s : suit;
  begin { InverseSuitOrd }
    s := Club;
    if n < 4 then
      for i := 1 to n do s := succ(s);
    InverseSuitOrd := s
  end { InverseSuitOrd } ;

function InverseValOrd(n : integer) : value;
  {
    InverseValOrd returns a value of type value such that ord(InverseValOrd(n)) = n.
    Thus InverseValOrd is the inverse function to ord applied to variables of type value.
  }
  var
    i : integer;
    v : value;
  begin { InverseValOrd }
    v := two;
    if n < 13 then
      for i := 1 to n do v := succ(v);
    InverseValOrd := v
  end { InverseValOrd } ;

procedure WriteCard(S : suit; V : value);
  {
    Writes the card with suit S and value V.
  }
  begin { WriteCard }
    case S of
        Club : write('C');
     Diamond : write('D');
       Heart : write('H');
       Spade : write('S')
    end { case } ;
    case V of
         two : write('2');
       three : write('3');
        four : write('4');
        five : write('5');
         six : write('6');
       seven : write('7');
       eight : write('8');
        nine : write('9');
         ten : write('T');
```

```
      Jack : write('J');
     Queen : write('Q');
      King : write('K');
       Ace : write('A')
    end { case } ;
    write(' ')
  end { WriteCard } ;

procedure deal(var sc : suitcards; var vc : valuecards);
  {
   Deals and writes a hand of 5 cards and remembers the number of each value dealt in
   the array vc and the number of each suit dealt (except for 2's) in the array sc.
  }
  var
    i, r, card : integer;
    s : suit;
    v : value;
  begin { deal }
    write('Hand number ', count : 1, ': ');
    for s := Club to Spade do sc[s] := 0;                        { Clear arrays }
    for v := two to Ace do vc[v] := 0;
    for i := 0 to 4 do
      begin
        r := ran(52-i) + i;                                      { Deal a card }
        card := d[r];
        d[r] := d[i];
        d[i] := card;
        s := InverseSuitOrd(card div 13);
        v := InverseValOrd(card mod 13);
        WriteCard(s, v);                                            { Write it }
        if v <> two then sc[s] := sc[s] + 1;           { Increment totals in arrays }
        vc[v] := vc[v] + 1
      end
  end { deal } ;

procedure evaluate(sc : suitcards; vc : valuecards);
  {
   Evaluates a poker hand based on the arrays vc and sc created by deal.
  }
  var
    OfaKind : array[0..5] of integer;
    i, wild, str : integer;
    s : suit;
    v, vtemp, vstr : value;
    flush, straight : Boolean;
  begin { evaluate }
    wild := vc[two];                                     { Number of wild cards }
    vc[two] := 0;
    for i := 0 to 5 do OfaKind[i] := 0;            { Count how many of each value }
    for v := three to Ace do OfaKind[vc[v]] := OfaKind[vc[v]] + 1;
    flush := false;                          { There is a flush if any suit + wild = 5 }
    for s := Club to Spade do Flush := Flush or (sc[s] + wild = 5);
    straight := false;
    v := Ace;
    while (v > four) and not straight do
      begin
        vtemp := v;                                        { Test for straight }
        if vc[vtemp] <> 0
          then str := 1
          else str := 0;
```

```
      for i := 2 to 5 do
        begin
          if vtemp > two then
            begin
              vtemp := pred(vtemp);
              if vc[vtemp] <> 0 then str := str + 1
            end
        end;
      straight := str + wild = 5;                          { or a wild card }
      vstr := v;
      v := pred(v)
    end;
  write('is ');                                     { Write the evaluation }
  if straight and flush and (vstr = Ace) then writeln('a royal flush.') else
  if straight and flush then writeln('a straight flush.') else
  if OfaKind[5 - wild] > 0 then writeln('five of a kind.') else
  if OfaKind[4 - wild] > 0 then writeln('four of a kind.') else
  if ((OfaKind[3] > 0) and (OfaKind[2 - wild] > 0))
    or ((OfaKind[2] = 2) and (wild > 0))
      then writeln('a full house.') else
  if flush then writeln('a flush.') else
  if straight then writeln('a straight.') else
  if OfaKind[3 - wild] > 0 then writeln('three of a kind.') else
  if (OfaKind[2] + wild > 1) then writeln('two pair.') else
  if OfaKind[2 - wild] <> 0
    then writeln('one pair.')
    else writeln('a bust.')
end { evaluate } ;

begin { main }
  write('How many hands do you want to generate? ');
  readln(hands);
  writeln;
  seed := 0.987654321;
  for i := 0 to 51 do d[i] := i;
  for count := 1 to hands do
    begin
      deal(sc, vc);
      evaluate(sc, vc)
    end
end { PokerHands } .
```

10.24 BRIDGE HAND

```
program BridgeHand(input, output);
  {
    Evaluates bridge hands read as input or generated randomly.
  }
  const
    printlimit = 18;                  { At least printlimit points to print a hand }
  type
    suit = (Club, Diamond, Heart, Spade);
    value = (two, three, four, five, six, seven, eight, nine, ten, Jack, Queen, King, Ace);
    hand = array[suit, value] of Boolean;
    deck = array[0..51] of integer;
    suitcards = array[suit] of integer;
    valuecards = array[value] of integer;
  var
    sc : suitcards;
    vc : valuecards;
    hands, count, points, i : integer;
    d : deck;
    South : hand;
```

```
  ch : char;
  DealHands : Boolean;
  PointSum, seed : real;

function InverseSuitOrd(n : integer) : suit;
  {
    InverseSuitOrd returns a value of type suit such that ord(InverseSuitOrd(n)) = n.
    Thus InverseSuitOrd is the inverse function to ord applied to variables of type suit.
  }
  var
    i : integer;
    s : suit;
  begin { InverseSuitOrd }
    s := Club;
    if n < 4 then
      for i := 1 to n do s := succ(s);
    InverseSuitOrd := s
  end { InverseSuitOrd } ;

function InverseValOrd(n : integer) : value;
  {
    InverseValOrd returns a value of type value such that ord(InverseValOrd(n)) = n.
    Thus InverseValOrd is the inverse function to ord applied to variables of type value.
  }
  var
    i : integer;
    v : value;
  begin { InverseValOrd }
    v := two;
    if n < 13 then
      for i := 1 to n do v := succ(v);
    InverseValOrd := v
  end { InverseValOrd } ;

procedure Deal(var sc : suitcards; var vc : valuecards; var South : hand);
  {
    Deals a bridge hand.  The card deck is stored as integers in the array d, and 13
    random cards are selected from d.  As these cards are entered into the South hand,
    the number of each suit and value is counted in sc and vc.
  }
  var
    i, r, card : integer;
    s : suit;
    v : value;

  function ranfrac : real;              { Declare and initialize seed in main program }
    begin seed := 1011.0*seed; seed := seed-trunc(seed); ranfrac := seed end;
  function ran(i:integer) : integer;  begin ran := trunc((i)*ranfrac) end;

  begin { Deal }
    for i := 0 to 12 do
      begin
        r := ran(52 - i) + i;                              { r will be between i and 51 }
        card := d[r];                                      { Switch card i with card r }
        d[r] := d[i];
        d[i] := card;
        s := InverseSuitOrd(card div 13);                                  { Get suit }
        v := InverseValOrd(card mod 13);                                  { and value }
        South[s, v] := true;                                { and put in South hand }
        sc[s] := sc[s] + 1;                                     { Count of each suit }
        vc[v] := vc[v] + 1                                     { Count of each value }
      end
  end { Deal };
```

```
procedure ReadHand(var sc : suitcards; var vc : valuecards; var South : hand);
  {
    A bridge hand is read from input. As these cards are read into the South hand, the
    number of each suit and value is counted in sc and vc.
  }
  var
    i : integer;
    s : suit;
    v : value;

  procedure ReadCard(var S : suit; var V : value);
    {
      Reads a card. Suit goes to S and value to V.
    }
    var
      ch : char;
    begin { ReadCard }
      read(ch);                                          { Reads suit }
      case ch of
        'C', 'c' : S := Club;
        'D', 'd' : S := Diamond;
        'H', 'h' : S := Heart;
        'S', 's' : S := Spade
      end { case } ;
      read(ch);                                          { Reads value }
      case ch of
             '2' : V := two;
             '3' : V := three;
             '4' : V := four;
             '5' : V := five;
             '6' : V := six;
             '7' : V := seven;
             '8' : V := eight;
             '9' : V := nine;
        'T', 't' : V := ten;                             { Uses "T" or "t" for 10 }
        'J', 'j' : V := Jack;
        'Q', 'q' : V := Queen;
        'K', 'k' : V := King;
        'A', 'a' : V := Ace
      end { case } ;
      if eoln then readln else read(ch)                  { Skips next character }
    end { ReadCard } ;

  begin { ReadHand }
    for i := 1 to 13 do
      begin
        ReadCard(s, v);                                  { Reads a card }
        South[s, v] := true;                             { Enters it into the South hand }
        sc[s] := sc[s] + 1;                              { Count of each suit }
        vc[v] := vc[v] + 1                               { Count of each value }
      end
  end { ReadHand };

procedure ResetHand(var sc : suitcards; var vc : valuecards; var South : hand);
  {
    Resets a hand to no cards and counts of cards to zero.
  }
  var
    s : suit;
    v : value;
```

```
begin { ResetHand }
  for s := Club to Spade do
    begin
      sc[s] := 0;                                          { Count of suits }
      for v := two to Ace do South[s, v] := false                  { Hand }
    end;
  for v := two to Ace do vc[v] := 0                       { Count of values }
end { ResetHand } ;

procedure evaluate(PrintLimit : integer; var TotalPoints : integer;
                   var sc : suitcards; var vc : valuecards);
  {
    Computes the point count of a hand as described in the problem statement as
    TotalPoints. Prints the hand and the results if Totalpoints >= PrintLimit.
  }
  var
    s : suit;
    HighCardPoints, DistPoints, Corrections : integer;

  procedure PrintHand(South : hand);
    {
      Prints a sorted hand with extra spaces between the suits.
    }
    var
      s : suit;
      v : value;

    procedure WriteCard(S : suit; V : value);
      {
        Writes a card of suit S and value V.
      }
      begin { WriteCard }
        case S of                                            { Writes suit }
           Club    : write('C');
          Diamond  : write('D');
           Heart   : write('H');
           Spade   : write('S')
        end { case } ;
        case V of                                           { Writes value }
             two : write('2');
           three : write('3');
            four : write('4');
            five : write('5');
             six : write('6');
           seven : write('7');
           eight : write('8');
            nine : write('9');
             ten : write('T');                         { Writes "T" for 10 }
            Jack : write('J');
           Queen : write('Q');
            King : write('K');
             Ace : write('A')
        end { case } ;
        write(' ')
      end { WriteCard } ;

    begin { PrintHand }
      writeln;
      if DealHands then write('Hand #', count : 1) else write('The hand');
      write(':          ');
```

```
      for s := Spade downto Club do
        begin
          for v := Ace downto two do
            if South[s, v] then WriteCard(s, v);            { Print a card if in hand }
          write('     ')                            { Write extra spaces between suits }
        end;
      writeln;
      writeln
    end { PrintHand } ;

  begin { evaluate }
    HighCardPoints := 4 * vc[Ace] + 3 * vc[King] + 2 * vc[Queen] + vc[Jack];
    DistPoints := 0;
    for s := Club to Spade do
      if sc[s] < 3 then DistPoints := DistPoints + 3 - sc[s];
    if vc[Ace] = 4 then Corrections := 1 else
    if vc[Ace] = 0 then Corrections := -1 else Corrections := 0;
    TotalPoints := HighCardPoints + DistPoints + Corrections;
    if TotalPoints >= PrintLimit then
      begin
        PrintHand(South);
        writeln('High-card points          = ', HighCardPoints : 2);
        writeln('Distributional points = ', DistPoints : 2);
        writeln('Corrections               = ', Corrections : 2);
        writeln('Total points              = ', TotalPoints : 2);
        writeln
      end
  end { evaluate } ;

begin { main }
  writeln('Do you want to evaluate (a) Hands you enter, or');
  writeln('                        (b) Random hands?');
  writeln;
  write('Enter "a" or "b": ');
  repeat
    readln(ch)
  until ch in ['A', 'B', 'a', 'b'];
  DealHands := ch in ['B', 'b'];
  writeln;
  if DealHands then
    begin
      seed := 0.987654321;
      write('How many hands do you want to generate? ');
      readln(hands);                                  { Get number of hands to do }
      writeln;
      for i := 0 to 51 do d[i] := i;                         { Create deck of cards }
      PointSum := 0;
      for count := 1 to hands do
        begin
          ResetHand(sc, vc, South);
          deal(sc, vc, South);
          evaluate(PrintLimit, points, sc, vc);
          PointSum := PointSum + points;
          if (count mod 10 = 0) or (count = hands) then    { Summarize every 10 hands }
          writeln('Average point count in ', count : 1, ' hands is ',
                  PointSum / count : 5 : 2, '.')
        end
    end else
    begin
      write('Enter a 13-card hand: ');
      while not eof do
        begin
```

```
        ResetHand(sc, vc, South);
        ReadHand(sc, vc, South);
        evaluate(0, points, sc, vc);
        write('Enter a 13-card hand: ')
      end
    end
end { BridgeHand } .
```

10.25 PASCAL'S TRIANGLE

```
program PascalTriangle(output);
  {
    Calculates and prints Pascal's Triangle with row and diagonal sums.
  }
  const
    size = 10;                                          { Last row to print }
    sizp = 11;                                          { Last row plus 1 }
  var
    i, j, rowsum, diagsum : integer;
    triangle : array[0..sizp, -1..sizp] of integer;     { To hold a border of 0's }
  begin                                                 { around it }
    for i := 0 to sizp do                               { Clear triangle and border }
      for j := -1 to sizp do
        triangle[i, j] := 0;
    triangle[0, 0] := 1;                                { Start with value at top }
    for i := 1 to size do                               { Generate the triangle }
      for j := 0 to i do
        triangle[i, j] := triangle[i - 1, j - 1] + triangle[i - 1, j];
    writeln(' ' : 3 * size - 1, 'Pascal''s Triangle');
    writeln('Diagonal', ' ' : 6 * sizp + 1, 'Row');
    writeln('Sums', ' ' : 6 * sizp + 4, 'Sums');
    diagsum := 1;                                       { First diagonal sums }
    for i := 0 to size do
      begin
        write(diagsum : 2, ' ' : 3 * (size - i) + 1);   { Leave space to start }
        diagsum := 0;
        rowsum := 0;
        for j := 0 to i do                              { triangle at proper place }
          begin
            write(triangle[i, j] : 6);
            rowsum := rowsum + triangle[i, j];          { Generate rowsum }
            diagsum := diagsum + triangle[i + 1 - j, j] { and next diagsum }
          end;
        writeln(' ' : 3 * (size - i) + 4, rowsum : 5)
      end
  end { PascalTriangle } .
```

10.26 SEVEN COME ELEVEN

```
program seven11(output);
  {
    "Throws" dice and records the results for comparison with theory.
  }
  const
    howmany = 360;                                      { The number of dice throws }
  var
    i, throw : integer;
    count : array[2..12] of integer;
    seed : real;

  function ranfrac : real;          { Declare and initialize seed in main program }
    begin seed := 1011.0*seed; seed := seed-trunc(seed); ranfrac := seed end;
  function ran(i:integer) : integer;  begin ran := trunc((i)*ranfrac) end;
```

```
begin { main }
  writeln;
  writeln('Seven-Come-Eleven -- The throwing of the dice ',
          howmany : 1, ' times.');
  writeln;
  writeln('Value  Theory  Actual');
  writeln('---------------------');
  seed := 0.654321;
  for i := 2 to 12 do count[i] := 0;                    { Initialize counts }
  for i := 1 to howmany do
    begin
      throw := ran(6) + ran(6) + 2;                     { Throw the dice }
      count[throw] := count[throw] + 1                  { and update the count }
    end;
  for i := 2 to 12 do                                   { Print results }
    writeln (i : 3, howmany div 6 - (howmany div 36) * abs(7 - i) : 8,
             count[i] : 8)
end { seven11 } .
```

10.27 WORDFINDER

```
program Wordfinder(input, output);
  {
    Finds words in a word puzzle which is a rectangular array of letters.
  }
  type
    puz = array[0..21, 0..71] of char;
    line = array[1..31] of char;
    str2 = array[1..2] of char;
  var
    puzzle : puz;
    i, j, len, rows, cols : integer;
    word : line;
    found, done : Boolean;
    direction : str2;

  function upper(c : char) : char;                      { ASCII version }
    begin if c in ['a'..'z'] then upper := chr(ord(c) - 32) else upper := c end;

  procedure readpuzzle(var rows, cols : integer; var puzzle : puz);
    {
      Reads the puzzle and returns the number of its rows and columns.
    }
    var
      c : char;
      i : integer;
    begin { readpuzzle }
      cols := 0;
      rows := 0;
      while not eoln do
        begin
          rows := rows + 1;                               { Count the rows }
          i := 0;
          while not eoln do
            begin
              i := i + 1;                                 { Count the columns }
              read(c);
              puzzle[rows, i] := upper(c)
            end;
          if rows = 1 then cols := i;         { Record the columns only the first time }
          readln
        end;
      readln
    end { readpuzzle } ;
```

```
procedure borderpuzzle(rows, cols : integer; var puzzle : puz);
  {
    Places a border around the puzzle for printing and for stoping searches.
  }
  var
    i : integer;
  begin { borderpuzzle }
    for i := 0 to cols + 1 do
      begin
        puzzle[0, i] := '-';                    { Place border at top and bottom }
        puzzle[rows + 1, i] := '-'
      end;
    for i := 1 to rows do
      begin
        puzzle[i, 0] := '|';                    { and at left and right }
        puzzle[i, cols + 1] := '|'
      end
  end { borderpuzzle } ;

procedure printpuzzle(rows, cols : integer; puzzle : puz);
  {
    Prints the puzzle in the center of the screen with a border.
  }
  var
    tab, i, j : integer;
  begin { printpuzzle }
    tab := (80-cols) div 2;                     { For centering }
    writeln; writeln(' ' : 35, 'The Puzzle');
    writeln; write(' ' : tab);
    for j := 1 to cols do if j div 10 = 0       { 1st digit of col # }
      then write(' ')
      else write(j div 10 : 1);
    writeln; write(' ' : tab);
    for j := 1 to cols do write(j mod 10 : 1);  { 2nd digit of col # }
    writeln;
    for i := 0 to rows + 1 do
      begin
        if (i > 0) and (i <= rows)
          then write(i : tab - 2, ' ')
          else write(' ' : tab - 1);
        for j := 0 to cols + 1 do write(puzzle[i, j]); writeln
      end
  end { printpuzzle } ;

procedure readwriteword(var word : line; var len : integer);
  {
    Reads a word and prints it at the beginning of a line. It returns the word and its
    length and reads the delimiter ending the word.
  }
  var
    i : integer;
  begin { readwriteword }
    i := 1;
    read(word[i]);
    while (word[i] <> ',') and (word[i] <> '.') do
      begin
        word[i] := upper(word[i]);
        write(word[i]);
        i := i + 1;
        read(word[i])
      end;
    len := i - 1
  end { readwriteword } ;
```

```
procedure prompt;
  {
    Issues the prompt for a line of words to find.
  }
  begin { prompt }
    writeln;
    writeln('Enter a line of words to find.');
    writeln('Use no blanks, but separate words with a comma.');
    writeln('End the line with a period.');
    writeln
  end { prompt };

procedure lookfor(w : line; L, row, col : integer;
                  var found : Boolean; var dir : str2; puzzle : puz);
  {
    Searches for word w of length L that starts at row, col in the puzzle. Returns a
    Boolean found which is true if the word was found and false if not. The direction
    in which a found word runs is returned in dir.
  }
  var
    i, j, k, iinc, jinc : integer;
    s, t : array[-1..1] of char;
    done : Boolean;
  begin { lookfor }
    s[-1] := 'N'; s[0] := ' '; s[1] := 'S';                 { Labels for the directions }
    t[-1] := 'W'; t[0] := ' '; t[1] := 'E';
    found := false;
    done := false;
    if puzzle[row, col] = w[1] then      { Do not look if first letter does not match }
      begin
        iinc := -1;                                          { Look first in NW direction }
        jinc := -1;
        while (not found) and (not done) do
          begin
            i := row;
            j := col;
            k := 1;
            while (k <= L) and (w[k] = puzzle[i, j]) do
              begin
                k := k + 1;
                i := i + iinc;
                j := j + jinc
              end;
            found := k > L;
            if not found then                                { Get next direction }
              begin
                jinc := jinc + 1;
                if (iinc = 0) and (jinc = 0) then jinc := 1;
                if jinc = 2 then
                  begin
                    jinc := -1;
                    iinc := iinc + 1;
                    done := iinc = 2
                  end
              end
          end;
        if found then
          begin
            dir[1] := s[iinc];                               { Record last direction used }
            dir[2] := t[jinc]
          end
      end
  end { lookfor } ;
```

```
begin { main }
  writeln(' ' : 35, 'Wordfinder');
  writeln;
  write('Enter the puzzle, one row at a time with no blanks.   ');
  writeln('Finish with an empty line.');
  writeln;
  readpuzzle(rows, cols, puzzle);
  borderpuzzle(rows, cols, puzzle);
  printpuzzle(rows, cols, puzzle);
  prompt;
  while not eof do
    begin
      while not eoln do
        begin                                   { Get a word and try to find it }
          readwriteword(word, len);
          found := false;
          done := false;
          i := 1;
          j := 1;
          while (not found) and (not done) do
            begin        { Search for word starting at each letter in the puzzle }
              lookfor(word, len, i, j, found, direction, puzzle);
              if found then
                begin                                          { Print results }
                  write(' found at row ',i : 1,' column ',j : 1,' going ');
                  if direction[1] <> ' ' then write(direction[1]);
                  if direction[2] <> ' ' then write(direction[2]);
                  writeln('.')
                end;
              j := j + 1;
              if j > cols then
                begin
                  j := 1;
                  i := i + 1;
                  if i > rows then done := true
                end
            end;
          if not found then writeln(' not found')
        end;
      readln;
      prompt
    end
end { Wordfinder } .
```

10.28 DUMBBELLS

```
program DumbbellsA(output);
  {
    Dumbbell packing iteratively.
  }
  const
    max = 10;
  var
    N, q : integer;
    A : array[-2..max, -3..max] of integer;
  begin
    writeln('The Dumbbell Table');
    writeln;
    write(' N \ q',0:5);
    for q:=1 to max do write(q:6);
    writeln; write('----+');
    for q:=0 to max do write('------');
    writeln;
```

```
  for N := -1 to max do                    { Clear the array which must have a border }
    for q := -3 to max do                  { of enough 0's to cover out-of-range }
      A[N, q] := 0;                        { values needed in the formula }
  A[0, 0] := 1;                            { Compute and print row 0 }
  writeln(0 : 2,'    |', A[0, 0] : 6);
  a[1, 0] := 1;                            { Compute and print row 1 }
  a[1, 1] := 1;
  writeln(1 : 2,'    |', a[1, 0] : 6, a[1, 1] : 6);
  for N := 2 to max do                     { Compute and print other rows }
    begin
      write(N : 2, '    |');
      for q := 0 to N do
        begin
          A[N, q] := A[N - 1, q] + 2 * A[N - 1, q - 1] + A[N - 2, q - 1]
                     - A[N - 3, q - 3];
          write(A[N, q] : 6)
        end;
      writeln
    end
end { DumbbellsA} .

program DumbbellsB(input, output);
  {
    Dumbbell packing recursively.
  }
  var
    N, q : integer;

  function A(N, q : integer) : integer;
    {
      Recursive function to evaluate the dumbbell formula.
    }
  begin { A }
    if (N < 0) or (q < 0) or (q > N) then A := 0 else
    if N < 2 then A := 1 else
      A := A(N-1, q) + 2 * A(N-1, q-1) + A(N-2, q-1) - A(N-3, q-3)
  end { A } ;

  begin { main }
    writeln('Dumbbells');
    writeln;
    write('Enter N and q: ');
    while not eof do
      begin
        readln(N, q);                                          { Read arguments }
        writeln('A[', N : 1, ',  ', q : 1, '] = ', A(N, q) : 1);  { Write answer }
        writeln;
        write('Enter N and q: ')
      end
  end { DumbbellsB } .
```

10.29 LINDSTEDT CUBES

```
program LindstedtCubes(input, output);
  {
    Computes the Lindstedt sum for randomly oriented 3 x 3 x 3 arrangements of dice and
    records the maximum and minimum sums found.
  }
  type
    three = 1..3; spots = 1..6;
    orientation = 'a'..'x';
    orientations = array[three, three, three] of orientation;
    cube = (up, front, right, back, left, down);
    die = array[cube] of spots;
    block = array[three, three, three] of die;
    table = array[orientation] of die;
  var
    dice : block;
    tbl : table;
    arrangement, maxarrangement, minarrangement : orientations;
    i, j, n, sums, count, upper, lower, max, min : integer;
    seed : real;

  function ranfrac : real;              { Declare and initialize seed in main program }
    begin seed := 1011.0*seed; seed := seed-trunc(seed); ranfrac := seed end;
  function ran(i:integer) : integer;  begin ran := trunc((i)*ranfrac) end;

  procedure MakeTable(var tbl : table);
    {
      Makes a table of the 24 possible orientations of a single die. These 24 orientations
      are labelled 'a' .. 'x'.
    }
    var
      c, d : char;
      opposite, face : cube;
    begin { MakeTable }
      tbl['a'][up] := 1; tbl['a'][front] := 2; tbl['a'][right] := 3;
      tbl['b'][up] := 1; tbl['b'][front] := 3; tbl['b'][right] := 5;
      tbl['c'][up] := 1; tbl['c'][front] := 5; tbl['c'][right] := 4;
      tbl['d'][up] := 1; tbl['d'][front] := 4; tbl['d'][right] := 2;
      tbl['e'][up] := 2; tbl['e'][front] := 4; tbl['e'][right] := 6;
      tbl['f'][up] := 2; tbl['f'][front] := 6; tbl['f'][right] := 3;
      tbl['g'][up] := 2; tbl['g'][front] := 3; tbl['g'][right] := 1;
      tbl['h'][up] := 2; tbl['h'][front] := 1; tbl['h'][right] := 4;
      tbl['i'][up] := 3; tbl['i'][front] := 5; tbl['i'][right] := 1;
      tbl['j'][up] := 3; tbl['j'][front] := 1; tbl['j'][right] := 2;
      tbl['k'][up] := 3; tbl['k'][front] := 2; tbl['k'][right] := 6;
      tbl['l'][up] := 3; tbl['l'][front] := 6; tbl['l'][right] := 5;
      d := 'x';
      for c := 'a' to 'l' do                          { Opposite faces sum to 7 }
        begin
          tbl[c][back] := 7 - tbl[c][front];
          tbl[c][left] := 7 - tbl[c][right];
          tbl[c][down] := 7 - tbl[c][up];
          face := up;              { Last 12 orientations are the first 12 upside down }
          for opposite := down downto up do
            begin
              tbl[d][opposite] := tbl[c][face];
              if face <> down then face := succ(face)
            end;
          d:=pred(d)
        end
    end { MakeTable } ;
```

```
procedure GetRandomArrangement( var a : orientations);
  {
    Creates a random arrangement for the block of 27 dice.
  }
  var
    i, j, k : three;
  begin { GetRandomArrangement }
    for i := 1 to 3 do                                  { For each of the dice }
      for j := 1 to 3 do
        for k := 1 to 3 do
          begin
            a[i, j, k] := chr(ran(24) + ord('a'));
            dice[i, j, k] := tbl[a[i, j, k]]
          end
  end { GetRandomArrangement } ;

function sum(dice : block) : integer;
  {
    Computes the Lindstedt sum for the given arrangement of dice.
  }
  var
    s, i, j, k : integer;
  begin { sum }
    s := 0;
    for i := 1 to 2 do
      for j := 1 to 3 do
        for k := 1 to 3 do
          s := s  + dice[i, j, k][right] * dice[i + 1, j, k][left]       { R-L planes }
                  + dice[j, i, k][down] * dice[j, i + 1, k][up]          { U-D planes }
                  + dice[j, k, i][back] * dice[j, k, i + 1][front];      { F-B planes }
    sum := s
  end { sum } ;

procedure print(a : orientations);
  {
    Prints a tableau showing an arrangement of the 27 dice.
  }
  var
    i, j, k : integer;
  begin { print }
    writeln;
    writeln('                 Front                   Middle',
          '                 Back');
    for i := 1 to 3 do
      begin
        for k := 1 to 3 do
          begin
            write('          ');
            for j := 1 to 3 do write('   [', a[i, j, k], ']')
          end;
        writeln
      end;
    writeln
  end { print } ;

procedure PrintTable(tbl : table);
  {
    Prints the table of arrangements for decoding the arrangement tableau.
  }
  var
    i, j, k : integer;
    c, d : char;
    face : cube;
```

```
  begin { PrintTable }
    writeln(' Orientation keys used above (Up, Front, Right,',
              ' Back, Left, Down)');
    writeln;
    writeln('        UFRBLD             UFRBLD             UFRBLD',
                   UFRBLD');
    c := 'a';
    for i := 0 to 5 do
      begin
        d := c;
        for j := 0 to 3 do
          begin
            write('  [', d, ']   ');
            for face := up to down do write(tbl[d][face] : 1);
            write('      ');
            if j < 3 then for k := 1 to 6 do d := succ(d)
          end;
        c:=succ(c);
        writeln
      end
  end { PrintTable };

begin { main }
  seed := 0.87654321;
  MakeTable(tbl);
  write('Enter the number of experiments to evaluate: ');
  readln(n);
  writeln;
  max := 0;                              { Initialize best sums found so far }
  min := 2000;
  for count := 1 to n do
    begin
      GetRandomArrangement(arrangement);
      sums := sum(dice);
      if sums > max then                              { New maximum sum }
        begin
          max := sums;
          maxarrangement := arrangement;
          writeln('New maximum on experiment #', count : 1, ' = ', sums : 1)
        end;
      if sums < min then                              { New minimum sum }
        begin
          min := sums;
          minarrangement := arrangement;
          writeln('New minimum on experiment #', count : 1, ' = ', sums : 1)
        end
    end;
  writeln;
  writeln(' The maximum sum found: ', max : 1);
  print(maxarrangement);
  writeln(' The minimum sum found: ', min : 1);
  print(minarrangement);
  PrintTable(tbl)
end { LindstedtCubes } .
```

10.30 BINGO

```
program bingo(input, output);
  {
    Plays Bingo on up to 32 cards.
  }
  type
    row = 1..5;
    col = (B, I, N, G, O);
    card = array[row, col] of 0..75;
    cards = array[1..32] of card;
    isabingo = array[1..32] of Boolean;
  var
    cc : cards;
    k, count, last, number, howmany : integer;
    c, ic, jc : col;
    list : array[1..75] of integer;
    anybingo : Boolean;
    bingo : isabingo;
    seed : real;

  function ranfrac : real;                  { Declare and initialize seed in main program }
    begin seed := 1011.0*seed; seed := seed–trunc(seed); ranfrac := seed end;
  function ran(i:integer) : integer;  begin ran := trunc((i)*ranfrac) end;

  function InverseOrd(n : integer) : col;
    {
      InverseOrd returns a value of type col such that ord(InverseOrd(n)) = n.
    }
    var
      i : integer;
      c : col;
    begin { InverseOrd }
      c := B;
      if n < 13 then for i := 1 to n do c := succ(c);
      InverseOrd := c
    end { InverseOrd } ;

  procedure makecard(var c : card);
    {
      Creates a random Bingo card.
    }
    var
        j, k, r : integer;
        h : col;
        list : array[1..15] of 1..75;
    begin { makecard }
      k := 1;
      for h := B to O do                                          { For each column }
        begin
          for j := 1 to 15 do
            begin
              list[j] := k;                        { List of numbers allowed for that column }
              k := k + 1
            end;
          for j := 1 to 5 do                        { Pick 5 random numbers from this list }
            begin
              r := 1 + ran(16 – j);
              c[j, h] := list[r];                                   { to store in this column }
              list[r] := list[16 – j]
            end
        end;
      c[3, N] := 0                                                { Center square is free }
    end { makecard } ;
```

```
procedure printcards(c : cards);
  {
    Prints the array of Bingo cards.
  }
  var
    j, k, first, last : integer;
    h : col;
  begin { printcards }
    first := 1; last := first + 3;                    { First and last cards on this row }
    while first <= howmany do                             { For all rows of output }
      begin
        if last > howmany then last := howmany;
        writeln;
        for k := first to last do
          begin
            write('      Card', k : 4, '       ');            { Write card numbers }
            if k < last then write('  ')
          end;
        writeln;
        for k := first to last do
          begin
            write('------------------- ');                         { Write border }
            if k < last then write('  ')
          end;
        writeln;
        for k := first to last do
          begin
            write('|  B  I  N  G  O | ');                         { Write BINGO }
            if k < last then write('  ')
          end;
        writeln;
        for k := first to last do
          begin
            write('|-----------------| ');                         { More border }
            if k < last then write('  ')
          end;
        writeln;
        for j := 1 to 5 do
          begin
            for k := first to last do
              begin
                write('|');
                for h := B to O do write(c[k][j, h] : 3);              { Numbers }
                write('  | ');
                if k < last then write('  ')
              end;
            writeln
          end;
        for k := first to last do
          begin
            write('------------------- ');                      { Bottom border }
            if k < last then write('  ')
          end;
        writeln;
        first := first + 4;
        last := first + 3
      end
  end { printcards } ;
```

```
procedure call(var c : col; var n : integer);
  {
    Issues the call for a Bingo move.
  }
  var
    t : integer;
  begin { call }
    t := 1 + ran(last);                          { Get a random number to select }
    n := list[t];                                { an unused number from the list }
    list[t] := list[last];
    list[last] := n;                             { Put it at end of list }
    c := InverseOrd((n - 1) div 15);             { Record the proper BINGO letter }
    last := last - 1                             { Shorten the list }
  end { call } ;

procedure entercall(c : col; n : integer; var anybingo : Boolean; var bingo : isabingo);
  {
    Enters a Bingo call on all cards and checks for any Bingo.
  }
  var
    row, col, h, j : integer;
    rowbingo, colbingo, maind, offd : Boolean;
  begin { entercall }
    for h := 1 to howmany do                     { For each card }
      begin
        row := 1;                                { Search for number on this row }
        while (row < 6) and (cc[h][row, c] <> n) do row := row + 1;
        if row < 6 then                          { Number was found }
          begin
            cc[h][row, c] := 0;                  { Zero it out }
            rowbingo := true;
            colbingo := true;
            maind := row = ord(c) + 1;
            offd := row + ord(c) = 5;
            ic := B;
            jc := O;
            for j := 1 to 5 do
              begin
                rowbingo := rowbingo and (cc[h][row, ic] = 0);   { Check row }
                colbingo := colbingo and (cc[h][j, c] = 0);      { Column }
                maind := maind and (cc[h][j, ic] = 0);           { and diagonals }
                offd := offd and (cc[h][j, jc] = 0);             { For BINGO }
                if ic <> O then
                  begin
                    ic := succ(ic);
                    jc := pred(jc)
                  end
              end;
            bingo[h] := rowbingo or colbingo or maind or offd    { BINGO? }
          end else bingo[h]:=false;                              { No }
        anybingo := anybingo or bingo[h]                         { Bingo on any card }
      end
  end { entercall } ;

begin { main }
  seed := 0.654321;
  for k := 1 to 75 do list[k] := k;              { Create list of numbers }
  last := 75;
  writeln('You may play up to 32 cards.');
  write('How many cards do you want to play? ');
  readln(howmany);
  writeln;
  for k := 1 to howmany do makecard(cc[k]);      { Make the cards }
```

```
    printcards(cc);writeln;                              { and print them }
    count := 0;
    anybingo := false;
    while not anybingo do                                { Continue until BINGO }
      begin
        call(c, number);                                 { Get a number }
        count := count + 1;
        case c of
           B: write('B');
           I: write('I');
           N: write('N');
           G: write('G');
           O: write('O')
        end;
        write('-',number : 1, '    ');                   { Print it }
        entercall(c, number, anybingo, bingo);           { Play the cards }
        if count mod 10 = 0 then                         { Show cards after 10 calls }
          begin
            writeln; writeln;
            printcards(cc);
            writeln; writeln
          end
      end;
    writeln; writeln; write('Bingo! on cards: ');       { BINGO! }
    for k := 1 to howmany do if bingo[k] then write(k : 3); writeln;
    printcards(cc)                                       { Show cards }
  end { bingo } .
```

10.31 LOGICAL BIT ADDITION

```
program LogicalBitAddition(input, output);
  {
    Program to display the progress of 6-bit binary 1's complement addition.
  }
  type
    sixbit = packed array[0..5] of Boolean;
  var
    add1, add2, total : sixbit;
    ov : Boolean;

  procedure readin(var a : sixbit);
    {
      Reads a 6-bit binary number, high order bit to low order bit, into a Boolean array
      where true is a 1-bit and false a 0-bit.
    }
    var
      i : integer;
      c : char;
    begin { readin }
      for i := 5 downto 0 do
        begin
          read(c);
          a[i] := c = '1'
        end;
      readln
    end { readin } ;

  function convert(a : sixbit) : integer;
    {
      Computes the value of a 6-bit number stored in a Boolean array.
    }
    var
      i, sum : integer;
```

```
  begin { convert }
    sum := 0;
    for i := 4 downto 0 do sum := 2 * sum + ord(a[i]);
    if a[5]
      then convert := sum - 31            { Negative, take 1's complement }
      else convert := sum
  end { convert } ;

procedure display(a : sixbit);
  {
    Prints a 6-bit number stored in a Boolean array.
  }
  var
    i : integer;
  begin
    for i := 5 downto 0 do write(chr(ord('0') + ord(a[i])))
  end { display } ;

procedure add(a, b : sixbit; var sum : sixbit; var overflow : Boolean);
  {
    Computes and prints the sum and carry of a + b and continues until there are no
    more carries.
  }
  var
    i : integer;
    carry : sixbit;
    carryflag : Boolean;
  begin { add }
    overflow := false;
    carryflag := true;
    while carryflag do                    { Continue until all carries are added in }
      begin
        carryflag := false;
        for i := 0 to 5 do
          begin
            sum[i] := a[i] <> b[i];                    { Sum is exclusive or ( <> ) }
            carry[(i + 1) mod 6] := a[i] and b[i];                   { Carry is and }
            carryflag := carryflag or carry[(i + 1) mod 6]
          end;
        overflow := overflow <> (carry[5] <> carry[0]);
        writeln;
        writeln('           ------');
        write('Sum        ');
        display(sum);                                          { Show the sums }
        if carryflag then                                  { and carries if any }
          begin
            writeln;
            write('Carry      ');
            display(carry);
            writeln
          end;
        a := sum;                            { Numbers to be added on next pass }
        b := carry
      end
  end { add } ;

begin { main }
  writeln('Enter two 6-bit numbers, one per line');
  writeln;
  write('First Number:  ');
```

```
    while not eof do
      begin
        readin(add1);
        write('Second Number: ');
        readin(add2);
        writeln;
        write(' ' : 8);
        display(add1);
        writeln(convert(add1) : 10);
        write(' ' : 8);
        display(add2);
        writeln(convert(add2) : 10);
        add(add1, add2, total, ov);
        if ov
          then writeln('           ***')
          else writeln(convert(total) : 10);
        writeln;
        writeln('Enter two 6-bit numbers, one per line');
        writeln;
        write('First Number:  ')
      end
  end { LogicalBitAddition } .
```

10.32 CORRELATION COEFFICIENTS

```
program correlation(input, output);
  {
    Correlation Coefficient calculator.
  }
  const
    n = 10;
  type
    vector = array[1..n] of real;
  var
    i, count : integer;
    x, y : vector;

  function CC(x, y : vector; n : integer) : real;
    {
      Returns the correlation coefficient of the n-element vectors x and y.
    }
    var
      i : integer;
      sumx, sumy, sumxx, sumyy, sumxy : real;
    begin { CC }
      sumx := 0; sumy := 0; sumxx := 0; sumyy := 0; sumxy := 0;
      for i := 1 to n do
        begin
          sumx := sumx + x[i];                          { Accumulate sums }
          sumy := sumy + y[i];
          sumxx := sumxx + x[i] * x[i];
          sumyy := sumyy + y[i] * y[i];
          sumxy := sumxy + x[i] * y[i]
        end;
      CC :=   (n * sumxy - sumx * sumy) /       { Compute correlation coefficient }
            sqrt((n * sumxx - sumx * sumx) * (n * sumyy - sumy * sumy))
    end { CC } ;

  begin { main }
    writeln('Correlation Coefficients');
    writeln;
    writeln('Enter up to ',n:1,' (x, y) pairs, one pair/line.');
    writeln;
```

```
  count := 0;
  while not eof do
    begin                                   { Read and count vector elements }
      count := count + 1;
      readln(x[count], y[count])
    end;
  writeln;
  writeln('Input Data');
  writeln;
  writeln('    i          x[i]                    y[i]');
  for i := 1 to count do writeln(I : 3, '    ', x[i] : 18, y[i] : 18);
  writeln;
  writeln('Correlation Coefficient: ', CC(x, y, count) : 18)
end { correlation } .
```

10.33 DNA

```
program DNA(input, output);
  {
    Reads a series of codons and uses table look-up to retrieve the amino acids generated
    by these codons.
  }
  type
    nucleotide = (T, C, A, G);
    amino = (phenylalanine, leucine, isoleucine, methionine, valine, serine, proline,
             threonine, alanine, tyrosine, period, histidine, glutamine, asparagine,
             lysine, asparaticacid, glutamicacid, cysteine, tryptophan, arginine, glycine);
    table = array[T..G, T..G, T..G] of amino;
  var
    i, j, k : nucleotide;
    ci, cj, ck : char;
    Tbl : table;
    done : Boolean;

  procedure FillTable(var genetic : table);
    {
      Creates the table of Genetic Codes.
    }
    var
      i : nucleotide;
    begin { FillTable }
      for i := T to C do
        begin
          genetic[T, T, i] := phenylalanine;
          genetic[T, A, i] := tyrosine;
          genetic[C, A, i] := histidine;
          genetic[A, A, i] := asparagine;
          genetic[G, A, i] := asparaticacid;
          genetic[T, G, i] := cysteine;
          genetic[A, G, i] := serine
        end;
      for i := A to G do
        begin
          genetic[T, T, i] := leucine;
          genetic[T, A, i] := period;
          genetic[C, A, i] := glutamine;
          genetic[A, A, i] := lysine;
          genetic[G, A, i] := glutamicacid;
          genetic[A, G, i] := arginine
        end;
      for i := T to G do
        begin
          genetic[C, T, i] := leucine;
          genetic[G, T, i] := valine;
```

```
        genetic[T, C, i] := serine;
        genetic[C, C, i] := proline;
        genetic[A, C, i] := threonine;
        genetic[G, C, i] := alanine;
        genetic[C, G, i] := arginine;
        genetic[G, G, i] := glycine
      end;
    for i := T to A do genetic[A, T, i] := isoleucine;
    genetic[A, T, G] := methionine;
    genetic[T, G, A] := period;
    genetic[T, G, G] := tryptophan
  end { FillTable } ;

procedure ShowNucleotide(x : nucleotide);
  {
    Prints a nucleotide.
  }
  begin { ShowNucleotide }
    case x of
      T : write('T' : 1);
      C : write('C' : 1);
      A : write('A' : 1);
      G : write('G' : 1)
    end { case }
  end { ShowNucleotide };

procedure ShowAmino(acid : amino);
  {
    Prints an amino acid.
  }
  begin { ShowAmino }
    case acid of
phenylalanine : write('phenylalanine' : 16);
      leucine : write('leucine' : 16);
   isoleucine : write('isoleucine' : 16);
   methionine : write('methionine' : 16);
       valine : write('valine' : 16);
       serine : write('serine' : 16);
      proline : write('proline' : 16);
    threonine : write('threonine' : 16);
      alanine : write('alanine' : 16);
     tyrosine : write('tyrosine' : 16);
       period : write('period' : 16);
    histidine : write('histidine' : 16);
    glutamine : write('glutamine' : 16);
   asparagine : write('asparagine' : 16);
       lysine : write('lysine' : 16);
asparaticacid : write('asparatic acid' : 16);
glutamicacid : write('glutamic acid' : 16);
     cysteine : write('cysteine' : 16);
   tryptophan : write('tryptophan' : 16);
     arginine : write('arginine' : 16);
      glycine : write('glycine' : 16)
    end { case }
  end { ShowAmino } ;
```

```
function nuc(ch : char) : nucleotide;
  {
    Returns the nucleotide corresponding to the character ch.
  }
  begin { nuc }
    case ch of
      'T', 't' : nuc := T;
      'C', 'c' : nuc := C;
      'A', 'a' : nuc := A;
      'G', 'g' : nuc := G
    end { case }
  end { nuc } ;

procedure dashes;
  {
    Writes a line of dashes.
  }
  var
    i : integer;
  begin { dashes }
    for i:=1 to 69 do write('-');
    writeln
  end { dashes } ;

begin { main }
  FillTable(Tbl);                                    { Make table of genetic codes }
  writeln('The Table of Amino Acids');               { Print the table }
  writeln;
  writeln('           T                C                A',
      '                G');
  dashes;
  for i := T to G do
    begin
      for k := T to G do
        begin
        if k = C then ShowNucleotide(i) else write('  ');
          for j := T to G do ShowAmino(Tbl[i, j, k]);
          write('    ');
          ShowNucleotide(k);
          writeln
        end;
      dashes
    end;
  write('Enter a string of codons: ');
  done := false;
  while not done do
    begin
      while (not eoln) and (not done) do
        begin
          read(ci, cj, ck);                          { Get a codon in character form }
          i := nuc(ci);                              { Convert characters to nucleotides }
          j := nuc(cj);
          k := nuc(ck);
          ShowNucleotide(i);                         { Print the codon }
          ShowNucleotide(j);
          ShowNucleotide(k);
          done := Tbl[i, j, k] = period;             { Stop if codon evaluates to period }
          ShowAmino(Tbl[i, j, k]);                   { Print the amino acid }
          writeln
        end;
      readln;
      writeln;
```

```
    if not done
      then write('Enter a string of codons: ')  { Get more codons }
      else writeln('Halt')                      { or stop }
  end
end { DNA } .
```

10.34 MAGIC SQUARES

```
program MagicSquares(input, output);
  {
    Generates a Magic Square using the De la Loubere algorithm. The resulting square is
    then tested for several magic properites.
  }
  type
    square = array[0..18, 0..18] of integer;
  var
    magic : square;
    i, j, m, n, row, col, A, B, C, D, nmrows, nmcols, nmdiags, sum :
integer;
    s : array[1..4] of integer;

  function MakeMagic(var magic : square; m, row, col, A, B, C, D : integer) : Boolean;
    {
      Generates a magic square from the rules given in problem statement.
    }
    var
      i, j, nrow, ncol, count, element, n : integer;
    begin { MakeMagic }
      MakeMagic := true;
      n := m + 1;
      while A < 0 do A := A + n;          { So that any mod operator will work }
      while B < 0 do B := B + n;
      while C < 0 do C := C + n;
      while D < 0 do D := D + n;
      for i := 0 to m do                  { Initialize magic square }
        for j := 0 to m do
          magic[i, j] := 0;
      element := 1;
      for i := 1 to n * n - 1 do          { Fill magic square with elements }
        begin
          magic[row, col] := element;
          element := element + 1;
          nrow := (row + B) mod n;        { Find next vacant slot }
          ncol := (col + A) mod n;
          if magic[nrow, ncol] = 0 then
            begin                         { Standard increments are ok }
              row := nrow;
              col := ncol
            end else
            begin                         { Must use alternative increments }
              count := 0;
              repeat
                  row := (row + D) mod n;
                  col := (col + C) mod n;
                  count := count + 1
              until (magic[row, col] = 0) or (count > n * n);
              if count > n * n then MakeMagic := false
            end
        end;
      magic[row, col] := element
    end { MakeMagic } ;
```

```
procedure print(magic : square;n : integer);
  {
    Prints a magic square.
  }
  var
    i, j : integer;
  begin { print }
    writeln;
    writeln('The ',n:1,' by ',n:1,' magic square');
    writeln;
    for i := n - 1 downto 0 do
      begin
        for j := 0 to n - 1 do write(magic[i, j] : 4);
        writeln
      end;
    writeln
  end { print } ;

function symmetric(a : square; k : integer) : Boolean;
  {
    Tests a magic square for symmetry.
  }
  var
    i, j, s : integer;
  begin { symmetric }
    symmetric := true;
    s := sqr(k + 1) + 1;
    for i := 0 to k do
      for j := 0 to k do
        begin
          if a[i, j] + a[k - i, k - j] <> s then symmetric := false
        end
  end { symmetric } ;

begin { main }
  repeat
    write('Enter size of square (an odd number between 3 and 19): ');
    readln(n)
  until n in [3, 5, 7, 9, 11, 13, 15, 17, 19];
  repeat
    write('Enter the coordinates of the starting square: ');
    readln(row, col)
  until (row > 0) and (col > 0) and (row <= n) and (col <= n);
  write('Enter the 4 increments: ');
  readln(A, B, C, D);
  writeln;
  writeln('Size of magic square is: ',n:1);
  writeln('Coordinates of starting square are row ',row:1,
        ' and column ',col:1);
  writeln('Increments are: ',A:1,' ',b:1,' ',c:1,' ',d:1);
  m := n - 1;          { Because we number rows and columns starting at 0, not 1 }
  col := col - 1;
  row := n - row;                          { and rows are numbered from top }
  if MakeMagic(magic, m, row, col, A, B, C, D) then    { Create magic square }
    begin
      print(magic, n);                              { Display the magic square }
      nmrows := 0;
      nmcols := 0;
      nmdiags := 0;
      sum := n * (n * n + 1) div 2;
```

```
      for i := 0 to m do
        begin
          for j := 1 to 4 do s[j] := 0;
          for j := 0 to m do
            begin
              s[1] := s[1] + magic[i, j];                      { Compute row sums, }
              s[2] := s[2] + magic[j, i];                           { Column sums, }
              s[3] := s[3] + magic[(i + j) mod n, j];                  { Major and }
              s[4] := s[4] + magic[(i + j) mod n, m - j]   { minor diagonal sums }
            end;
          if s[1] = sum then nmrows := nmrows + 1;  { Bump counters if sums }
          if s[2] = sum then nmcols := nmcols + 1;
          if s[3] = sum then nmdiags := nmdiags + 1;                { are magic }
          if s[4] = sum then nmdiags := nmdiags + 1
        end;
      writeln('Number of Magic Rows:                    ', nmrows : 2);
      writeln('Number of Magic Columns:                 ', nmcols : 2);
      writeln('Number of Magic Diagonals:               ', nmdiags : 2);
      write ('Symmetric?                              ');
      if symmetric(magic, m) then writeln('Yes') else writeln(' No')
    end else
    begin
      writeln; writeln('Cannot make magic square from this input')
    end
  end { MagicSquares } .
```

10.35 CROSSWORD PUZZLE

```
program Crossword(input, output);
  {
    Create and print a crossword puzzle including spaces for the across and down
    definitions.
  }
  const
    rowmax = 50;
    colmax = 25;
    nmax   = 99;
    white  =  0;
    black  = -1;
  var
    puzzle : array[0..rowmax, 0..colmax] of integer;
    across, down : array[1..nmax] of integer;
    r, c : integer;                                    { User-chosen size limits }
    aindex, dindex : integer;      { Control variables for across and down arrays }

  procedure DefinePuzzle;
    {
      Creates a crossword puzzle based on input. To simplify the procedure, a border of
      black squares will be placed around the puzzle.
    }
    var
      row, col : integer;                           { Local loop control variables }
    begin { DefinePuzzle }
      write('Enter row & column size limits: ');
      readln(r, c); writeln;
      for row := 1 to r do                  { Initialize all puzzle squares to white }
        for col := 1 to c do
          puzzle[row, col] := white;
      for col := 1 to c do                            { Color border squares black }
        begin
          puzzle[ 0, col] := black;
          puzzle[r + 1, col] := black
        end;
```

```
  for row := 1 to r do
    begin
      puzzle[row, 0 ] := black;
      puzzle[row, c + 1] := black
    end;
  for row := 1 to r do                    { Get coordinates of black squares }
    begin
      write('Enter column numbers of black squares in row ',
              row : 1, ': ');
      while not eoln do
        begin
          read(col);
          puzzle[row, col] := black
        end;
      readln
    end
  end { DefinePuzzle } ;

procedure NumberSquares;
  {
    Numbers the squares in a crossword puzzle.
  }
  var
    n, row, col : integer;
  begin { NumberSquares }
    n := 1;                                              { Initialize }
    aindex := 0;
    dindex := 0;
    for row := 1 to r do
      for col := 1 to c do
        begin
          if puzzle[row, col] = white then        { Check left and right neighbors }
            if (puzzle[row, col - 1] < 0) and (puzzle[row, col + 1] = white) then
              begin
                puzzle[row, col] := n;                   { Number the square }
                aindex := aindex + 1;
                across[aindex] := n
              end;
          if puzzle[row, col] >= 0 then         { Check top and bottom neighbors : }
            if (puzzle[row - 1, col] < 0) and (puzzle[row + 1, col] = white) then
              begin
                puzzle[row, col] := n;                   { Number the square }
                dindex := dindex + 1;
                down[dindex] := n
              end;
          if puzzle[row, col] > 0 then n := n + 1  { Inc n if square has been numbered }
        end
  end { NumberSquares } ;

procedure PrintPuzzle;
  {
    Prints the puzzle including across and down square numbers and spaces for
    definitions.
  }
  var
    i, j, row, col : integer;
  begin { PrintPuzzle }
    writeln;
    for j := 1 to 7 * c + 1 do write('-');
    writeln;
```

```
      for row := 1 to r do
        begin
          for i := 1 to 3 do
            begin
              for col := 1 to c do
                begin
                  write(' | ');
                  if puzzle[row, col] < 0 then write('******') else
                  if (puzzle[row, col] > 0) and (i = 1)
                    then write(puzzle[row, col] : 2, '        ')
                    else write('          ')
                end;
              writeln(' | ')
            end;
          for j := 1 to 7 * c + 1 do write('-');
          writeln
        end;
      writeln;                                 { Print space for Across and Down entries }
      writeln;
      writeln('      Across');
      writeln;
      for i := 1 to aindex do
        begin
          write(across[i] : 3, '    ');
          for j := 1 to 75 do write('_');
          writeln
        end;
      writeln;
      writeln;
      writeln('      Down');
      writeln;
      for i := 1 to dindex do
        begin
          write(down[i] : 3, '    ');
          for j := 1 to 75 do write('_');
          writeln
        end
    end { PrintPuzzle } ;

  begin { main }
    DefinePuzzle;
    NumberSquares;
    PrintPuzzle
  end { Crossword } .
```

10.36 GRAY CODE

```
program GrayCode(input, output);
  {
    Prints an N-bit table of the binary integers converted to Gray code and then back to
    binary. N, the number of bits for the table, is requested as input and it can be in the
    range 1 to 8.
  }
  type
    bitstring = packed array[1..8] of char;
  var
    s1, s2, s3 : bitstring;
    i, j, k, n, number, power : integer;
```

```
procedure BinaryToGray(a : bitstring;n : integer; var b : bitstring);
  {
    Converts a bitstring from binary to Gray code.
  }
  var
    i : integer;
  begin { BinaryToGray }
    b[1] := a[1];
    for i := 2 to n do                        { Exclusive or ( <> ) of adjacent bits }
      if a[i] <> a[i - 1] then b[i] := '1' else b[i] := '0'
  end { BinaryToGray } ;

procedure GrayToBinary(a : bitstring; n : integer; var b : bitstring);
  {
    Converts a bitstring from Gray code to binary.
  }
  var
    i : integer;
    flag : Boolean;
  begin { GrayToBinary}
    flag := false;              { flag is false when number of 1-bits so far is even }
    for i := 1 to n do
      begin
        if a[i] = '1' then flag := not flag;        { Change flag if new 1-bit found }
        if flag then b[i] := '1' else b[i] := '0'
      end
  end { GrayToBinary} ;

begin { main }
  write('Enter the number of bits for the table (1 to 8): ');
  readln(n); writeln;
  writeln('Decimal   Binary ----> Gray ----> Binary');
  writeln('----------------------------------------');
  power := 1;
  for i := 1 to n do power := power * 2;              { The number of lines is 2^n }
  for k := 0 to power - 1 do
    begin
      number := k;
      for j := n downto 1 do                   { Convert n to its binary digits into s1 }
        begin
          if (number mod 2) = 0 then s1[j] := '0' else s1[j] := '1';
          number := number div 2
        end;
      write(k : 4);
      for i := 1 to 9 - n div 2 do write(' ');
      for i := 1 to n do write(s1[i]);
      BinaryToGray(s1, n, s2);                           { Convert to Gray into s2 }
      write(' ' : 12 - n);
      for i := 1 to n do write(s2[i]);
      GrayToBinary(s2, n, s3);                    { Convert back to binary into s3 }
      write(' ' : 12 - n);
      for i := 1 to n do write(s3[i]);
      writeln
    end
end { GrayCode } .
```

10.37 HEADS OR TAILS

```
program HeadsOrTails(input, output);
  {
    Tosses a coin randomly and counts numbers of heads and tails and runs of heads and
    tails.
  }
```

```
type
  coin = (head, tail);
  tosscounter = array[coin] of integer;
  runcounter = array[1..10, coin] of integer;
var
  i, n : integer;
  heads : runcounter;
  total, run : tosscounter;
  seed : real;

procedure flip(n : integer; var total : tosscounter; var heads : runcounter);
  {
    Flips a coin n times and records the total number of heads and tails in total, and the
    number of runs of each length in heads.
  }
  var
    run : tosscounter;
    i, runlength : integer;
    up, down : coin;

  procedure clear(var run, total : tosscounter; var heads : runcounter);
    {
      Clears the arrays used for summarizing the results.
    }
    var
      i : integer;
      face : coin;
    begin { clear }
      for face := head to tail do
        begin                                                    { Clear tables }
          run[face] := 0; total[face] := 0;
          for i := 1 to 10 do heads[i, face] := 0
        end
    end { clear } ;

  function ranfrac : real;              { Declare and initialize seed in main program }
    begin seed := 1011.0*seed; seed := seed–trunc(seed); ranfrac := seed end;
  function ran(i : integer) : integer;  begin ran := trunc((i)*ranfrac) end;

  begin { flip }
    clear(run, total, heads);
    for i := 1 to n do
      begin
        if ran(2) = 0              { Get the random up and down face of a coin toss }
          then begin up := head; down := tail end
          else begin up := tail; down := head end;
        total[up] := total[up] + 1;                          { Add toss to total }
        if run[down] <> 0 then                 { If counting run of face opposite up }
          begin                                  { end it and record the count }
            if run[down] > 9 then runlength := 10 else runlength := run[down];
            heads[runlength, down] := heads[runlength, down] + 1;
            run[down] := 0                               { run[up] will also be 0 }
          end;
        run[up] := run[up] + 1                  { Increment count of run of up face }
      end;
    if run[up] > 9 then runlength := 10 else runlength := run[up];
    heads[runlength, up] := heads[runlength, up] + 1  { Mop up count of last run }
  end { flip } ;

begin { main }
  seed := 0.654321;
  writeln;
  write('Enter the number of trials: ');
  readln(n);
```

```
    writeln;
    flip(n, total, heads);                              { Flip the coin n times }
    writeln('                    Heads    Tails    Total');   { Print results }
    writeln;
    writeln(total[head] : 18, total[tail] : 8, total[head] + total[tail] : 8);
    writeln;
    for i := 1 to 9 do
      writeln('Runs of ', i : 2, heads[i, head] : 8, heads[i, tail] : 8,
    heads[i, head] + heads[i, tail] : 8);
    writeln('Runs >  10', heads[10, head] : 8, heads[10, tail] : 8,
             heads[10, head] + heads[10, tail] : 8)
  end { HeadsOrTails } .
```

10.38 MULTIPLICATION

```
program multiplication(input, output);
  {
   Displays the product of two integers in worksheet form. All numbers are kept as
   character arrays so that large integers can be multiplied. The multiplier and
   multiplicand must each be 40 or fewer digits long and must be on one line with *
   separating them and terminated with the end-of-line.
  }
  var
    zero, carry, prod, i, j, k, L1, L2, L3, L4, temp : integer;
    product : array[1..40] of integer;
    multiplier, multiplicand, subprod : packed array[0..41] of char;
  begin
    zero := ord('0');
    for i:=0 to 41 do subprod[i]:=' ';
    writeln('High precision multiply');
    writeln;
    writeln('Enter the numbers to be multiplied.');
    write('Use the form  xxxxxx*yyyyy  with no blanks: ');
    while not eof do
      begin
        multiplier[0] := 'x';
        multiplicand[0] := 'x';
        L1 := 0;
        L2 := 0;
        while multiplier[L1] <> '*' do                   { Read multiplier }
          begin
            L1 := L1 + 1;
            read(multiplier[L1])
          end;
        while not eoln do                                { Read multiplicand }
          begin
            L2 := L2 + 1;
            read(multiplicand[L2])
          end;
        readln;
        writeln;
        writeln;
        L3 := L2 + 1;
        L1 := L1 - 1;
        if L1 > L3 then L3 := L1;
        write(' ' : 40 - L1);                            { Write multiplier }
        for i := 1 to L1 do write(multiplier[i]);
        writeln;
        write(' ' : 39 - L2);                            { Write multiplicand }
        for i := 0 to L2 do write(multiplicand[i]);
        writeln;
        write(' ' : 40 - L3);                            { Write line under numbers }
        for i := 1 to L3 do write('-');
```

```
      writeln;
      for i := 1 to 40 do product[i] := 0;
      for i := L2 downto 1 do
        begin
          if subprod[41 - L2 + i] = 'x'                          { If 'x' in subproduct }
            then subprod[41 - L2 + i] := '0'                      { replace it with 0 }
            else for j := 41 - L2 + i to 40 do subprod[j] := ' ';      { else clear }
          if (L2 <> 1) and (multiplicand[i] = '0')         { multiplicand digit is 0. }
            then subprod[40 - L2 + i] := 'x'          { Store 'x' and skip this digit }
              else                                         { Multiply by this digit }
              begin
                carry := 0;
                L4 := 40 - L2 + i;
                for j := 1 to 39 - L2 + i do subprod[j] := ' '; { Clear subproduct }
                for j := L1 downto 1 do
                  begin
                    prod := (ord(multiplicand[i]) - zero) * (ord(multiplier[j]) - zero)
                              + carry;                              { Multiply digits }
                    temp := prod mod 10;                { Get low order digit of result }
                    subprod[L4] := chr(zero + temp);            { Store in subproduct }
                    product[L4] := product[L4] + temp;           { and in product line }
                    L4 := L4 - 1;
                    carry := prod div 10                             { Compute carry }
                  end;
                if carry <> 0 then subprod[L4] := chr(zero + carry);   { Add last carry }
                product[L4] := product[L4] + carry;
                for j := 1 to 40 do write(subprod[j]);         { Print last subproduct }
                writeln
              end
        end;
      for i := 40 downto 2 do                  { Normalize product to digits in 0..9 }
        begin
          temp := product[i];
          product[i] := temp mod 10;
          product[i - 1] := product[i - 1] + temp div 10
        end;
      i := 1;                                                 { Write product line }
      while (product[i] = 0) and (i < 41 - L3) do
        begin
          write(' ');
          i := i + 1
        end;
      for j := i to 40 do write('-');
      writeln;
      i := 1;
      while (product[i] = 0) and (i < 40) do
        begin
          write(' ');
          i := i + 1
        end;
      for j := i to 40 do write(product[j] : 1);
      writeln;
      writeln;
      writeln('Enter the numbers to be multiplied.');
      write('Use the form  xxxxxx*yyyyy  with no blanks: ')
    end
  end { multiply } .
```

10.39 LONG DIVISION

```
program LongDivision(input, output);
  {
    Displays the quotient of two integers in worksheet form.
  }
  var
    dividend, divisor, quotient, remainder, prod, diff, tier, k : integer;
    ch : char;

  function sizeof(k : integer) : integer;
    {
      Returns number of decimal digits in k.
    }
    begin { sizeof }
      if k = 0 then sizeof := 1 else sizeof := trunc(1 + ln(k) / ln(10))
    end { sizeof } ;

  function digit(num, n : integer) : integer;
    {
      Returns the nth digit from the right of num.
    }
    begin { digit }
      if n = 1 then digit := num mod 10 else digit := digit(num div 10, n - 1)
    end { digit } ;

  function div10n(num, n : integer) : integer;
    {
      Returns num div (10^n).
    }
    begin { div10n }
      if n = 0 then div10n := num else div10n := div10n(num, n - 1) div 10
    end { div10n } ;

  begin { main }
    write('Enter dividend and divisor: ');
    while not eof do
      begin
        readln(dividend, divisor);
        writeln;
        quotient := dividend div divisor;                    { Compute quotient }
        remainder := dividend mod divisor;                     { and remainder }
        writeln(quotient : sizeof(divisor) + sizeof(dividend)      { Write them }
                  + 3, ' R ', remainder : sizeof(remainder));
        write(' ' : sizeof(divisor) + 1);
        for k := 1 to sizeof(dividend) + 2 do
          write('*');                                 { Place *'s under quotient }
        writeln;                      { Write divisor and dividend with * between }
        writeln(divisor : sizeof(divisor), ' * ', dividend : sizeof(dividend));
        tier := sizeof(quotient);
        diff := div10n(dividend, tier - 1);             { Compute first subtrahend }
        while tier > 0 do       {Form as many tiers as there are digits in quotient }
          begin
            prod := digit(quotient, tier) * divisor;           { Compute a product }
            if tier = sizeof(quotient)
              then ch := '*' else ch := ' ';             { Place *'s under divisor }
            for k := 1 to sizeof(divisor) + 2 do write(ch);               { Indent }
            writeln(prod : sizeof(dividend) + 2 - tier);       { Write the product }
            for k := 1 to sizeof(divisor) + sizeof(dividend) + 4 - sizeof(prod) - tier do
              write(' ');                                  { Indent proper amount }
            for k := 1 to sizeof(prod) do write('-');   { and then form dotted line }
            writeln;
            diff := diff - prod;                            { Compute a difference }
```

```
        write(diff : sizeof(divisor) + sizeof(dividend) + 4 – tier);      { Write it }
        if tier > 1 then              { For all but last tier, bring down another digit }
          repeat
            write(digit(dividend, tier – 1) : 1);          { Write it next to difference }
            diff := 10 * diff + digit(dividend, tier – 1);        { Integrate difference }
            if diff < divisor
              then tier := tier – 1                 { Short circuit, quotient has a 0 }
          until (tier = 1) or (diff >= divisor);
        writeln;
        tier := tier – 1
      end;
    writeln;
    write('Enter dividend and divisor: ')
  end
end { LongDivison }.
```

10.40 THE PLOT THICKENS

```
program PlotThickens(input, output);
  {
    Plots two functions, f(x) and g(x), to show that the plot program of the text has
    been generalized to allow the user to specify the range of x and y values used. The plot
    function uses the standard Pascal feature of allowing function names to be passed as
    parameters. Some Pascal compilers (for example Turbo Pascal 3.0) do not allow this.
  }
  const
    prompt = 'Enter xmin, delta-x, ymin, delta-y: ';
    plotchar = '*';
    xlim = 80;                                  { Number of screen columns to use }
    ylim = 21;                                     { Number of screen rows to use }
    x1 = 6;                                           { Column location of y-axis }
    y1 = 1;                                              { Row location of x-axis }
    sl = 35;                                          { Maximum length of title }
    ftitle = 'exp(-x/8) * cos(x)                  ';
    gtitle = '3 * sin(x) * (1 + x^2 * exp(-x))    ';
  type
    str = packed array[1..sl] of char;
  var
    screen : array[y1..ylim, x1..xlim] of char;                   { Screen image }
    xmin, xmax, ymin, ymax : real;                                     { Limits }
    deltax, deltay : real;                                 { x and y increments }
    i : integer;
    r : real;

  function f(x : real) : real;
    {
      First sample function to be plotted.
    }
    begin { f }
      f := exp(–x / 8) * cos(x)
    end { f } ;

  function g(x : real) : real;
    {
      Second sample function to be plotted.
    }
    begin { g }
      g := 3 * sin(x) * (1 + x * x * exp(–x))
    end { g } ;
```

```
procedure plot(function f(x : real) : real;
                    xmin, deltax, ymin, deltay, xtitle, ytitle : real; title : str);
  {
    Plots f(x).
  }
  const
    xinc = 5;                                          { Label every 5th x inc }
    yinc = 2;                                          { Label every 2nd y inc }
  var
    i, j : integer;                                    { Screen coordinates }
    iha : integer;                                     { Index of horizontal axis }
    x, y : real;                                       { Function coordinates }
    xmax, ymax : real;                                 { Maximum x and y }
    xt, yt : integer;
    a, b : real;

  begin { plot }
    writeln; writeln;
    xt := round(xtitle); yt := round(ytitle);
    iha := ylim;                                       { Places horizontal axis at bottom }
    xmax := xmin + deltax * ((xlim - x1) div xinc);
    ymax := ymin + deltay * ((ylim - y1) div yinc);
    a := (ylim - y1) / (ymin - ymax);
    b := y1 - a * ymax;
    for i := y1 to ylim do
      for j := x1 to xlim do
        screen[i, j] := ' ';                           { Blank out the plot area }
    for j := x1 to xlim do                             { Draw horizontal axis }
      if (j - x1 + 1) mod xinc = 1 then
        screen[iha, j] := '|' else screen[iha, j] := '-';
    for i := y1 to ylim do screen[i, x1] := '|';       { Draw vertical axis }
    for j := 1 to 35 do screen[xt, yt + j - 1] := title[j];
    for j := x1 to xlim - 1 do
      begin
        x := xmin + (j - x1) * (xmax - xmin) / (xlim - x1);    { Relate x to index j }
        y := f(x);
        if (y >= ymin) and (y <= ymax) then
          begin
            i := round(a * y + b);                     { Relate y to appropiate row index i }
            screen[i, j] := plotchar                   { Place a plot character at that point }
          end
      end;
    for i := y1 to ylim do
      begin
        if i mod yinc = 1 then
          begin
            write(ymax - (i - 1) * deltay / yinc : x1 - 1 : 1);
            screen[i, x1 + 1] := '-'
          end else write(' ' : x1 - 1);
        for j := x1 to xlim - 1 do write(screen[i, j]);  { Print a row of characters }
          writeln
      end;
    writeln;
    j := x1;                                           { Label the x-axis }
    x := xmin;
    write(' ' : x1 - 4);
    repeat
      write(x : xinc : 1 );
      j := j + xinc;
      x := x + deltax
    until j > xlim;
    writeln
  end { plot } ;
```

```
begin { main }
  writeln('Plot Demo Program');
  writeln;
  xmin := 0; ymin := -1;
  deltax := 0.5; deltay := 0.2;
  plot(f, xmin, deltax, ymin, deltay, 8, 30, ftitle);
  writeln;
  write('Press "Return" for second plot: ');
  readln;
  xmin := 0; ymin := 0;
  deltax := 0.2; deltay := 0.5;
  plot(g, xmin, deltax, ymin, deltay, 12, 33, gtitle)
end { PlotThickens } .
```

10.41 SUBVECTOR

```
program subvector(input, output);
  {
    Test program for procedure subvecsum.
  }
  const
    max = 100;
  type
    vector = array[1..max] of integer;
  var
    A : vector;
    lim : 1..max;
    i, L, R, sum, count : integer;

  procedure subvecsum(var A : vector; L, R : integer; var left, right, sum : integer);
    {
      Finds the subvector of A[L..R] of largest sum and sets left and right to index
      values that mark where that subvector is located within A.
    }
    var
      k, tleft, tright, tsum, t : integer;
    begin { subvecsum }
      if L = R
        then                          { The obvious subvector serves as an anchor }
          begin
            left := L;
            right := R;
            sum := A[L]
          end
        else                 { Obtain the max subvector of array to right of A[L] }
          begin
            subvecsum(A, L + 1, R, tleft, tright, tsum);          { Its sum is tsum }
            t := 0;                              { Perhaps sum of A[L] thru A[tright] }
            for k := L to tright do t := t + A[k];              { forms a greater sum }
            if (A[L] > tsum) and (A[L] > t) then
              begin              { or A[L] alone may be greater than either tsum or t }
                left := L;
                right := L;
                sum := A[L]
              end else
            if t > tsum then
              begin
                left := L; right := tright; sum := t
              end else
              begin
                left := tleft; right := tright; sum := tsum
              end
          end
    end { subvecsum } ;
```

```
begin { main }
  writeln('Subvector Tester');
  writeln;
  write('Enter vector size from 1 to ', max, ': ');
  while not eof do
    begin
      readln(lim);
      writeln;
      writeln('Enter ', lim : 1, ' integer values');
      writeln;
      for i := 1 to lim do read(A[i]);
      readln;
      writeln;
      subvecsum(A, 1, lim, L, R, sum);
      writeln('From L = ', L : 1, ' to R = ', R : 1, ' the sum is ',
              sum : 1, ' for subvector: ');
      writeln;
      count := 0;
      for i := L to R do
        begin
          write(A[i] : 6);
          count := count + 1;
          if count mod 10 = 0 then writeln                { 10 items / line }
        end;
      writeln;
      writeln;
      write('Enter vector size from 1 to ', max, ': ')
    end
end { subvector } .
```

CHAPTER 11 — RECORDS, SETS, AND FILES

You have just a bit of work to do before teaching this chapter and one decision to make. The work is to investigate how large a set may be in your Pascal (so you can tell students what to enter for that limit in Appendix I), and to be prepared to show exactly how Pascal file names are articulated to external operating system names. (You may have done the latter earlier on if your op system didn't provide I/O redirection with respect to the standard files.) If your Pascal offers a *close* procedure, teach its proper use and, whether it does or not, explain the danger of failure to close an external output file. (The text recommends use of *reset* as a synthetic close procedure.)

The decision has to do with your attitude toward variant records. There are at least three possibilities:

1. Time is of the essence, so to hell with them.

2. They have occasional application in data processing (the use that Wirth apparently intended), so cover them once over lightly and tell students never to use a free-union variant record. (To criticize a student who forgets, give 'em the old Bob Uecker line: "He missed the tag! He missed the tag!")

3. Variant records are a powerful tool to thwart Pascal's strong typing. They let us "get at the bits".

Frustrated hackers (and there is some of that in at least one of us) love to tinker in the spirit of option 3, but we now admit that, at least with Turbo Pascal, there is no need to use free-union variants because we can do the same thing with Turbo's "absolute" directive.

SUGGESTED TEST QUESTIONS

Multiple-Choice Questions (Correct answers are indicated by •)

1. The statement*writeln*(*myfile*) is not valid if *myfile* has type

   a **file of** *integer*;
   b **file of** *real*;
   c **file of array**[1..10] **of** *integer*;
   d **file of record** *a,b* : *real* **end**;
   •e none of the above are valid

2. A sensible Pascal record

   a must have a fixed part
   b must have a variant part
   c may have a variant part only if it has a fixed part
   •d must have one or the other or both of a fixed and variant part
   e none of the above is true with respect to a record

3. An operator such as + that has a context-dependent meaning is said to be

   •a overloaded
   b overworked
   c ambiguous
   d two-faced
   e none of the above

4. Which of the following is not a legal set type?

   a **set of** *Boolean*
   b **set of** *char*
   •c **set of** *real*
   d **set of** (*red, white, blue*)
   e all are legal

5. The cardinality of the set [1..5, 4..7, 5, 6] is

   a 4
   b 5
   c 6
   •d 7
   e 11

6. The expression four.zero might have the value

   a 4.0
   b '4.0'
   c 'four.zero'
   d -73
   •e any of the above

7. The set constructor operator is

   a **set of**
   •b [ ]
   c ( )
   d { }
   e none of the above

8. Given that *s* is of type set of 'A'..'Z' and *ch* is of type char, consider:

```
s := ['O'];
for ch := 'A' to 'Z' do
   if (ord(ch) – ord('A')) mod 4 = 0 then s := s + [ch];
s := s – ['M', 'Q'];
```

Which of the following is now true about set *s*?

a The set will still contain only the single letter 'O'
b The set will contain all uppercase letters
c The set will contain all uppercase letters except for 'M' and 'Q'
•d The set will consist of the vowels ['A', 'E', 'I', 'O', 'U', 'Y']
e The set will contain five unknown letters

9. If *f* is declared to be a **file of** *sometype*, the declaration is legal provided that *sometype* is

a any type at all
b any structured type or any simple type other than real
c any type except a record type
d any type except a set type
•e any type except another file type

10. If your Pascal does not have a close statement, the best way to close an external output file of any type is

a rewrite it
•b reset it
c write an end-of-file marker to it
d deliberately abort the program
e reassign its name to a different operating system name

11. Consider the assignment statement *B* := *input*^ where *B* is of type char. The best description of what is happening is

•a *B* is assigned the next unread character in the input buffer
b *B* is assigned a copy of the last character read by a prior read statement
c *B* is assigned an eoln character
d *B* is assigned an eof character
e nothing; the statement is syntactically incorrect

12. Given :

1) *A* and *B* are sets whose elements have the same type
2) the statement *write*(*A* + *B* = *A* * *B*) prints TRUE.

Then we can conclude that

a If *A* is null ([ ]), then so is *B*.
b *A* = *B*
c each set has the same number of elements
d *A* – *B* = [ ]
•e all of the above are true

13. Writing a given number of real numbers to a file of real takes less time than writing them to a textfile because

a floating-point arithmetic is faster than integer arithmetic
b the computer uses faster mass storage devices for files of type real
•c doing so avoids conversion from real to ASCII representation
d all of the above
e none of a through c is true

Programming Questions

1. A certain external file — a Pascal source program, perhaps — consists of lines of text each of which may start with an unknown number of blanks, i.e., some lines may start with 3 blanks, some with 17, some with none at all. We want to create a compressed file with the same information except that each line of the created file should start with `m\` where `m` is the number of blanks, perhaps 0, that started the corresponding line of the original file but which are not copied to the revised file. The backward slash, '\', is used to separate blank counts from the next valid character in the file.

   Example: A line which starts `-------program zilch;` {where the '-'s represent blanks} would be saved as `7\program zilch;` (which happens to save five characters).

   Write a program to do the above. Let your user specify the names of the original and compressed files at run time.

2. Given

```
type
  inches = real;
  lbs = real;
  person = record
    name: string[30];
    height : inches;
    weight : lbs
  end;
```

   Given also that file `PEOPLE.TXT` contains an unknown number of records of the type shown. Write a program that reads the file and prints out the record of all persons whose weight exceeds twice their height.

3. Assume that you have access to **function** *ran*(*n*) that returns a random integer in the range 0 to $n - 1$. Write a program that fills a two-dimensional array of dimensions 0..9, 0..9 with random integers in the range 0..9, displays the array as it is being filled, and then prints the index of all rows and columns that contain all ten values 0..9. As indexes are printed, identify each as to whether it is a row index or a column index. Use set operations to determine whether a row or column contains all of the digits.

4. A file whose name is to be specified as input contains English words, one per line, some of which are capitalized and some of which are not. The first few words in a typical file might be

```
ace
America
Azores
baseball
Brazil
```

   Write a program that reads such a file and that writes all capitalized words to external file UC.TXT and all other words to external file LC.TXT.

5. Given

```
type gizmo = record
      { stuff }
    end;

var f, g : file of gizmo;
```

   Assume that file *f* is an existing file that contains an unknown number of records (and therefore possibly an odd number). Write a program that copies file *f* to file *g*, but with each successive pair of records reversed. If there is a record left over, just tack it on to the end of *g*. Assign files *f* and *g* to particular names of your invention. Open and close both files properly and be careful with your end of file test.

6. Two files LC.TXT and UC.TXT each contain one English word per line and are in alphabetic order. All of the words in LC.TXT are made up only of lower case letters and those in UC.TXT have their first letter (only) capitalized. The first few words in each of these files might be

LC.TXT	UC.TXT
`ace`	`America`
`arcade`	`Azores`
`baseball`	`Brazil`
`bright`	`Britain`

Write a program that reads such files, merges them into one alphabetized file, and writes that file to an external file whose name is specified as input.

7. Given **type** *AllCharacters* = **set of** *char*;

Write **procedure** *ReadUntilAllFound*(**var** *n* : *integer*); that reads lines of varying length of text, keeps track of all the different characters found in a variable of type *AllCharacters*, and continues until all the different characters have been found. It should then set *n* to the total number of characters read.

8. As an aid to a quack psychologist who is studying ESP, write a program to do the following:

Randomly shuffle a deck of 100 cards each containing a single symbol [25 cards for each of the following four symbols: * (star) o (circle) + (plus) – (minus)].

Deal the cards one at a time but do not display them. Request the subject to enter one of the four symbols as a guess as to the symbol on the card just dealt. Keep track of each symbol dealt and the subject's response to that symbol in an array of type *results* where

```
type
  symbol = (star, circle, plus, minus);
  results = array[symbol, symbol] of integer;
```

Use rows for the symbol on the card and columns for the response. When all 100 cards have been dealt and the responses recorded, write the array of results and count the correct guesses (the sum of all the diagonal elements of the array) and the total number of times each symbol was selected by the subject (the sums of each of the columns of the array).

9. Given

```
type
  bit = 0..1;
  dual = record
    case tag : bit of
      0 : (letter : char);
      1 : (number : integer)
    end;
var
  f : file of dual;
```

Write a program that asks the user to specify the actual name of existing file *f*. Assign the file, open it, read and print each of its records, and close it.

SOLUTIONS TO PROGRAMMING EXERCISES

11.9 HIDDEN MESSAGES

```
program HiddenMessages(input, output, inf);
  {
    Reads a hidden-message square and tests procedures used to extract messages.
  }
  const
    maxsize = 676;
    maxmessages = 160;
    maxlength = 64;
  type
    cell = record
        number : integer;
        letter : char
    end;
    puzzle = array[1..maxsize] of cell;
    str = packed array[1..maxlength] of char;
  var
    A : puzzle;
    i, j, rows, cols : integer;
    inf : text;

  procedure ReadPuzzle(var a : puzzle; var rows, cols : integer);
    {
      Reads the puzzle as a linear array of records. Size of array is determined by the input
      which will be found in the file MESSAGES.DAT. This file must have the numbers
      on odd numbered lines and the letters on even numbered lines. Each number or letter
      shoud be right adjusted in a field width of 3 characters.
    }
    var
      i, j : integer;
    begin { ReadPuzzle }
      i := 0;
      j := 0;
      rows := 0;                                          { To count the rows }
      cols := 0;                                          { To count the columns }
      while not eof(inf) do
        begin
          while not eoln(inf) do
            begin
              i := i + 1;
              read(inf, a[i].number)      { Numbers come on odd numbered lines }
            end;
          if cols = 0 then cols := i;            { Set columns only the first time }
          readln(inf);                                    { End line of numbers }
          while not eoln(inf) do
            begin                         { Letters come on even numbered lines }
              j := j + 1;
              read(inf, a[j].letter);              { Two blanks before each letter }
              read(inf, a[j].letter);
              read(inf, a[j].letter)
            end;
          rows := rows + 1;
          readln(inf)
        end
    end { ReadPuzzle } ;
```

```
procedure Display(A : puzzle;rows, cols : integer);
  {
    Prints the message puzzle.
  }
  var
    i, j, margin : integer;
  begin { Display }
    writeln(' ' : 35, 'The Puzzle');
    writeln;
    margin := 38 - 3 * cols div 2;                    { Length of margin }
    for i := 1 to rows do
      begin
        write(' ' : margin);                       { Write a line of numbers }
        for j := 1 + cols * (i - 1) to cols * i do write(A[j].number : 3);
        writeln;
        write(' ' : margin);                         { Write a line of letters }
        for j := 1 + cols * (i - 1) to cols * i do write('  ', A[j].letter);
        writeln
      end
  end { Display } ;

procedure ReadMess(a : puzzle;rows, cols, MessNo : integer);
  {
    Displays message number MessNo in puzzle a.
  }
  var
    i : integer;
  begin { ReadMess }
    write('Message #', MessNo : 1, ': ');
    for i := 1 to rows * cols do
      if a[i].number = MessNo then write(a[i].letter);
    writeln
  end { ReadMess } ;

procedure ReadAll(a : puzzle;rows, cols : integer);
  {
    Copies all messages into the message array and then displays them.
  }
  var
    i, MessNo : integer;
    message : array[1..maxmessages] of str;
    size : array[1..maxmessages] of integer;
  begin { ReadAll }
    for MessNo := 1 to maxmessages do size[MessNo] := 0;
    for i := 1 to rows * cols do                       { Collect the messages }
      begin
        MessNo := a[i].number;
        size[MessNo] := size[MessNo] + 1;
        message[MessNo, size[MessNo]] := a[i].letter
      end;
    for MessNo := 1 to maxmessages do                         { Print them }
      if size[MessNo] > 0 then
        begin
          write('Message #', MessNo : 1, ': ');
          for i := 1 to size[MessNo] do write(message[MessNo, i]);
          writeln;
          writeln
        end
  end { ReadAll } ;
```

```
begin { main }
  reset(inf, 'MESSAGES.DAT');
  ReadPuzzle(A, rows, cols);                         { Read the puzzle }
  Display(A, rows, cols);                            { Display the puzzle }
  writeln;
  writeln('*** Test of ReadMess ***');
  writeln;
  for i := 9 downto 0 do                             { Will show all messages from }
    begin                                            { 9 down to 0 that are in the puzzle}
      ReadMess(A, rows, cols, i);
      writeln
    end;
  writeln;
  writeln('*** Test of ReadAll ***');
  writeln;
  ReadAll(A, rows, cols)                             { Shows all messages in the puzzle }
end { messages } .
```

11.10 BOWLING SCORES

```
program bowling(input, output, inf);
  {
    Displays lines of bowling scores based on pins/roll input.
  }
  const
    NameMax = 15;
  type
    frame = record
      mark1, mark2, mark3 : char;
      score : integer
    end;
    str = packed array[1..NameMax] of char;
    line = record
      name : str;
      score : array[1..10] of frame
    end;
  var
    row : line;
    i, j, FirstRoll, SecondRoll, ExtraRoll, total : integer;
    keep : array[1..21] of integer;
    foul : Boolean;
    inf : text;

  procedure ReadName( var s : str);
    {
      Reads a bowler's name into s and fills s with trailing blanks.
    }
    var
      i, j : integer;
    begin { ReadName }
      i := 0;
      repeat
        i := i + 1;
        read(inf, s[i])
      until s[i] = ' ';
      for j := i + 1 to NameMax do s[j] := ' '
    end { ReadName } ;
```

```
procedure GetRoll(var Roll : integer; var mark : char; LastRoll : integer;
                  var foul : Boolean);
  {
    Reads the next Roll from input file. Uses LastRoll to determine any mark for this
    Roll and sets foul if there has been a foul.
  }
  var
    first : Boolean;
  begin { GetRoll }
    mark := ' ';
    read(inf, Roll);
    j := j + 1;
    first := LastRoll = -1;
    if LastRoll = -1 then LastRoll := 0;
    if Roll > 10 then foul := true else
      if first and (Roll = 10) then mark := 'X' else
        if Roll + LastRoll > 10 then foul := true else
          if Roll + LastRoll = 10 then mark := '/' else
    mark := chr(ord('0') + Roll);
    if foul then keep[j] := 0 else keep[j] := Roll
  end { GetRoll } ;

procedure LineOf(c : char);
  {
    Writes a line of the character c.
  }
  var
    k : integer;
  begin { LineOf }
    for k := 1 to NameMax + 50 do write(c);
    writeln
  end { LineOf } ;

procedure WriteRow(Row : line; n : integer);
  {
    Writes the output for one bowler.
  }
  var
    i, j : integer;
  begin { WriteRow }
    with row do
      begin
        LineOf('=');
        write('Frame', ' ' : NameMax - 5);                 { Writes frame numbers }
        for i := 1 to 10 do write(i : 5);
        writeln;
        LineOf('-');
        write(' ' : NameMax);                                       { Writes marks }
        for i := 1 to n - 1 do write('      ', score[i].mark1, score[i].mark2);
        if n = 10
          then writeln('    ', score[10].mark1, score[10].mark2, score[10].mark3)
          else writeln;
        LineOf('-');
        write(name);                                                { Writes name }
        i := 0; j := 1;
        total := 0;
        while i < n do                                               { and scores }
          begin
            i := i + 1;
            if (keep[j] = 10) or (keep[j] + keep[j + 1] = 10)
              then total := total + keep[j] + keep[j + 1] + keep[j + 2]
              else total := total + keep[j] + keep[j + 1];
            if foul and (i = n) then write(' Foul') else write(total : 5);
```

```
          if keep[j] = 10 then j := j + 1 else j := j + 2
        end;
      writeln
    end
  end { WriteRow } ;

begin { main }
  reset(inf, 'BOWLING.DAT');
  while not eof(inf) do
    begin
      ReadName(row.name);                                    { Read a name }
      i := 0; j := 0; foul := false;
      while (i < 10) and (not foul) do                    { For each frame }
        begin
          i := i + 1;
          GetRoll(FirstRoll, row.score[i].mark1, -1, foul);       { Get first roll }
          if FirstRoll = 10
            then row.score[i].mark2 := ' '              { and second if not strike }
            else GetRoll(SecondRoll, row.score[i].mark2, FirstRoll, foul)
        end;
      if FirstRoll = 10 then            { Two more rolls needed in 10th frame strike }
        begin
          GetRoll(ExtraRoll, row.score[10].mark2, -1, foul);
          if row.score[10].mark2 = 'X'
            then GetRoll(ExtraRoll, row.score[10].mark3, -1, foul)
            else GetRoll(ExtraRoll, row.score[10].mark3, ExtraRoll, foul)
        end else
      if FirstRoll + SecondRoll = 10  { One more roll needed if 10th frame spare }
        then GetRoll(ExtraRoll, row.score[10].mark3, 0, foul)
        else row.score[10].mark3 := ' ';
      readln(inf);
      WriteRow(row, i)
    end;
  LineOf('=')
end { bowling }.
```

11.11 VANNA

```
program Vanna(input, output, message);
  {
    Prints a phrase with hidden letters. The player select letters to make the hidden ones visible.
  }
  const
    rows = 5; cols = 20;                                            { Array size }
  type
    cell = record
      ch : char;
      visible : Boolean                      { Indicates whether this character is visible }
    end;
    grid = array[1..rows, 1..cols] of cell;
  var
    board : grid;
    c, letter : char;
    message : text;

  function upper(c : char) : char;                              { ASCII version }
    begin if c in ['a'..'z'] then upper := chr(ord(c) - 32) else upper := c end;
```

```
procedure fill(var A : grid);
  {
    Reads the message file and fills the grid.  Only upper case letters are visible.
  }
  var
    i, j : integer;
    s : string[20];
  begin { fill }
    write('Message file? ');          { Get file name — a Turbo string is used }
    readln(s);
    reset(message, s);
    for i := 1 to rows do
      begin
        for j := 1 to cols do
          begin
            if not eoln(message) then read(message, c) else
              begin      { Because some compilers don't read eoln chars as blanks }
                readln(message); c := ' '
              end;
            A[i, j].visible := c in [' ', 'A'..'Z'];
            A[i, j].ch := upper(c)                   { Always store upper case letters }
          end
      end
  end { fill } ;

procedure display(var A : grid);
  {
    Show the grid (visible letters only).
  }
  var
    i, j : integer;
  begin { display }
    writeln;
    for i := 1 to rows do
      begin
        write('                    ');
        for j := 1 to cols do
          if A[i, j].visible then write(A[i, j].ch) else write('.');
        writeln
      end
  end { display } ;

procedure turn(L : char; var A : grid);
  {
    Make all letters L in grid visible.
  }
  var
    i, j : integer;
  begin { turn }
      for i := 1 to rows do
        for j := 1 to cols do
          if A[i, j].ch = upper(L) then A[i, j].visible := true
  end { turn } ;
```

```
begin { main }
  fill(board);
  display(board);
  write('Letter? ');
  while not eof do
    begin
      readln(letter);
      turn(letter, board);
      display(board);
      write('Letter? ')
    end
end { Vanna }.
```

11.12 RECORD MERGE

```
program filemergeDriver(input, output, f1, f2, f3);
  type
    employee = record
      name : packed array[1..5] of char;
      id : integer
    end;
    testfile = file of employee;
  var
    f1, f2, f3  : testfile;
    emp : employee;

  procedure filemerge(var a, b, c : testfile);
    {
      Merges the records in ordered files a and b and places them in file c.
    }
    begin
      reset(a); reset(b); rewrite(c);
      while (not eof(a)) or (not eof(b)) do
        begin
          if eof(a)  then read(b, emp) else
          if eof(b)  then read(a, emp) else
          if a^.id < b^.id then read(a, emp) else read(b, emp);
          write(c, emp)
        end { while }
    end { filemerge };

  begin { main }
    rewrite(f1);
    emp.name := 'Laine';
    emp.id := 1234;
    write(f1, emp);
    emp.name := 'Adams';
    emp.id := 2345;
    write(f1, emp);
    emp.name := 'Baker';
    emp.id := 3456;
    write(f1, emp);
    emp.name := 'Hatch';
    emp.id := 4567;
    write(f1, emp);
    emp.name := 'Drake';
    emp.id := 5678;
    write(f1, emp);
    rewrite(f2);
    emp.name := 'Evans';
    emp.id := 2000;
    write(f2, emp);
    emp.name := 'Marks';
```

```
    emp.id := 2500;
    write(f2, emp);
    emp.name := 'Slade';
    emp.id := 3000;
    write(f2, emp);
    emp.name := 'Tonks';
    emp.id := 3500;
    write(f2, emp);
    emp.name := 'Brown';
    emp.id := 4000;
    write(f2, emp);
    emp.name := 'Jones';
    emp.id := 4500;
    write(f2, emp);
    emp.name := 'Lampe';
    emp.id := 5000;
    write(f2, emp);
    emp.name := 'Green';
    emp.id := 5500;
    write(f2, emp);
    filemerge(f1, f2, f3);
                              { Now we've prepared and merged two ordered files }
                                     { Let's see if filemerge did its job correctly }
    reset(f3);
    while not eof(f3) do
      begin
        read(f3, emp);
        writeln(emp.id : 4, '    ', emp.name)
      end
  end { FileMergeDriver } .
```

11.13 STORAGE PACKS

```
program StoragePacks(input, output);
  {
    Displays the storage representation of different data types.
  }
  type
    bit = 0..1;
    byte = 0..255;
    choice = 0..6;
    types = record
      case choice of
        0 : ( int : integer);
        1 : ( B : packed array[0..15] of Boolean);
        2 : ( bt : packed array[0..15] of bit);
        3 : ( s : set of 0..15);
        4 : ( by : packed array[0..1] of byte);
        5 : ( ch : packed array[1..2] of char);
        6 : ( cz : packed array[0..1] of char)
      end;
  var
    all : types;
    i, j, n : integer;
    c : char;
```

```
procedure option(var n : integer);
  {
    Displays options and reads choice to n.
  }
  begin { option }
    writeln;
    writeln('      Options');
    writeln;
    writeln('0     Integer');
    writeln('1     Boolean [0..15]');
    writeln('2     Bit [0..15]');
    writeln('3     Set of 0..15');
    writeln('4     Byte [0..1]');
    writeln('5     Char [1..2]');
    writeln('6     Char [0..1]');
    writeln('7     End program');
    writeln;
    write('To select an option, enter 0..7: ');
    readln(n);
    writeln
  end { option } ;

begin { main }
  writeln('Storage Pack');
  option(n);                                    { Select an option }
  while (n >= 0) and (n < 7) do
    begin
      write('Enter ');                { Provide the data for that data type }
      case n of
        0: begin
             write('an integer: ');
             readln(all.int)
           end;
        1: begin
             writeln('16 Boolean values each as T or F',
                     ' with no spaces between them: ');
             for i := 0 to 15 do
               begin
                 read(c);
                 all.B[i] := (c = 'T') or (c = 't')
               end;
             readln
           end;
        2: begin
             writeln('16 bits with spaces between them: ');
             for i := 0 to 15 do read(all.bt[i]);
             readln
           end;
        3: begin
             writeln('the members of 0..15 that are in the set.');
             all.s := [];
             while not eoln do
               begin
                 read(i);
                 all.s := all.s + [i]
               end;
               readln
           end;
        4: begin
             writeln('Enter 2 integers in [0..255].');
             readln(all.by[0], all.by[1])
           end;
```

```
        5: begin
             write('Enter 2 characters: ');
             readln(all.ch[1], all.ch[2])
           end;
        6: begin
             write('Enter 2 characters: ');
             readln(all.cz[0], all.cz[1])
           end
        end { case };
      writeln;                                          { Write all the data types }
      writeln('Integer:        ', all.int);
      write('Boolean:       ');
      for i := 0 to 15 do if all.B[i] then write('T ') else write('F ');
      writeln;
      write('Bit:            ');
      for i := 0 to 15 do
        if all.bt[i] in [0,1] then write(all.bt[i]:2) else write('  ?');
      writeln;
      write('Set:            ');
      for i := 0 to 15 do if i in all.s then write(i : 1, ' ');
      writeln;
      writeln('Byte:            ', all.by[0] : 1, '  ', all.by[1] : 1);
      writeln('Characters: "', all.ch[1], all.ch[2], '"');
      writeln('Characterz: "', all.cz[0], all.cz[1], '"');
      option(n)
    end
  end { StoragePacks } .
```

11.14 LETTER SETS

```
program LetterSets(input, output);
  {
    Reads a rows by cols grid of letters and lists the row pairs that contain the same letters
    and those that have no letters in common.
  }
  const
    rows = 5;                                                   { Size of grid }
    cols = 5;
  type
    grid = array[1..rows, 1..cols] of 'A'..'Z';
  var
    G : grid;

  procedure fillgrid(var G : grid);
    {
      Reads letters to fill the grid.
    }
    var
      r, c : integer;
      ch : char;

    function upper(c : char) : char;                          { ASCII version }
      begin if c in ['a'..'z'] then upper:=chr(ord(c) -32) else upper:=c end;
```

```
begin { fillgrid }
  for r := 1 to rows do
    begin
      for c := 1 to cols do
        begin
          read(ch);
          G[r, c] := upper(ch)
        end;
      readln
    end
end { fillgrid } ;

procedure showgrid(G : grid);
  {
    Displays the grid.
  }
  var
    r, c : integer;
  begin { showgrid }
    writeln;
    writeln('The Grid');
    writeln;
    for r:=1 to rows do
      begin
        for c:=1 to cols do write(G[r, c]);
        writeln
      end;
    writeln
  end { showgrid } ;

procedure rowcompare(var G : grid);
  {
    Puts letters from each row into a set for that row and then compares row set pairs to
    see if they are the same or contain no common elements.
  }
  var
    r, c, k : integer;
    s : array[1..rows] of set of 'A'..'Z';          { Set of letters used on each row }
  begin
    for r := 1 to rows do
      begin
        s[r] := [ ];                                          { Initialize to null set }
        for c := 1 to cols do s[r] := s[r] + [ G[r, c] ]      { Include letters on row }
      end;
    for r := 1 to rows - 1 do
      for k := r + 1 to rows do                               { For all row pairs }
        if s[r] = s[k] then
          writeln('Rows', r : 2, ' and', k : 2, ' use the same letters.') else
        if s[r] * s[k] = [ ] then
          writeln('Rows', r : 2, ' and', k : 2, ' have no letter in common.')
  end { rowcompare };

begin { main }
  writeln('Enter the letters in the ', rows : 1, ' x ', cols : 1, ' grid ');
  writeln;
  fillgrid(G);
  showgrid(G);
  rowcompare(G)
end { LetterSets }.
```

11.15 PRIME SIEVE

```
program primefind(output);
  {
    Forms and prints a set of all primes <= maxsetsize.
  }
  const
    maxsetsize = 255;
  type
    intset = set of 0..maxsetsize;
  var
    primes : intset;
    i, j : integer;

  procedure printset(var s : intset);
    {
      Prints a list of all integers in the set s.
    }
    var
      i, count : integer;
    begin { printset }
      count := 0;
      for i := 1 to maxsetsize do
        begin
          if i in s then
            begin
              write(i : 6);
              count := count + 1;
              if count mod 10 = 0 then writeln          { For 10 primes per line }
            end
        end;
      writeln
    end { printset } ;
  begin { main }
    writeln('Table of primes less than ', maxsetsize + 1 : 1);
    writeln;
    primes := [2];                   { Initialize to a set containing the only even prime }
    i := 3;
    while i <= maxsetsize do    { Add to primes all odd numbers from 3 to maxsetsize }
      begin
        primes := primes + [i];
        i := i + 2
      end;
    j := 3;
    while j < 16 do
      begin
        while not (j in primes) do j := j + 2;                  { Find a prime }
        i := j * j;                               { Delete all its multiples from primes }
        while i < maxsetsize do
          begin
            primes := primes - [i];
            i := i + 2 * j
          end;
        j := j + 2
      end;
    printset(primes)
  end { primefind } .
```

11.16 FILE JOIN

```
program FileJoin(input, output, infile1, infile2, outfile);
  {
    Two text files (names requested as input) are joined by appending the second file to the
    first. The output file name is also requested and cannot be the same as either of the input
    files. Each of the files is listed on the screen as a check. Turbo Pascal strings are used.
  }
  var
    line : string[255];
    inf1, inf2, outf : string[20];
    infile1, infile2, outfile : text;

  begin
    writeln('File Join Program');
    writeln;
    write('Enter name of first input file: ');        { Read file names }
    readln(inf1);
    writeln;
    write('Enter name of second input file: ');
    readln(inf2);
    writeln;
    write('Enter name of output file: ');
    readln(outf);
    writeln;
    reset(infile1, inf1);                              { Open files }
    reset(infile2, inf2);
    rewrite(outfile, outf);
    writeln('Reading from "', inf1, '": ');
    while not eof(infile1) do
      begin
        readln(infile1, line);                         { Read from infile1 }
        writeln(line);                                 { Print a line on screen }
        writeln(outfile, line)                         { and write to outfile }
      end;
    writeln; writeln('Reading from "', inf2, '": ');
    while not eof(infile2) do
      begin
        readln(infile2, line);                         { Read from infile1 }
        writeln(line);                                 { Print a line on screen }
        writeln(outfile, line)                         { and write to outfile }
      end;
    writeln;
    close(outfile);                                    { Close output file }
    reset(outfile, outf);                              { and reopen for reading }
    writeln('This is the joined file "', outf, '": ');
    while not eof(outfile) do
      begin
        readln(outfile, line);
        writeln(line)
      end
  end { FileJoin } .
```

11.17 SINGLE SPACE

```
program SingleSpace(input, output, f2, f1);
  {
    Reads a multispaced text file and writes it to an output file with all empty lines omitted.
  }
  var
    ch : char;
    f1, f2 : text;
    filespec1, filespec2 : string[20];
  begin
    write('Enter name of multi-spaced input file: ');
    readln(filespec1);
    write('Enter name of single-spaced output file: ');
    readln(filespec2);
    reset(f1, filespec1);                                    { Open files }
    rewrite(f2, filespec2);
    writeln;
    writeln('Reading "', filespec1, '"');
    writeln;
    writeln('Writing "', filespec2, '"');
    writeln;
    while not eof(f1) do
      begin
        while eoln(f1) and not eof(f1) do readln(f1);       { Skip null lines of f1 }
        if not eof(f1) then
          begin                                              { Copy non-null lines to f2 }
            while not eoln(f1) do
              begin
                read(f1, ch);
                write(f2, ch)
              end;
            readln(f1);
            writeln(f2)
          end
      end;
    close(f1);                                               { Close files }
    close(f2);
    writeln('Done', chr(7))
  end { SingleSpace } .
```

11.19 REAL QUICK

```
program RealQuick(realfile, textfile, output);
  {
    Reads and writes files of real and text files and times these operatons.
  }
  const
    limit = 10000;                       { The number of reals to read and write }
  var
    x : real;
    i, time1, time2, time3 : integer;
    realfile : file of real;
    textfile : text;

  function clock : integer;
    {
      A dummy function to be replaced by one that reads your clock.
    }
    begin { clock }
      clock := 0
    end { clock } ;
```

```
begin { main }
  writeln('File Timing Program');
  writeln;
  x := 1.0;
  time1 := clock;                                          { Get start time }
  rewrite(realfile, 'real');
  for i := 1 to limit do                                   { Write to file of real }
    begin
      write(realfile, x);
      x := x + 1.0
    end;
  close(realfile);
  reset(realfile, 'real');                                 { Read them back }
  for i := 1 to limit do read(realfile, x);
  close(realfile);
  time2 := clock;                                          { Get finish time }
  writeln('The time to read and write ', limit : 1,
    ' reals in a file of real is ', time2 - time1 : 1, ' time units.');
  x := 1.0;
  time1 := clock;                                          { Get start time }
  rewrite(textfile, 'text');
  for i := 1 to limit do                                   { Write to text file }
    begin
      writeln(textfile, x); x := x + 1.0
    end;
  close(textfile);
  reset(textfile, 'text');
  x := 1.0;
  for i := 1 to limit do read(textfile, x);                { Read them back }
  close(textfile);
  time2 := clock;                                          { Get finish time }
  writeln('The time to read and write ', limit : 1,
    ' reals in a textfile is ', time2 - time1 : 1, ' time units.')
end.
```

11.20 ELECTORAL VOTE

```
program ElectoralVote(infile, output);
  {
    Computation of the number of electoral votes for each state and the District of Columbia
    based on state names and population figures in the text file US.POP.  The share
    of votes for each state is computed as a real number including a fractional part.  When
    the fraction is removed from each state's share, the resulting total number of votes will
    be less that 435.  An additional vote is then awarded to states based on the largest
    unused fractional part of the share until all 435 votes have been allocated.
  }
  const
    states = 50;
  type
    state = record
      name : packed array[1..14] of char;
      population : real;
      votes : integer;
      fraction : real
    end;
    union = array[1..states] of state;
    IndexList = array[1..states] of integer;
  var
    US : union;
    infile : text;
```

```
procedure ReadPop(var US : union);
  {
    Reads state names and population figures.
  }
  var
    i, j : integer;
  begin { ReadPop }
    reset(infile, 'US.POP');
    for i := 1 to states do
      begin
        for j := 1 to 14 do read(infile, US[i].name[j]);
        readln(infile, US[i].population)
      end
  end { ReadPop } ;

procedure apportion(var US : union);
  {
    Apportions votes to each of the states pased on population entries in US array.
  }
  var
    i, totalvotes : integer;
    totalpop, share : real;
    Index : IndexList;
  procedure SelectionIndexSort(var Index : IndexList);
    {
      A selection sort that sorts by an index list a into the global array US.
    }
    var
      i, j, maxdex, temp : integer;
      max : real;
    begin { SelectionIndexSort }
      for i := 1 to states do Index[i] := i;                     { Initialize index list }
      for i := 1 to states - 1 do                                { Do ith pass }
        begin
          max := US[Index[i]].fraction;                   { Initialize max as first number }
          maxdex := i;                                                  { and its index }
          for j := i + 1 to states do             { Search through array for a larger one }
            if US[Index[j]].fraction > max then              { Each time we find one, }
              begin
                max := US[Index[j]].fraction;                          { Keep its value }
                maxdex := j                                                 { and index }
              end;
          temp := Index[maxdex];                                          { Switch it }
          Index[maxdex] := Index[i];                     { with first number not yet sorted }
          Index[i] := temp                                     { so it is in its proper place }
        end
    end { SelectionIndexSort } ;

  begin { apportion }
    totalpop := 0;                                            { Compute total population }
    for i := 1 to states do totalpop := totalpop + US[i].population;
    totalvotes := 0;
    for i := 1 to states do
      begin
        share := 435 * US[i].population / totalpop;              { Share for each state }
        US[i].votes := trunc(share);                           { Whole number of votes }
        if US[i].votes = 0 then US[i].votes := 1;                         { Cannot be 0 }
        US[i].fraction := share - US[i].votes;                        { Unused fraction }
        totalvotes := totalvotes + US[i].votes                      { Votes given so far }
      end;
```

```
    SelectionIndexSort(Index);                { Index will show order of fractions }
    for i := 1 to 435 – totalvotes do         { Give neediest states 1 more until 435 }
      US[Index[i]].votes := US[Index[i]].votes + 1;               { have been given }
    for i := 1 to states do
      US[i].votes := US[i].votes + 2                          { Each state gets 2 more }
  end { apportion } ;

procedure show(US : union);
  {
    Print the array of states, populations, and votes.
  }
  var
    i, j, totalvotes, minvotes : integer;
  begin { show }
    writeln('State           Population Votes'); writeln;
    minvotes := US[1].votes; totalvotes := 0;
    for i := 1 to states do
      begin
        writeln(US[i].name, US[i].population : 10 : 0, US[i].votes : 6);
        totalvotes := totalvotes + US[i].votes;                 { Count the votes }
        if US[i].votes < minvotes then minvotes := US[i].votes { Find minimum }
      end;
    writeln('D. C.', minvotes : 25);                   { Give D. C. the minimum }
    totalvotes := totalvotes + minvotes;
    writeln; writeln('Total Electoral Votes', totalvotes : 9)
  end { show } ;

begin { main }
  writeln('Computation of Electoral Votes by State');
  writeln;
  ReadPop(US);
  apportion(US);
  show(US)
end { ElectoralVote } .
```

CHAPTER 12 — POINTERS

This chapter is likely to be either the last one you will cover during your first semester or the first one you will cover during your second. In either case, the care and feeding of pointers is usually something that students find somewhat unnatural and difficult to master. One well-known computer scientist, Anthony Hoare (who invented the case statement), believes that the whole concept of a pointer is a big mistake. He says that pointers are to data structures as **goto** is to language structure, and you know what most computer scientists think of that four-letter word. (Lisp gets along quite nicely without explicit mention of pointers; they're there, but kept hidden as a good example of information hiding.) Nonetheless, no Pascal course is complete without coverage of pointers; hence Chapter 12.

Whatever else you do, make your students run the "finger-walking" example. After that, we recommend that you cover the various kinds of linked lists and the section on binary trees in the order presented. Some of the exercises are a bit difficult, so you may want to assign those that are based on an existing program that is to be modified rather than those that make the student write a pointer-based program from scratch. You know your students; challenge them, but don't destroy them. If you really are in the final stages of the first semester, leave something for the data structures teacher to do next term. But if you are just beginning the data structures course, then, by all means, spend a good bit of time on this chapter and assign several of the exercises.

SUGGESTED TEST QUESTIONS

Multiple-Choice Questions (Correct answers are indicated by •)

1. Which of the following data types may be returned as the value of a Standard Pascal function?

 a array
 b record
 c set
 d file
 •e pointer

2. Which of the following is not a Standard Pascal reserved word?

 a nil
 •b otherwise
 c packed
 d set
 e with

3. A Pascal record that has no name is said to be

 a illegal
 •b anonymous
 c orphaned
 d incognito
 e none of the above

4. The memory space currently used to hold nodes created by new statements is called

 a available space
 •b the heap
 c the stack
 d a buffer
 e none of the above

5. If $A\text{^} = B$ and $B\text{^} = A$ then which of the following must be true?

 a $A = B$
 b $A\text{^} = B\text{^}$
 •c $A\text{^^} = A$
 d all of the above
 e none of a through c is true

6. The seven nodes of a certain complete binary tree are named A to G in breadth-first order. The nodes listed by postorder traversal would be

 a ABCDEFG
 b GFEDCBA
 c ABDECFG
 d DBEAFCG
 •e DEBFGCA

7. If $p\text{^} = q\text{^}$, which of the following is necessarily true?

 a $p = q$
 b p and q have the same type
 c $p\text{^}$ and $q\text{^}$ are nodes in the same linked structure
 d all of the above
 •e none of a through c is necessarily true

 { Note to instructor: (b) is "almost" true, but if $p\text{^}$ is 5 and $q\text{^}$ is 5.0, then $p\text{^} = q\text{^}$ even though p and q have different types.}

8. At a time when pointer *P* is pointing to the second node of a 3-node DLLL, these two statements are executed:

```
P^.left^.right := nil;
P^.right^.left := nil;
```

The structure is now indistinguishable from

a three isolated nodes
b a 3-node SLLL
c a 3-node SLCL
d a 3-node DLCL
• e a complete binary tree of height 1

Programming Questions

1. Complete a recusive definition of

function *identical(L1,L2 : ptr) : Boolean;*

that returns *true* iff *L1* and *L2* point to SLLLs that are identical. Each list is composed of nodes that have fields called *info* and *link.* (By "identical" is meant that corresponding nodes of the lists have identical *info* parts; we don't expect their connective links to be identical.) If the lists are not identical, their lengths may (or may not) differ. Either or both may be **nil**. If both are **nil**, consider them identical.

2. Consider the binary trees shown below:

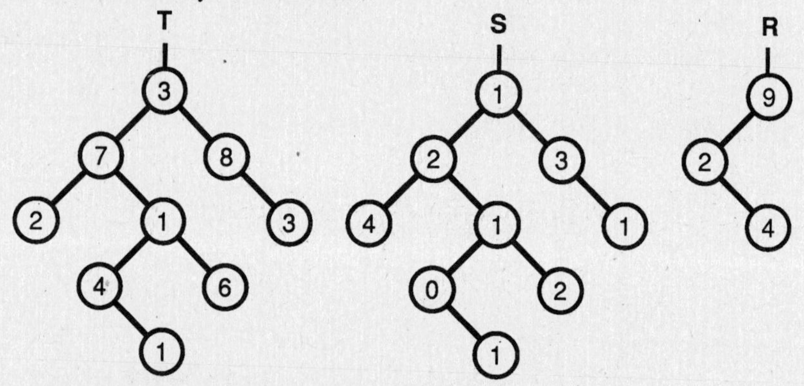

Tree T is called *congruent* to tree S because they have the same shape. Tree S is called *sumequal* to tree R because the sum of the integers in all nodes in S is the same as the corresponding sum for tree R.

Write a recursive function *treecongruent(T, S)* that returns *true* if trees *T* and *S* are congruent and *false* otherwise.

Write recursive function *treesumequal(T, S)* that returns *true* if trees *T* and *S* are sumequal and *false* otherwise.

3. Write Pascal **function** *leaves(T : tree) : integer* that returns as its value the number of leaves in the tree *T*.

4. Write Pascal **function** *biggest(T : nodeptr) : nodeptr;* that returns as its value a pointer to the node with the largest *info* field (which is of type *integer*) in the binary tree *T*. If there is more than one node with the same largest value, return a pointer to any one of them. If there are no nodes in the list, return **nil**.

5. Write a recursive Pascal **procedure** *prune*(*L* : *list*) that deletes the last node from the nonempty linear linked list *L*. Issue an error message if the list is **nil**.

6. You are given an arithmetic expression in the form of a binary tree. The *info* part of each of the nodes is either a dyadic operator (+ – * /) or an integer operand. Example: 3 + 4 * 5 / (7 – 5) can be represented as follows:

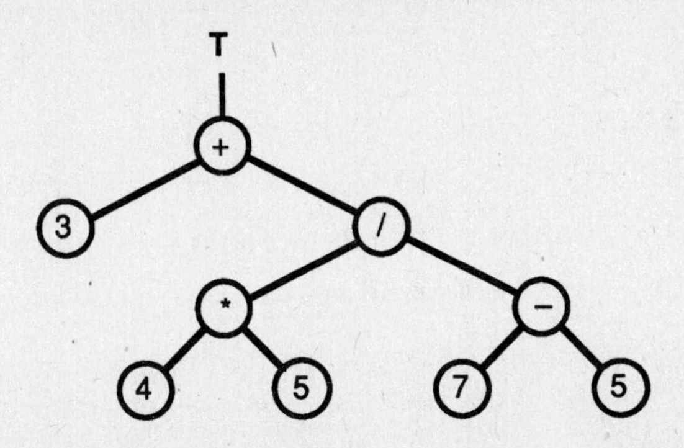

Write a type definition for **type** *node* and then **function** *value*(*T* : *tree*) : *integer*; that returns the numerical value of the expression represented by tree *T* (this would be 13 for the above expression).

7. Write Pascal **procedure** *advance*(**var** *L* : *list*; *i*, *j* : *integer*) where *L* points to an SLLL. This procedure should modify the SLLL so that the *i*th item has been moved *j* positions toward the beginning of the list.

Original list:

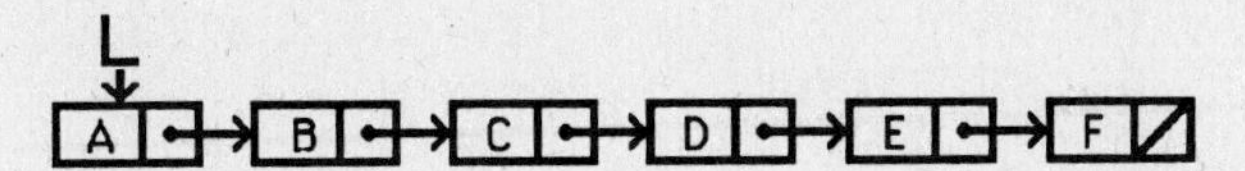

List after calling *advance*(5,2):

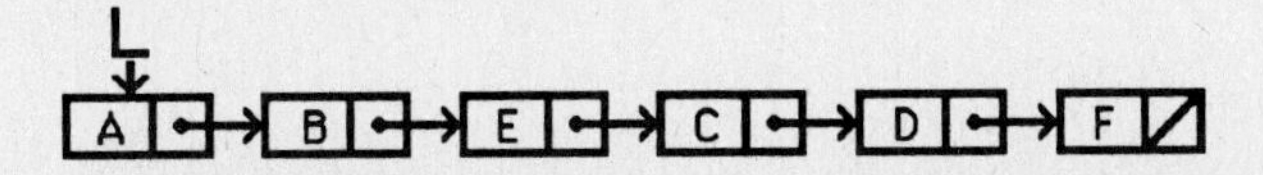

8. A programmer believes he has built a DLLL pointed to by *L* of type *ptr*. All of its right links are set properly, but some of its left links are defective. Write recursive **procedure** *fix*(**var** *L* : *ptr*); that fixes list *L* so that it is truly a DLLL.

9. Given that *L* is pointing to a SLCL, write **procedure** *linearize*(**var** *L* : *ptr*); that turns list *L* into a SLLL.

10. Linked lists where each node consists of only a pointer field and no information part are ususally thought to be of no practical use. However it would be possible to represent nonnegative integers with lists of this form, with nil representing 0 and an n-node list representing the integer n. This is really a form of the unary number system where the information part of each node is supressed since its value would always be 1. For example, in this system the integer 5 is represented by the list:

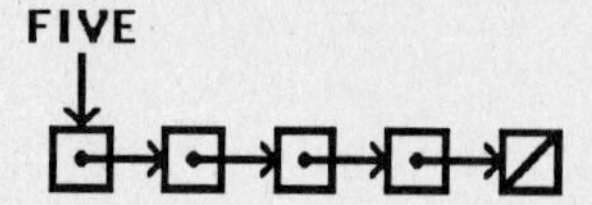

Define a type *intnode* using Pascal pointers that describes nodes of this type, and then write the following Pascal functions and procedures (at least one of these must be recursive and at least one must be iterative — indicate which is which):

Function *convert*(n) which converts the integer n to a list of n *intnode*s and returns a pointer to this list.

Function *subtract*(M, N). Here M and N are pointers to lists representing the integers m and n. The result should be a pointer to a list of new nodes that represents the difference of the larger integer and the smaller. The lists M and N should be unchanged.

Procedure *output*(N). This procedure should print the integer n that is represented by the list N.

SOLUTIONS TO PROGRAMMING EXERCISES

12.9 LAUNDERED LIST

```
program SLLL(input, output);
  {
    Builds an initial SLLL of [presumably] alphabetized names and then allows additional
    names to be spliced in at their proper places and names already in the list to be deleted.
  }
  type
    str = string[20];
    nodeptr = ^node;
    node = record
      name : str;
      link : nodeptr
    end;
  var
    list : nodeptr;
    inf : text;

  procedure buildlist(var L : nodeptr);
    {
      Reads names presumed to be in alphabetic order and organizes them as a SLLL
      pointed to by L.
    }
    var
      p : nodeptr;
    begin { buildlist }
      reset(inf, 'SLLL.DAT');
      new(L);                     { Create a new node, pointed at by L to start list }
      readln(inf, L^.name);                                      { Fill the name field }
      p := L;                   { Make a copy of L for advancing through the list }
      while not eof(inf) do
        begin
          new(p^.link);           { Create a new node pointed at by p's link field }
          p := p^.link;                                     { p now points at new node }
          readln(inf, p^.name)                         { Read a name into its name field }
        end { while };
      p^.link := nil                           { Set the link of the final node to nil }
    end { buildlist } ;

  procedure printlist(L : nodeptr);
    {
      Prints nodes of a SLLL beginning with the node pointed to by L.
    }
    var
      p : nodeptr;
    begin { printlist }
      p := L;
      while p <> nil do
        begin
          writeln(p^.name);
          p := p^.link                                              { Find next node }
        end;
      writeln
    end { printlist } ;

  procedure insert(newname : str; var L : nodeptr);
    {
      Inserts newname into the SLLL pointed to by L, maintaining alphabetic order.
    }
    var
      p : nodeptr;
      firstnode : Boolean;
```

```
    begin { insert }
      if L = nil
        then firstnode := true
        else firstnode := newname <= L^.name;
      if firstnode then
        begin
          new(p);
          p^.name := newname;
          p^.link := L;
          L := p
        end
      else insert(newname, L^.link)
    end { insert } ;

  procedure delete(oldname : str; var L : nodeptr);
    {
      Delete node containig oldname from list L.
    }
    var
      p : nodeptr;
    begin { delete }
      if L = nil then writeln('Name  ', oldname, ' not in list') else
        if oldname = L^.name then
          begin
            p := L;
            L := L^.link;
            dispose(p)
          end else delete(oldname, L^.link)
    end { delete } ;

  begin { main }
    writeln('Program to test delete procedure');
    writeln;
    buildlist(list);
    writeln('Original list');
    writeln;
    printlist(list);
    insert('Garvey', list);
    insert('Aaron', list);
    insert('Zysmanski', list);
    writeln('List with additions');
    writeln;
    printlist(list);
    delete('Garvey', list);
    delete('Aaron', list);
    delete('Zysmanski', list);
    writeln('List with deletions');
    writeln;
    printlist(list)
  end { SLLL } .
```

12.11 HEAD TO TAIL

```
program HeadToTail(input, output);
  {
    Builds two random lists and appends the second one to the end of the first.
  }
  type
    nodeptr = ^node;
    node = record
      info : integer;
      link : nodeptr
    end;
```

```
var
  L1, L2 : nodeptr;
  count, limit, i, j : integer;
  seed : real;

procedure PrintList(L : nodeptr);
  {
    Print the list L.
  }
  var
    p : nodeptr;
  begin { PrintList }
    if L = nil then writeln('  nil') else
      begin
        p := L;
        while p <> nil do
          begin
            write(p^.info : 4);
            p := p^.link
          end;
        writeln
      end
  end { PrintList } ;

function ranfrac : real;                    { Declare and initialize seed in main program }
  begin seed := 1011.0*seed; seed := seed-trunc(seed); ranfrac := seed end;
function ran(i:integer) : integer;  begin ran := trunc((i)*ranfrac) end;

procedure insert(i : integer; var L : nodeptr);
  {
    Insert a new node with value i as first node of L.
  }
  var t : nodeptr;
  begin { insert }
    new(t);
    t^.info := i;
    t^.link := L;
    L := t
  end { insert } ;

procedure append(var L, M : nodeptr);
  {
    Appends list M to the end of list L.
  }
  var
    temp : nodeptr;
  begin { append }
    if L = nil then L := M else
    if M <> nil then
      begin
        temp := L;
        while temp^.link <> nil do temp := temp^.link;            { Find end of L }
        temp^.link := M
      end
  end { append } ;
```

```
begin { main }
  write('How many pairs of random lists do you want to append? ');
  readln(count);
  seed := 0.654321;
  for j := 1 to count do
    begin
      L1 := nil;                                          { Make first list }
      limit := ran(7);                                    { of random length }
      for i := 1 to limit do insert(ran(100), L1);
      L2 := nil;                                          { Make second list }
      limit := ran(7);
      for i := 1 to limit do insert(ran(100), L2);
      writeln;
      writeln('Case #', j : 1);
      writeln;
      write('   First List   ');                          { Print the lists }
      PrintList(L1);
      write('  Second List   ');
      PrintList(L2);
      writeln;
      append(L1, L2);                                     { Append L2 to L1 }
      write('Combined List   ');                          { and print result }
      PrintList(L1);
      writeln
    end
end { HeadToTail } .
```

12.12 LIST MERGE

```
program ListMerge(input, output);
  {
    Creates random sorted lists and merges them.
  }
  type
    nodeptr = ^node;
    node = record
      info : integer;
      link : nodeptr
    end;
  var
    L1, L2 : nodeptr;
    count, limit, next, i : integer;
    seed : real;

  procedure PrintList(L : nodeptr);
    {
      Print the list L.
    }
    var
      p : nodeptr;
    begin { PrintList }
      if L = nil then writeln('  nil') else
        begin
          p := L;
          while p <> nil do
            begin
              write(p^.info : 4);
              p := p^.link
            end;
          writeln
        end
    end { PrintList } ;
```

```
function ranfrac : real;                    { Declare and initialize seed in main program }
  begin seed := 1011.0*seed; seed := seed–trunc(seed); ranfrac := seed end;
function ran(i:integer) : integer;  begin ran := trunc((i)*ranfrac) end;

procedure MakeSortedList(var L : nodeptr);
  {
    Makes a list of random sorted integers of random length.
  }
  var
    temp : nodeptr;
    limit, next, i : integer;

  procedure MakeNextNode(i : integer; var L : nodeptr);
    {
      Creates a node with value i and name L.
    }
    begin { MakeNextNode }
      new(L);
      L^.info := i;
      L^.link := nil
    end { MakeNextNode } ;

  begin { MakeSortedList }
    L := nil;
    limit := ran(9);                                                   { Get length }
    next := 0;
    for i := 1 to limit do
      begin
        next := next + ran(8) + 3;                  { Insures that they will be sorted }
        if L = nil then
          begin
            MakeNextNode(next, L);
            temp := L
          end else
          begin
            MakeNextNode(next, temp^.link);
            temp := temp^.link
          end
      end
  end { MakeSortedList } ;

procedure merge(var L, M : nodeptr);
  {
    Merges lists L and M back into list L.
  var
    temp : nodeptr;
  begin { merge }
    if L = nil then L := M else
    if M <> nil then
      begin
        if L^.info < M^.info
          then merge(L^.link, M)
          else
            begin
              temp := M^.link;
              M^.link := L;
              L := M;
              merge(L, temp)
            end
      end;
    M := nil
  end { merge } ;
```

```
begin { main }
  write('How many pairs of lists do you want to merge? ');
  readln(count);
  seed := 0.654321;
  for i := 1 to count do
    begin
      writeln;
      writeln('Case #', i : 1);
      writeln;
      MakeSortedList(L1);
      write('First List  ');
      printlist(L1);
      MakeSortedList(L2);
      write('Second List ');
      printlist(L2);
      writeln;
      merge(L1, L2);
      write('Merged List ');
      printlist(L1);
      writeln
    end
end { ListMerge } .
```

12.13 ALTERNATE KNIGHTS

```
program AlternateKnights(input, output);
  {
    For input values m and k, eliminate every kth knight of m knights sitting at the
    round table until only one remains. Alternate the counting direction each time that a
    knight is eliminated. Print the result.
  }
  type
    nodeptr = ^knight;
    knight = record
      number : integer;
      left, right : nodeptr
    end;
  var
    m : integer;                                   { Number of knights }
    k : integer;                                   { Elimination cycle }
    t : nodeptr;

  function survivor(m, k : integer) : nodeptr;
    {
      Computes the survivor with m knights and elimination cycle of k.
    }
    var
      L, t : nodeptr;
      i, j : integer;

    procedure seat(m : integer; var L : nodeptr);
      {
        Seats m knights at a circular table (DLCL).
      }
      var
        p, q : nodeptr;
        i : integer;
      begin { seat }
        new(L);
        p := L;
        p^.number := 1;
```

```
      for i := 2 to m do
        begin
          new(q);
          q^.left := p;
          q^.number := i;
          p^.right := q;
          p := q
        end;
      p^.right := L;                                  { Make list circular }
      L^.left := p;
      L := p                                          { Set L to point to last knight }
    end { seat } ;

  begin { survivor }
    seat(m, L);                                       { Seat the knights }
    while L <> L^.left do
      begin
        for i := 1 to k - 1 do L := L^.right;         { Skip k - 1 knights }
        L^.right := L^.right^.right;                  { Remove the kth knight }
        t := L^.right;
        t^.left := L;
        L := t;
        if L <> L^.left then                          { Go other way if not done }
          begin
            for i := 1 to k - 1 do L := L^.left;      { Skip k - 1 knights }
            L^.left := L^.left^.left;                 { Remove the kth knight }
            t := L^.left;
            t^.right := L;
            L := t
          end
      end;
    survivor := L                                     { Bind function's name }
  end { survivor } ;

begin { main }
  write('Enter number of knights (m) and cycle (k): ');
  while not eof do
    begin
      readln(m, k);
      t := survivor(m, k);
      write('For m = ', m : 1, ' and k = ', k : 1,
            ' the survivor is knight no. ');
      writeln(t^.number : 1);
      writeln;
      write('Enter number of knights (m) and cycle (k): ')
    end
end { AlternateKnights } .
```

12.14 DLLL

```
program DLLL(input, output, inf, trans);
  {
  Builds an initial DLLL of alphabetized names and then allows addition of new names or
  deletion of current ones. Insertion or deletion of a name that is to the left of the point of
  the last transaction is made by searching either forward from the head of the list or
  backward from the current point depending on an estimate of which search is likely to
  be shorter. The original list of alphabetized names is in DLLL.DAT and the transaction
  file is DLLLTRAN.DAT. Names in the transaction file may be in any order; each name
  is preceded by either 'I ' (for an Insertion) or 'D ' (for a Deletion).
  }
```

```
const                      { When testing is true, left and right movement in search }
  testing = true;          { of an insertion point is indicated by output of <- or -> }
                           { Search movements during deletion are marked by L or R }
type
  str = string[20];
  nodeptr = ^node;
  node = record
    left : nodeptr;
    name : str;
    right : nodeptr
  end;
var
  list, lastref : nodeptr;
  inf , trans : text;

procedure buildlist(var L : nodeptr);
  {
    Reads names presumed to be in alphabetic order and organizes them as a DLLL
    pointed to by L.
  }
  var
    p : nodeptr;
  begin { buildlist }
    reset(inf, 'DLLL.DAT');
    new(L);                    { Create a new node, pointed at by L to start list }
    readln(inf, L^.name);                                    { Fill the name field }
    L^.left := nil;                 { Set left link to nil since it's the first node }
    p := L;                   { Make a copy of L for advancing through the list }
    while not eof(inf) do
      begin
        new(p^.right);            { Create a new node pointed at by p's right link }
        p^.right^.left := p;    { Make new node point back to the preceding node }
        p := p^.right;                         { Update p to point to the new node }
        readln(inf, p^.name)                      { Read a name into its name field }
      end { while };
    p^.right := nil;                { Set the right link of the final node to nil }
    lastref := L
  end { buildlist } ;

procedure printlist(L : nodeptr);
  {
    Prints nodes of a DLLL beginning with the node pointed to by L.
  }
  var
    p : nodeptr;
  begin { printlist }
    p := L;
    while p <> nil do
      begin
        writeln(p^.name);
        p := p^.right                                            { Find next node }
      end;
    writeln
  end { printlist };

procedure insert(newname : str; var L : nodeptr);
  {
    Inserts newname into list L. Updates global pointer lastref.
  }
  var
    PFL : char;
```

```
procedure insertright(newname : str; var L : nodeptr);
  {
    Moves right to insert newname into list L.  Updates global pointer lastref.
  }
  var
    p : nodeptr;
    firstnode, pointfound : Boolean;
  begin { insertright }
    if testing and (L <> nil) then writeln('-> checking ', L^.name);
    if L = nil
      then firstnode := true
      else firstnode := newname <= L^.name;
    if firstnode then
      begin
        new(p);
        p^.left := nil;
        p^.name := newname;
        p^.right := L;
        L^.left := p;
        L := p;
        lastref := p
      end
    else
      begin
        if L^.right = nil
          then pointfound := true
          else pointfound := newname <= L^.right^.name;
        if pointfound then
          begin
            new(p);
            p^.left := L;
            p^.name := newname;
            p^.right := L^.right;
            if L^.right <> nil then L^.right^.left := p;
            L^.right := p;
            lastref := p
          end
        else insertright(newname, L^.right)
      end
  end { insertright } ;

procedure insertleft(newname : str; var L : nodeptr);
  {
    Moves left to insert newname into list L.  Updates global pointer lastref.
  }
  var
    p : nodeptr;
    firstnode : Boolean;
  begin { insertleft }
    if testing and (L <> nil) then writeln('<- checking ', L^.name);
    if L = nil
      then firstnode := true
      else firstnode := L^.left = nil;
    if firstnode then
      begin
        new(p);
        p^.left := nil;
        p^.name := newname;
        p^.right := L;
        if L <> nil then L^.left := p;
        L := p;
        lastref := p
      end
```

```
      else if newname >= L^.left^.name then
        begin
          new(p);
          p^.left := L^.left;
          p^.name := newname;
          p^.right := L;
          if L^.left <> nil then L^.left^.right := p;
          L^.left := p;
          lastref := p
        end
      else insertleft(newname, L^.left)
    end { insertleft } ;

  begin { insert }
    if L = nil then insertright(newname, L) else
    if newname >= lastref^.name then insertright(newname, lastref) else
      begin          { Compute probable first letter of midpoint of list to the left }
        PFL := chr((ord(list^.name[1]) + ord(lastref^.name[1])) div 2);
        if newname[1] <= PFL
          then insertright(newname, list)
          else insertleft(newname, lastref)
      end
  end { insert };

procedure delete(name : str; var L : nodeptr);
  {
    Deletes name from list L. Updates global pointer lastref.
  }
  var
    PFL : char;

  procedure del(name : str; var L : nodeptr; dir : char);
    {
      Moves in direction dir to delete newname from list L. Updates global pointer lastref.
    }
    var
      p : nodeptr;
    begin { del }
      if testing and (L <> nil) then writeln(dir, '   checking ', L^.name);
      if L = nil then writeln('*** ', name, ' not found ***') else
        if name = L^.name then
          if L^.left = nil then
            begin                      { Node is found with no nodes to the left }
              p := L;
              L := L^.right;
              if L <> nil then L^.left := nil;
              lastref := L;
              dispose(p)
            end else
              begin                    { Node is found with nodes to the left }
                p := L;
                p^.left^.right := p^.right;
                if p^.right <> nil then
                  begin
                    p^.right^.left := p^.left;
                    lastref := p^.right
                  end else lastref := p^.left;
                dispose(p)
              end else          { Node not found, so delete from proper sublist }
                case dir of
                  'L' : del(name, L^.left, 'L');
                  'R' : del(name, L^.right, 'R')
                end
  end { del };
```

```
  begin { delete }
    if L = nil then writeln(name, ' not found') else
      if name >= lastref^.name then del(name, lastref, 'R') else
        begin            { Compute probable first letter of midpoint of list to the left }
          PFL := chr((ord(list^.name[1]) + ord(lastref^.name[1])) div 2);
          if name[1] <= PFL
            then del(name, list, 'R')
            else del(name, lastref, 'L')
        end
  end { delete };

procedure update(var L : nodeptr);
  {
    Updates list L using file DLLLTRAN.DAT.
  }
  var
    name : str;
    command, blank : char;
  begin { update }
    reset(trans, 'DLLLTRAN.DAT');
    while not eof(trans) do
      begin
        readln(trans, command, blank, name);
        if testing then writeln(command, ' ', name);
        if not (command in ['I', 'D']) then
          writeln('Bad transaction: ', command, name) else
        case command of
          'I' : insert(name, L);
          'D' : delete(name, L)
        end;
        if testing then
          begin
            printlist(list);
            write('Press "Return" for next transaction ');
            readln;
            writeln
          end
      end
  end { update };

begin { main }
  buildlist(list);
  writeln('The List Before the Transactions'); writeln;
  printlist(list);
  write('Press "Return" to perform updates ');
  readln; writeln;
  update(list); writeln;
  writeln('The Final List'); writeln;
  printlist(list)
end { DLLL } .
```

12.16 THREE WAY TRIP
12.17 NODE SUMS
12.23 SIBLINGS

```
program TreeTraversalsDriver(input, output);
  {
    Tests TreeTraversals.
  }
  var
    n : integer;                                    { Number of nodes in tree }
    seed : real;

  procedure TreeTraversals(n : integer);
    {
      Forms a binary tree of n random integers, prints its traversals, and computes the sum
      of the nodes. A sib pointer is included in each node so problem 12.23 can be included.
    }
    type
      nodeptr = ^node;
      node = record
        left, right, sib : nodeptr;
        val : integer
      end;
    var
      tree : nodeptr;
      i, count, sum : integer;

    function ranfrac : real;              { Declare and initialize seed in main program }
      begin seed := 1011.0*seed; seed := seed–trunc(seed); ranfrac := seed end;
    function ran(i:integer) : integer; begin ran := trunc((i)*ranfrac) end;

    procedure insert(item : integer; var T : nodeptr);
      {
        Inserts item into tree T.
      }
      begin { insert }
        if T = nil then                                   { Create root }
          begin
            new(T);
            T^.sib := nil;
            T^.val  := item;
            T^.left :=  nil;
            T^.right := nil
          end else
        if item < T^.val
          then insert(item, T^.left)
          else insert(item, T^.right)
      end { insert } ;

    procedure siblings(t : nodeptr);
      {
        This procedure uses the fact that in any tree traversal, the nodes on any level occur
        in their proper left-right order. However it calls procedure sibs which is a
        backwards (right to left) preorder traversal and so the nodes on a given level occur
        in their right to left order. The array nodekeeper keeps a pointer to the last node
        found on each level. As the nodes are "visited", each one is set to point at the node
        on that level in nodekeeper and nodekeeper is reset.
      }
      var
        i : integer;
        nodekeeper : array[0..100] of nodeptr;
```

```
    procedure sibs(t : nodeptr; level : integer);
      begin { sibs }
        if t <> nil then
          begin                                                    { Visit the root }
            t^.sib := nodekeeper[level];                          { Set sib pointer }
            nodekeeper[level] := t;                           { Update nodekeeper }
            sibs(t^.right, level + 1);   { Do recursive reverse preorder traversals }
            sibs(t^.left, level + 1)
          end
      end { sibs } ;

    begin { siblings }
      for i := 0 to 100 do nodekeeper[i] := nil;     { Initialize nodekeeper array }
      sibs(t, 0)
    end { siblings } ;

  procedure print(a : integer);
    {
      Prints integer a (starting on new line if count of length of current line is 10).
    }
    begin { print }
      if count = 10 then
        begin                                                      { Start new line }
          writeln; count := 0
        end;
      count := count + 1;
      write(a : 7)
    end { print } ;

  { The four traversals that follow visit a node by both printing its val field and adding
    that val field to a global sum }

  procedure preorder(T : nodeptr);
    begin
      if T <> nil then
        begin { preorder }
          sum := sum + T^.val;
          print(T^.val);
          preorder(T^.left);
          preorder(T^.right)
        end
    end { preorder } ;

  procedure inorder(T : nodeptr);
    begin { inorder }
      if T <> nil then
        begin
          inorder(T^.left);
          sum := sum + T^.val;
          print(T^.val);
          inorder(T^.right)
        end
    end { inorder } ;

  procedure postorder(T : nodeptr);
    begin { postorder }
      if T <> nil then
        begin
          postorder(T^.left);
          postorder(T^.right);
          sum := sum + T^.val;
          print(T^.val)
        end
    end { postorder } ;
```

```
procedure BFT(T : nodeptr);
  var
    p, first : nodeptr;
  begin { BFT }
    if T <> nil then
      begin
        p := T;
        first := nil;
        repeat                                      { For all nodes on this level }
          sum := sum + p^.val;                                      { Add to sum }
          print(p^.val);                                            { Print value }
          if first = nil then                  { Find first child on next level }
            if p^.left <> nil
              then first := p^.left
              else first := p^.right;
          p := p^.sib
        until p = nil;
        BFT(first)
      end
  end { BFT } ;

begin { TreeTraversals }
  tree := nil;                          { Create root of a new binary search tree }
  for i := 1 to n do insert(ran(100), tree);               { Fill it with n nodes }
  siblings(tree);                     { Fill in sibling pointers for problem 12.23 }
  count := 0;
  sum := 0;
  writeln('Preorder');                                   { Print the traversals }
  preorder(tree);
  writeln; writeln('Sum of nodes = ',sum : 1); writeln;
  count := 0;
  sum := 0;
  writeln('Inorder');
  inorder(tree);
  writeln; writeln('Sum of nodes = ',sum : 1); writeln;
  count := 0;
  sum := 0;
  writeln('Postorder');
  postorder(tree);
  writeln; writeln('Sum of nodes = ',sum : 1); writeln;
  count := 0;
  sum := 0;
  writeln('Breadth First Order');
  BFT(tree);
  writeln; writeln('Sum of nodes = ',sum : 1); writeln
end { TreeTraversals };

begin { main }
  seed := 0.987654321;
  writeln('Traversals and Sums of Random Trees'); writeln;
  write('Number of nodes for tree? ');                       { Issue a prompt }
  while not eof do
    begin
      readln(n);
      writeln;
      TreeTraversals(n);              { Create tree and print traversals and sums }
      writeln;
      write('Number of nodes for tree? ')               { Reissue the prompt }
    end
end { TreeTraversalsDriver } .
```

12.18 FAREY FRACTIONS

```
program FareyFractions(output);
  {
    Program to compute the Farey Fractions of all orders that will fit on one line of output.
  }
  const
    MaxLineLength = 80;            { Maximum numbers of characters on one line }
  type
    nodeptr = ^node;
    node = record
      numerator, denominator : integer;
      link : nodeptr
    end;
  var
    order, LineLength : integer;
    fractions : nodeptr;

  procedure print(F : nodeptr);
    {
      Print the fractions contained in the linked list F.
    }
    var
      t : nodeptr;
    begin { print }
      writeln;
      write('    ');
      t := F;
      while t <> nil do                              { Print the numerators }
        begin
          if t^.denominator > 9   { Use 2 or 3 columns depending on denominator }
            then write(t^.numerator : 3)
            else write(t^.numerator : 2);
          t := t^.link
        end;
      writeln;
      write(order : 2, '  ');
      t := F;
      while t^.link <> nil do                        { Print the fraction bars }
        begin
          if T^.denominator > 9
            then write('--,')
            else write('-,');
          t := t^.link
        end;
      writeln('-');
      write('    ');
      t := F;
      while t <> nil do                              { Print the denominators }
        begin
          if t^.denominator > 9
            then write(t^.denominator : 3)
            else write(t^.denominator : 2);
          t := t^.link
        end;
      writeln
    end { print };
```

```
procedure init(var F : nodeptr; var order, LineLength : integer);
  {
    Initialize the fraction list F to the first order fractions.
  }
  begin { init }
    new(F);
    F^.numerator := 0;
    F^.denominator := 1;
    new(F^.link);
    F^.link^.numerator := 1;
    F^.link^.denominator := 1;
    F^.link^.link := nil;
    LineLength := 8;
    order := 1
  end { init } ;

procedure NextOrder(F : nodeptr; var order, LineLength : integer);
  {
    Modify the fraction list F by adding nodes of the next order. Also compute the
    LineLength needed to print this new fraction list.
  }
  var
    t : nodeptr;
  begin { NextOrder }
    order := order + 1;
    LineLength := 5;
    while F^.link <> nil do
      begin
        if F^.denominator + F^.link^.denominator = order then
          begin                                              { Insert new node }
            new(t);
            t^.numerator := F^.numerator + F^.link^.numerator;
            t^.denominator := order;
            t^.link := F^.link;
            F^.link := t
          end;
        F := F^.link;
        if F^.denominator > 9
          then LineLength := LineLength + 3
          else LineLength := LineLength + 2
      end
  end { NextOrder } ;

begin { main }
  write(' ' : (MaxLineLength - 19) div 2); writeln('Farey Fractions'); writeln;
  writeln('Ord Fraction');
  init(fractions, order, LineLength);
  while LineLength <= MaxLineLength do
    begin
      print(fractions);
      NextOrder(fractions, order, LineLength)
    end
end { FareyFractions } .
```

12.19 OWNER'S MANUAL

```
program OwnersManual(input, output);
  {
    Demo of insert, print, and delete routines for DLCLs with owner pointer.
  }
  type
    str = packed array[1..8] of char;
    nodeptr = ^node;
    node = record
      info : str;
      left, right, owner : nodeptr
    end;
  var
    L : nodeptr;
    s : str;

  function reading(var s : str) : Boolean;
    {
      A gerund function that reads s and returns true if there is at least one character in s
      and false otherwise.
    }
    var
      i, j : integer;
    begin { reading }
      j := 0;
      while not eoln do
        begin
          j := j + 1;
          read(s[j])                                    { Read jth character of string }
        end;
      for i := j + 1 to 8 do s[i] := ' '; readln;
      reading := j <> 0          { Return function value which depends on length of s }
    end { reading } ;

  procedure print(L : nodeptr);
    {
      Prints the list L.
    }
    var
      t : nodeptr;
    begin { print }
      writeln(L^.info, '  ', L^.owner^.info);
      t := L^.right;
      while t <> L do                                   { Stop when circle is complete }
        begin
          writeln(t^.info, '  ', t^.owner^.info);
          t := t^.right
        end
    end { print } ;

  procedure init(s : str; var L : nodeptr);
    {
      Starts a new list with owner node.
    }
    begin { init }
      new(L);
      L^.info := s;
      L^.left := L;
      L^.right := L;
      L^.owner := L
    end { init } ;
```

```
procedure Insert(s : str; L : nodeptr);
  {
    Inserts a node into L in proper position. Procedure Insert1 is used so that original
    list pointer L can be remembered during recursive calls.
  }
  procedure Insert1(s : str; L, u : nodeptr);
    {
      Insert s into L at position u or further.
    }
    var
      t : nodeptr;
      nextnode : Boolean;
    begin { Insert1 }
      if u^.right = L                              { Do we insert after this node? }
        then nextnode := true
        else nextnode := s < u^.right^.info;
      if nextnode then                             { Yes, do insertion }
        begin
          new(t);
          t^.info := s;
          t^.owner := u^.owner;
          t^.left := u;
          t^.right := u^.right;
          t^.right^.left := t;
          u^.right := t
        end else insert1(s, L, u^.right)           { else insert in rest of list }
    end { Insert1 } ;

  begin { Insert }
    insert1(s, L, L)
  end { Insert } ;

function deleting(s : str; L : nodeptr) : Boolean;
  {
    A gerund function that deletes node containing s from L if it is there. Returns
    true if deletion was successful otherwise false. Procedure Deleting1 is used so
    that original list pointer L can be remembered during recursive calls.
  }

  function deleting1(s : str; L, u : nodeptr) : Boolean;
    {
      Delete s from L at position u or further.
    }
    var
      t : nodeptr;
    begin { deleting1 }
      if u^.right = L then deleting1 := false else
        if s = u^.right^.info then                 { Delete node }
          begin
            deleting1 := true;
            t := u^.right;
            u^.right := t^.right;
            t^.right^.left := u;
            dispose(t)
          end else deleting1 := deleting1(s, L, u^.right)  { Delete from rest of list }
    end { deleting1 } ;

  begin { deleting }
    if L^.info = s then
      begin
        deleting := true;
        writeln('Cannot delete owner node.')
      end else deleting := deleting1(s, L, L)
  end { deleting } ;
```

```
begin { main }
  write('Enter an owner string of up to 8 characters: ');
  while not reading(s) do writeln('List must have owner node.');
  writeln;
  init(s, L);                                      { Open list with owner }
  write('Enter a string of up to 8 characters to insert or',
        ' "Return" when done: ');
  while reading(s) do                                  { Read an entry }
    begin
      if not deleting(s, L)                    { If already in list, delete }
        then insert(s, L);                             { otherwise insert }
      writeln;    { Show updated list }
      writeln('Node        Owner');
      print(L);
      writeln;
      writeln('To insert into list, enter a string not in list.');
      writeln('To delete from list, enter a string in list.');
      write('Enter a string of up to 8 characters or "Return"',
            ' when done: ')
    end
end { OwnersManual } .
```

12.20 MIRROR IMAGE

```
program MirrorImage(input, output);
  {
    Creates random binary search trees and reflects them to get the mirror image tree.
  }
  type
    nodeptr = ^node;
    node = record
      info : integer;
      left, right : nodeptr
    end;
  var
    limit, count, i, j : integer;
    tree : nodeptr;
    seed : real;

  function ranfrac : real;              { Declare and initialize seed in main program }
    begin seed := 1011.0*seed; seed := seed-trunc(seed); ranfrac := seed end;
  function ran(i:integer) : integer;  begin ran := trunc((i)*ranfrac) end;

  procedure insert(item : integer; var T : nodeptr);
    {
      Inserts item into tree T
    }
    begin { insert }
      if T = nil then                                        { Create root }
        begin
          new(T);
          T^.info  := item;
          T^.left := nil;
          T^.right := nil
        end else
      if item < T^.info
        then insert(item, T^.left)
        else insert(item, T^.right)
    end { insert } ;
```

```
procedure reflect(T : nodeptr);
  {
    Replaces tree T with its mirror image.
  }
  var
    t1, t2 : nodeptr;
  begin { reflect }
    if T <> nil then
      begin
        t1 := T^.left; reflect(t1);                    { Reflect the subtrees }
        t2 := T^.right; reflect(t2);
        T^.left := t2;                                  { and reverse them }
        T^.right := t1
      end
  end { reflect } ;

procedure preorder(t : nodeptr);
  begin { preorder }
    if t <> nil then
      begin
        write(t^.info : 4);
        preorder(t^.left);
        preorder(t^.right)
      end
  end { preorder } ;

procedure inorder(t : nodeptr);
  begin { inorder }
    if t <> nil then
      begin
        inorder(t^.left);
        write(t^.info : 4);
        inorder(t^.right)
      end
  end { inorder } ;

begin
  write('How many random trees do you want to generate? ');
  readln(count);
  seed := 0.654321;
  for j := 1 to count do
    begin
      tree := nil;
      limit := ran(10) + 5;
      for i := 1 to limit do insert(ran(100), tree);
      writeln;
      writeln('Original Tree #', j : 1);
      write('Pre order    ');
      preorder(tree); writeln;
      write('In order     ');
      inorder(tree); writeln;
      reflect(tree);
      writeln;
      writeln('Reversed Tree #', j : 1);
      write('Pre order    ');
      preorder(tree); writeln;
      write('In order     ');
      inorder(tree); writeln;
      writeln
    end
end { MirrorImage } .
```

12.21 TREE CONSTRUCTION

```
program TreeConstruction(input, output);
  {
    Creates a tree from its preorder and inorder traversals.
  }
  type
    nodeptr = ^node;
    node = record
      info : char;
      left, right : nodeptr
    end;
    str = packed array[1..26] of char;
  var
    i, number, size : integer;
    tree : nodeptr;
    pre, inn : str;

  procedure preorder(T : nodeptr);
    begin { preorder }
      if T <> nil then
        begin
          write(T^.info);
          preorder(T^.left);
          preorder(T^.right)
        end
    end { preorder } ;

  procedure inorder(T : nodeptr);
    begin { inorder }
      if T <> nil then
        begin
          inorder(T^.left);
          write(T^.info);
          inorder(T^.right)
        end
    end { inorder } ;

  procedure postorder(T : nodeptr);
    begin { postorder }
      if T <> nil then
        begin
          postorder(T^.left);
          postorder(T^.right);
          write(T^.info)
        end
    end { postorder } ;

  function construct(n : integer; pre : str; i : integer; inn : str; j : integer) : nodeptr;
    {
      Function to create a tree with n nodes. The preorder traversal of this trree is stored
      in pre and starts at pre[i]. The inorder traversal of this tree is stored in inn and
      starts at inn[j]
    }
    var
      t : nodeptr;
      k : integer;
    begin { Construct }
      if n < 1 then construct := nil else
        begin
          new(t);                                         { Node needed for the root }
          t^.info := pre[i];  { info field of root is first character in preorder traversal }
          k := 0;
```

```
      while inn[j + k] <> pre[i] do k := k + 1;  { Find root in inorder traversal }
                                                 { Everything to left is left subtree }
      t^.left := construct(k, pre, i + 1, inn, j);
                                                 { Everything to right is right subtree }
      t^.right := construct(n - k - 1, pre, i + k + 1, inn, j + k + 1);
      construct := t
    end
  end { construct } ;

begin { main }
  number := 1;                                   { ID number for tree }
  write('Enter Preorder traversal of tree ', number : 1, ': ');
  while not eof do
    begin
      size := 0;                                 { Will become size of this tree }
      while not eoln do
        begin
          size := size + 1;
          read(pre[size])
        end;
      readln;
      write('Enter  Inorder traversal of tree ', number : 1, ': ');
      for i := 1 to size do read(inn[i]);        { Sizes of pre and inn must be equal }
      readln;
      tree := construct(size, pre, 1, inn, 1);   { Make tree }
      writeln;
      write(' Preorder traversal of new tree ', number : 1, ': ');
      preorder(tree);                            { and show traversals }
      writeln;
      write('  Inorder traversal of new tree ', number : 1, ': ');
      inorder(tree);
      writeln;
      write('Postorder traversal of new tree ', number : 1, ': ');
      postorder(tree);
      writeln; writeln;
      number := number + 1;
      write('Enter Preorder traversal of tree ', number : 1, ': ')
    end
end { TreeConstruction } .
```

12.23 SIBLINGS — See 12.16

12.24 TIMBER!

```
program Timber(input, output);
  {
    A program to test and measure the creation and erasure of binary search trees.
  }
  var
    n : integer;                                 { Number of nodes in tree }
    seed : real;

  procedure BuildAndErase(n : integer);
    {
      Forms a binary search tree of random integers and then erases it. It also prints the
      amount of space used in this process.
    }
    type
      nodeptr = ^node;
      node = record
        left, right : nodeptr;
        val : integer
      end;
```

```
var
  tree : nodeptr;
  i , before, during, after : integer;

procedure insert(item : integer; var T : nodeptr);
  {
    Inserts item into tree T.
  }
  var
    p : nodeptr;
  begin { insert }
    if T = nil then                                          { Create root }
      begin
        new(T);
        T^.val  := item;
        T^.left :=  nil;
        T^.right := nil
      end else
    if item < T^.val
      then insert(item, T^.left)
      else insert(item, T^.right)
  end { insert } ;

function ranfrac : real;          { Declare and initialize seed in main program }
  begin seed := 1011.0*seed; seed := seed–trunc(seed); ranfrac := seed end;
function ran(i:integer) : integer;  begin ran := trunc((i)*ranfrac) end;

function space : integer;
  {
    A Turbo Pascal function to compute the space available in the heap. Replace this
    with the proper function for your compiler.
  }
  begin { space }
    space := MemAvail                    { MemAvail is a built-in Turbo function }
  end { space };

procedure erasetree(var T : nodeptr);
  {
    Disposes of all nodes in the binary tree T.
  }
  begin
    if T <> nil then
      begin
        erasetree(T^.left);                                  { Erase left subtree }
        erasetree(T^.right):                                 { Erase right subtree }
        dispose(T)                                             { Dispose of root }
      end
  end { erasetree };

begin { BuildAndErase }
  tree := nil;
  before := space;
  writeln('Memory available before creating tree = ', before : 1, '.');
  for i := 1 to n do insert(ran(1000), tree);
  during := space;
  write('Memory available after creating tree  = ', during : 1);
  writeln('.    ', before – during : 1, ' space units used.');
  erasetree(tree);
  after := space;
  write('Memory available after deleting tree  = ', after : 1);
  writeln('.    ', after – during : 1, ' space units released.')
end { BuildAndErase };
```

```
begin { main }
  seed := 0.987654321;
  write('Number of integers in tree: ');              { Issue a prompt }
  while not eof do
    begin
      readln(n);
      writeln;
      BuildAndErase(n);           { Create and then erase tree, showing heap size }
      writeln; write('Number of integers in tree: ')
    end
end { Timber } .
```

CHAPTER 13 — DATA STRUCTURES

From its length, it is obvious that we consider this a very important chapter, the centerpiece of the second semester. Despite the length, there are just two fundamental concepts: the difference between an abstract data structure and its storage structure, and the principle of information hiding. Everything else is flesh on those bones. Nonetheless, the chapter is worth several lectures and perhaps an exam in its own right. Don't be in too much of a hurry to move on.

As promised back in Chapter 9, we now try to show how recursion is implemented. We exhibit a synthetically-recursive version of factorial in the sense that it uses a homemade stack rather than the implicit one that a truly recursive version would use. We leave it to you to explain, and perhaps show with some other example, that if the function had had local variables in addition to its formal parameter, they too would have had to be pushed and popped.

The presentation of generalized lists and tries is somewhat unusual in an introductory text. But we persist in thinking that we are writing for computer science students, not (just) Pascal programmers. With regard to the tries, we thought it interesting to point out that a control structure (nested case statements) can simultaneously be a data structure. Has anyone else told you that?

We believe that many of the programming exercises are original (some would say bizarre.) Will a student really enjoy building the outline of a soccer ball out of nodes and pointers? Please let us know. For those of you who don't care to find out, there are plenty of conventional problems to use.

SUGGESTED TEST QUESTIONS

Multiple-Choice Questions (Correct answers are indicated by •)

1. The declaration **type** *gizmo* = **array**[...] **of** *sometype* is legal provided that *sometype* is not

   a an array type
   b a record type
   c a set type
   •d a file type
   e a pointer type

2. Which of the following was not classified as an elastic data structure?

   a stack
   b queue
   c deque
   •d linked list
   e variable-length string

3. Which of the following was not classified as a dynamic data structure?

   a set
   b linked list
   c tree
   d graph
   •e none, i.e., all were classified as dynamic

4. Which Pascal data type is dynamic even though it does not use nodes and pointers?

   a array
   b record
   •c set
   d file
   e all of the above are dynamic

5. A 1-ary tree would essentially be

   a a shrub
   b a complete tree
   c a queue
   d a deque
   •e an SLLL

6. The number of nodes in a complete trinary (3-ary) tree of height n is

   a 3^n
   b 3^{n+1}
   c $3^{n+1} + 1$
   d $3^{n+1} - 1$
   •e $(3^{n+1} - 1)$ div 2

7. A nonrecursive program is using a stack and no other variables other than *ch* of type *char* that receives input letters only via *read(ch)*. If the program reads the six letters A to F in that order, which, if any, of the following output sequences is impossible?

   a FEDCBA
   •b FEDBAC
   c DEFCBA
   d BDFECA
   e BADCFE

8. Consider the complete graph of four vertices labeled A through D. Because each vertex is connected to the other three, the adjacency-list representation of this graph would normally use 12 nodes. If the adjacency lists were stored in the most economical way possible, what is the fewest number of nodes you would need?

   a 1
   b 2
   c 4
   •d 8
   e 12, no economy is possible

Programming Questions

1. You have access to a queue *Q* only through the following:

   The procedure *clear(Q)* clears queue *Q*.
   The function *empty(Q)* returns *true* iff the queue is empty.
   The procedure *enter(item, Q)* puts *item* into the end of the queue.
   The procedure *leave(Q, item)* removes the front of the queue to *item*.

   Write recursive Pascal procedure *invert(Q : queue)*. The argument *Q* is the name of a queue and *invert(Q)* should reverse the order of items in that queue. You should use no other explicit data structures in your procedure other than the queue *Q*.

2. Given

```
type
    ptr = ^node;
    net = ptr;
    node = record
        r, c : integer;
        down, right : ptr
    end;
```

   Nodes are connected to form a data structure called a *net* that looks like this:

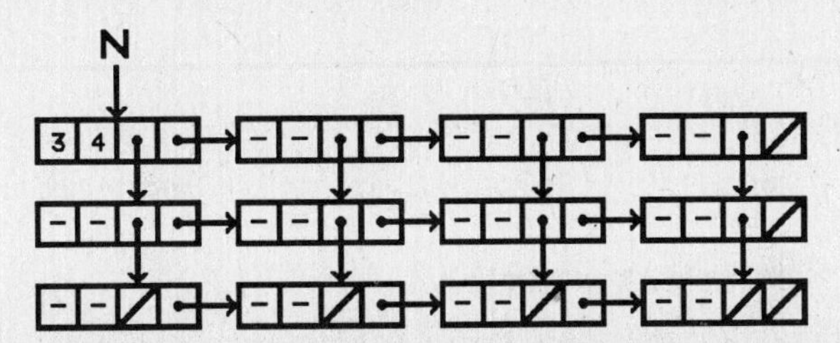

   The net may change in size but must maintain a rectangular arrangement of nodes.
   The top left node must always contain the current number of rows and columns.
   The dashes represent integer information that is irrelevant to this problem.

   One of the operations to be performed on a net is to delete any one of its columns (other than the first, which is a reference column). To allow this, complete the following procedure:

```
procedure DeleteColumn(var N : net; whichcol : integer);
  {
    If N is nil or whichcol is 1 or whichcol exceeds the number of columns,
    no action is taken. Otherwise, column number whichcol is deleted from the
    net whose top left node is pointed to by N, and that top left node is updated
    accordingly.
  }
```

3. Write **procedure** *makeAM*(**var** *AL* : *AdjacencyList*; **var** *AM* : *AdjacencyMatrix*); that inspects adjacency list *AL* and creates and prints adjacency matrix *AM*. Assume that the nodes of the graph are labeled with capital letters 'A' to the letter *ch* (less than or equal to 'Z' — i.e., no more than 26 nodes). Assume these declarations:

```
const
   ch = 'Z'; { or whatever the last node is named }
type
   alpha = 'A'..ch;
   list = ^node;
   node = record
      nodename : alpha;
      link : list
   end;
   AdjacencyList = array[alpha] of list;
   AdjacencyMatrix = array[alpha, alpha] of 0..1;
```

4. Write **procedure** *makeAL*(**var** *AM* : *AdjacencyMatrix*; **var** *AL* : *AdjacencyList*); that inspects adjacency matrix *AM* and creates and prints adjacency list *AL*. Assume that the nodes of the graph are labeled with capital letters 'A' to the letter *ch* (less than or equal to 'Z' — i.e., no more than 26 nodes). Assume these declarations:

```
const
   ch = 'Z'; { or whatever the last node is called }
type
   alpha = 'A'..ch;
   list = ^node;
   node = record
      nodename : alpha;
      link : list
   end;
   AdjacencyList = array[alpha] of list;
   AdjacencyMatrix = array[alpha, alpha] of 0..1;
```

5. Given that these stack operations are already defined for use on stack *s* of type *stack*:

   The function *empty*(*s*) returns true if stack *s* is empty.
   The procedure *push*(*item*, *s*) pushes *item* into stack *s*.
   The procedure *pop*(s, *item*) pops the top of stack *s* to *item*.

   Given also that **type** *three* = 0..3 and that *item* is of type *integer*, complete the definition of

```
procedure reorder(var s : stack; a, b, c : three);
  {
    This procedure rearranges either the top two or the top three items in stack s.
    It pops the top three items and then pushes them back in the order c, b, a
    where a, b, c is a permutation of 1, 2, 3 that cites the stack positions of
    original items.  The position called c may be 0, in which case the only
    sensible call to reorder would be reorder(s, 2, 1, 0) which exchanges the
    top two items in the stack.  Other examples are

    reorder(s, 1, 2, 3);   (* leaves the stack alone *)
    reorder(s, 3, 2, 1);   (* reverses the order of the top three items *)
    reorder(s, 3, 1, 2);   (* makes the old 3rd item the new top item *)

    The procedure prints an error message if the stack has fewer than two items
    when c is 0, fewer than 3 items when c > 0, or if either a or b is 0.
  }
```

The procedure *push*(*item*, *s*) pushes an *item* into the stack.
The procedure *pop*(*s*, *item*) pops the top of the stack to *item*.

6. All valid sentences in a certain language consist of arbitrarily long sequences of letters (either case), and may optionally contain embedded parentheses ( ), brackets [ ], or braces { } provided that they are balanced. Some legal sentences are

```
abc
a(bc)
[a(bc()[dE]){fg{H}}]
```

Some illegal ones are

```
[a}
ab]
]
```

Write a program that reads lines of input until *eof*, echoes the sequence, and then prints on the next line either "is legal" or "is not legal". Use stack operations to analyze each sequence. Assume that *s* is of type *stack*, *item* is of type *char*, and that the following routines are already defined:

The procedure *clear(s)* clears stack *s*.
The function *empty(s)* returns *true* iff the stack is empty.

7. There are several Pascal compilers available that do not implement the *dispose* procedure. In its place, some of them use routines named *mark* and *release*. It is not necessary for you to know what these routines do, but it is enough to say that they won't do the job in many cases. Assume that you are working with such a system on a project that has only one kind of node defined as:

```
type
  nodeptr = ^node;
  node = record
    info : integer;
    link : nodeptr
  end;
```

Since there is no *dispose* and no satisfactory substitute, you want to create your own *dispose* procedure. Show how you would do this by keeping your own collection of disposed nodes and then implement *dispose(p)*. Show how the standard function *new* would interface with your *dispose* and define any other procedures that you think would be necessary to make your system work.

8. You are part of a team working on an atlas program for a personal computer. When the name of a major city anywhere in the world is entered, this program will display a portion of a world map with a dot used to indicate the position of that city. There will also be a display that shows the following information about that city and the state or country within which it lies:

For cities in the US:
- City Name
- City Population
- State Name
- State Population
- Area of State
- State Capital
- Date the State Entered the Union
- Rank of when State entered Union

For all other cities
- City Name
- City Population
- Country Name
- Country Population
- Area of Country
- Capital of Country
- Name of Currency
- Value in US dollars of Currency
- Language of Country

Design a data structure suitable for easy storage and retrieval of information from a database designed around your data structure and write procedure *WriteInfo*(*CityName*) that writes the data listed above for any *CityName* in the world. Note: For the sake of this exercise, assume that no *CityName* will occur more than once in the database. Also, design your data structure so that it is not necessary to duplicate all of the state or country information as many times as there are cities in that state or country.

SOLUTIONS TO SELECTED PROGRAMMING EXERCISES

13.6 TREE STORAGE

```
program TreeStorage(input, output);
  {
    Constructs an n-ary tree from its traversals and prints it in generalized list form.
  }
  type
    nodeptr = ^node;
    node = record
      info : char;
      left, right : nodeptr
    end;
    str = packed array [1..26] of char;
  var
    i, num, size : integer;
    tree : nodeptr;
    pre, post : str;

  function construct(n : integer; pre : str; i : integer; post : str; j : integer) : nodeptr;
    {
      Creates a binary tree that is the representation of an n-ary tree with n nodes. The
      preorder traversal of this n-ary tree is found in the character array pre starting at
      pre[i]. The inorder traversal is found in post and starts at post[j].
    }
    var
      t : nodeptr;
      k : integer;
    begin { construct }
      if n < 1 then construct := nil else
        begin
          new(t);                                          { New node for root }
          t^.info := pre[i];          { info part of root is first character in preorder traversal }
          k := 0;
          while post[j + k] <> pre[i] do k := k + 1;      { Find root in postorder traversal }
          t^.left := construct(k, pre, i + 1, post, j);   { Everything to left is left subtree }
                                                     { Everything to right is right subtree }
          t^.right := construct(n - k - 1, pre, i + k + 1, post, j + k + 1);
          construct := t
        end
    end { construct } ;

  procedure WriteGL(T : nodeptr);
    {
      Displays the n-ary tree T (represented as a binary tree) in generalized list form.
    }
    begin { WriteGL }
      if T <> nil then
        begin
          write('  (', T^.info);                          { Write '(' then root }
          T := T^.left;                                    { Find eldest child }
          while T <> nil do                                { For all children }
            begin
              WriteGL(T);                                  { Print child's tree }
              T := T^.right                                { Find next child }
            end;
          write(') ')                       { Write ')' to end list of children }
        end
    end { WriteGL } ;
```

```
begin { main }
  num := 1;                                              { ID number for tree }
  write('Enter  Preorder traversal of n-ary tree #', num : 1, ': ');
  while not eof do
    begin
      size := 0;                                   { Will become size of this tree }
      while not eoln do
        begin
          size := size + 1;
          read(pre[size])
        end;
      readln;
      write('Enter Postorder traversal of n-ary tree #', num : 1, ': ');
      for i := 1 to size do read(post[i]);   { Sizes of pre & post must be the same }
      readln;
      writeln;
      tree := construct(size, pre, 1, post, 1);                        { Make tree }
      writeln('N-ary tree #', num : 1, ' in generalized list form: ');
      writeln;
      WriteGL(tree);
      writeln;
      writeln;
      num := num + 1;
      write('Enter  Preorder traversal of n-ary tree #', num : 1, ': ')
    end
end { TreeStorage } .
```

13.9 IQ TEST

```
program IQTest(input, output);
  {
    Plays the IQ Test game with nails on a triangular board and computes the average IQ
    for random play. The game board will be represented by a square array in which the
    triangular array is embedded. Enough empty holes are added around the border so that
    no edge tests are necessary in determining legal moves.
  }
  const
    victory = 13;
  type
    MoveRecord = record
      i, j, iinc, jinc : integer
    end;
    board = array [-1..7, -1..7] of Boolean;              { Game board and border }
    MoveArray = array [1..20] of MoveRecord;
    table = array [1..14] of integer;
  var
    i, LegalMoves, StartRow, StartCol, gameno, count, games, ScoreI, scoresum
          : integer;
    game : board;
    move : MoveRecord;
    moves, PossibleMoves : MoveArray;
    tally : table;
    seed : real;

  function ranfrac : real;             { Declare and initialize seed in main program }
    begin seed := 1011.0*seed; seed := seed - trunc(seed); ranfrac := seed end;
  function ran(i : integer) : integer;  begin ran := trunc((i)*ranfrac) end;
```

```
procedure initialize(var game : board; var tally : table; var seed : real);
  {
    The one-time-only initialization.
  }
  var
    i, j : integer;
  begin { initialize }
    for i := -1 to 7 do                                    { Clear board and border }
      for j := -1 to 7 do game[i, j] := false;
    for i := 1 to 14 do tally[i] := 0;                     { Clear tally table }
    seed := 0.87654321                                     { Initialize random seed }
  end { initialize } ;

procedure InitGame(var game : board; var row, col : integer);
  {
    Initializes the board to start a new game. If row = 0, a new empty starting hole is
    created at a random row and col. If row <> 0, row and col are used as the empty
    hole so a winning game can be reconstructed.
  }
  var
    i, j, start : integer;
  begin { InitGame }
    for i := 1 to 5 do                                     { Fill all holes with nails }
      for j := 1 to i do game[i, j] := true;
    if row = 0 then                        { If new empty starting hole in needed, }
      begin                                                { get a random one }
        start := ran(15) + 1;
        case start of
                        1 : begin row := 1; col := 1 end;
                     2, 3 : begin row := 2; col := start - 1 end;
                  4, 5, 6 : begin row := 3; col := start - 3 end;
              7, 8, 9, 10 : begin row := 4; col := start - 6 end;
       11, 12, 13, 14, 15 : begin row := 5; col := start - 10 end
        end { case }
      end;
    game[row, col] := false                    { Remove nail from empty starting hole }
  end { InitGame } ;

procedure GetMoves(game : board; var PossibleMoves : MoveArray;
                          var LegalMoves : integer);
  {
    Finds all legal moves on the game board and stores them in PossibleMoves and
    counts them in LegalMoves.
  }
  var
    move : MoveRecord;
  begin { GetMoves }
    LegalMoves := 0;
    with move do
      begin
        i := 1;
        while i < 6 do                                     { Search through all rows }
          begin
            j := 1;
            while j <= i do                                { and cols of game to find }
              begin
                if not game[i, j] then                     { an empty hole to move to }
                  begin
                    iinc := -1;
                    while iinc < 2 do                      { Then look for nails }
                      begin
                        jinc := -1;
```

```
                    while jinc <2 do                    { that can move there }
                      begin
                        if (iinc + jinc <> 0) and game[i + iinc, j + jinc]
                          and game[i + 2 * iinc, j + 2 * jinc] then
                          begin                          { If one is found, }
                            LegalMoves := LegalMoves + 1;        { add to count }
                            PossibleMoves[LegalMoves] := move  { Store move }
                          end;
                        jinc := jinc + 1
                      end;
                    iinc := iinc + 1
                  end
              end;
            j := j + 1
          end;
        i := i + 1
      end
    end
  end { GetMoves } ;

procedure MakeMove(var game : board; move : MoveRecord);
  {
    Makes a move on the game board.
  }
  begin { MakeMove }
    with move do
      begin
        game[i + 2 * iinc, j + 2 * jinc] := false;              { Move nail from here }
        game[i + iinc, j + jinc] := false;
        game[i, j] := true                                          { to there }
      end
  end { MakeMove } ;

procedure show;
  {
    Print the game board.
  }
  var
    i, j : integer;
  begin { show }
    for i := 5 downto 1 do
      begin
        for j := 1 to 7 - i do write(' ');
        for j := 1 to i do if game[i, j] then write('T ') else write('o ');
        writeln
      end
  end { show } ;

function score(i : integer) : integer;
  {
    Computes score when i nails are left.
  }
  begin { score }
    if i = 1 then score := 160 else
    if i = 2 then score := 140 else
    if i = 3 then score := 120 else score := 100
  end { score } ;

begin { main }
  initialize(game, tally, seed);
  write('How many games do you want to play? ');
  readln(games);
  writeln;
```

```
for gameno := 1 to games do
  begin
    count := 0;                                        { To count the moves made }
    StartRow := 0;                                     { To start new game }
    InitGame(game, StartRow, StartCol);
    repeat
      GetMoves(game, PossibleMoves, LegalMoves);       { Get all legal moves }
      if LegalMoves > 0 then
        begin
          move := PossibleMoves[ran(LegalMoves) + 1];  { Select one randomly }
          count := count + 1;
          moves[count] := move;                        { Keep it in case of victory }
          MakeMove(game, move)                         { Make the move }
        end
    until LegalMoves = 0;                              { Stop when there are no more moves }
    tally[14 - count] := tally[14 - count] + 1;  { Record the number of nails left }
    if count = victory then                            { If victory }
      begin
        writeln('Victory in Game #', gameno : 1);
        writeln;
        InitGame(game, StartRow, StartCol);            { Restart game }
        show;
        for i := 1 to count do                         { to display each move }
          begin
            writeln;
            move := moves[i];
            with move do
              writeln(' [', 6 - (i + 2 * iinc) : 1, ',', j + 2 * jinc : 1,
                      '] to [', 6 - i : 1, ',', j : 1, ']');
            writeln;
            MakeMove(game, move);
            show
          end;
        writeln;
        writeln('End of game #', gameno : 1);
        writeln
      end
  end;
writeln('Nails Left  Count  Score');   { Print summary after last game }
writeln('----------  -----  -----');
scoresum := 0;
for i := 1 to 14 do
  begin
    ScoreI := tally[i] * score(i);
    scoresum := scoresum + ScoreI;
    if tally[i] <> 0 then writeln(i : 6, tally[i] : 9, ScoreI : 8)
  end;
writeln;
writeln('Average score is: ', scoresum / games : 5 : 1)
end { IQTest } .
```

13.15 SILLY SENTENCES

```
program SillySentences(inf, output);
  {
    Generates random sentences based on the nouns, verbs and adjectives in the
    table words. There may be up to maxwords of each of the word types in the
    table.
  }
  const
    sentences = 20;                       { Number of sentences to generate }
    maxwords = 40;
```

```
type
  word = packed array [0..15] of char;
  wordlist = record
    noun, verb, adjective : array [0..maxwords] of word;
    max : -1..maxwords
  end;
var
  count : integer;
  words : wordlist;
  inf : text;
  seed : real;

function ranfrac : real;              { Declare and initialize seed in main program }
  begin seed := 1011.0*seed; seed := seed - trunc(seed); ranfrac := seed end;
function ran(i : integer) : integer; begin ran := trunc((i)*ranfrac) end;

procedure ReadWordTable(var words : wordlist);
  {
    Reads words from SILLY.DAT into the wordlist. words.max will be a count
    of the number of each word type.
  }

  procedure GetWord(var w : word);
    {
      Gets one word from the input file.
    }
    var
      length : integer;
    begin { GetWord }
      repeat                                           { Skip leading blanks }
        read(inf, w[1])
      until w[1] <> ' ';
      length := 1;
      repeat                                    { Get all characters in a word }
          length := length + 1;
          read(inf, w[length])
      until (w[length] = ' ') or eoln(inf);
      if w[length] = ' ' then length := length - 1;         { Erase trailing blank }
      w[0] := chr(length)                          { Length is kept as 0th character }
    end { GetWord } ;

  begin { ReadWordTable }
    with words do
      begin
        reset(inf, 'SILLY.DAT');
        max := -1;
        while not eof(inf) do
            begin
              max := max + 1;
              GetWord(noun[max]);
              GetWord(verb[max]);
              GetWord(adjective[max]);
              readln(inf)
            end
        end
    end { ReadWordTable } ;
```

```
procedure WriteSentence(words : wordlist);
  {
    Writes a Silly Sentence by randomly selecting words from the wordlist.
  }
  var
    wd : word;

  procedure WriteWord(var w : word);
    {
      Writes word w. Its length is in w[0].
    }
    var
      i : integer;
    begin { WriteWord }
      for i := 1 to ord(w[0]) do write(w[i])
    end { WriteWord } ;

begin { WriteSentence }
  with words do
    begin
      write('The ');
      WriteWord(adjective[ran(max)]);
      write(' ');
      WriteWord(noun[ran(max)]);
      write(' ');
      WriteWord(verb[ran(max)]);
      write(' a');
      wd := adjective[ran(max)];
      if wd[1] in ['a', 'e', 'i', 'o', 'u', 'A', 'E', 'I', 'O', 'U'] { Select "a" or "an" }
        then write('n ')
        else write(' ');
      WriteWord(wd);                              { before second adjective }
      write(' ');
      WriteWord(noun[ran(max)]);
      writeln('.')
    end
end { WriteSentence } ;

begin { main }
  writeln(sentences : 1, ' Silly Sentences');
  writeln;
  seed := 0.987654321;
  ReadWordTable(words);
  for count := 1 to sentences do WriteSentence(words)
end { SillySentences } .
```

13.20 POLYNOMIALS

```
program polynomials(input, output);
  {
    Implements the polynomial calculator described in the text.
  }
  const
    maxperline = 5;
  type
    nodeptr = ^node;
    node = record                                  { A term in a polynomial }
      coef : real;
      exp : integer;
      link : nodeptr
    end;
```

```
  polynomial = nodeptr;
  stacknodeptr = ^stacknode;
  stacknode = record                    { A stack item that points at a polynomial }
      item : polynomial;
      slink : stacknodeptr
  end;
  stack = stacknodeptr;
var
  poly, poly1, poly2 : polynomial;
  ch : char;
  x : real;
  st : stack;
  ok : Boolean;

procedure polyread(var poly : polynomial; var ok : Boolean);
  {
    Reads a polynomial and creates the corresponding linked structure.
  }
  var
    s, t : nodeptr;
    coefficient, exponent, lastexp : integer;
  begin { polyread }
    poly := nil;                                    { Initialize the polynomial to 0 }
    lastexp := maxint;                                         { Maximum exponent }
    while not eoln do
      begin
        read(coefficient);                                    { Read the coefficient }
        exponent := -1;                                 { To indicate error if at eoln }
        if not eoln then read(exponent);                         { Read the exponent }
                      { There should be no zero coefficients or negative exponents }
                                              { and exponents must be decreasing }
        if (coefficient = 0) or (exponent < 0) or (exponent >= lastexp) then
          begin
            writeln('Illegal input syntax');
            ok := false;
            poly := nil
          end else                                                    { Input is ok }
          begin
            lastexp := exponent;        { Remember to check against next exponent }
            new(t);                                                { Make a new node }
            t^.coef := coefficient;
            t^.exp := exponent;
            t^.link := nil;
            if poly = nil then poly := t else s^.link := t;          { and splice it in }
            s := t
          end
      end
  end { polyread } ;

  procedure polywrite(poly : polynomial);
  {
    Writes a polynomial using its linked representation.
  }
  var
    first : Boolean;
    online : integer;
  begin { polywrite }
    first := true;                       { Signs are handled differently for first term }
    online := 0;                                { Number of terms on this line so far }
    if poly = nil then write('0') else
```

```
  while poly <> nil do
    begin
      if (poly^.coef < 0)                                          { If negative term }
        then if first then write('-') else write(' - ')                  { write - sign }
        else if not first then write(' + ');                        { else write + sign }
                               { Write coefficient unless it is 1 (or exponent is 0) }
      if (abs(poly^.coef) <> 1) or (poly^.exp = 0)
        then write(abs(poly^.coef) : 1 : 0);
      if poly^.exp > 0 then write('x');             { Write variable x unless exp = 0 }
      if poly^.exp > 1 then write('^', poly^.exp : 1);           { Write exp if > 1 }
      first := false;                                           { No longer first term }
      online := online + 1;                { Increment number of terms on this line }
      if online >= maxperline then begin writeln; online := 0 end;
      poly := poly^.link                                         { Point to next term }
    end;
  writeln
end { polywrite } ;

function add(poly1, poly2 : polynomial) : polynomial;
  {
    Returns a pointer to a new list that represents the sum of poly1 and poly2.
  }
  var
    t : nodeptr;
    sum : real;
  begin { add }
    if poly1 = nil then add := poly2 else                         { If one poly is zero, }
      if poly2 = nil then add := poly1 else                       { the result is the other }
        if poly1^.exp = poly2^.exp then                      { If terms are same degree }
          begin
            sum := poly1^.coef + poly2^.coef;                         { add coefficients }
            if sum = 0 then add := add(poly1^.link, poly2^.link) else
              begin                                    { and add to result unless 0 term }
                new(t);
                t^.coef := sum;
                t^.exp := poly1^.exp;
                t^.link := add(poly1^.link, poly2^.link);
                add := t
              end
          end else                                { Otherwise put larger term in result }
        if poly1^.exp > poly2^.exp then
          begin
            new(t);
            t^.coef := poly1^.coef;
            t^.exp := poly1^.exp;
            t^.link := add(poly1^.link, poly2);                  { and add remaining lists }
            add := t
          end else
          begin
            new(t);
            t^.coef := poly2^.coef;
            t^.exp := poly2^.exp;
            t^.link := add(poly1, poly2^.link);
            add := t
          end
  end { add } ;
```

```
function gencopy(poly : polynomial; c : real; e : integer) : polynomial;
  {
    Returns a pointer to a generalized copy of poly ( poly multiplied by the term
    c * x^e).
  }
  var
    t : nodeptr;
  begin { gencopy }
    if poly = nil then gencopy := nil else
      begin
        new(t);                                                        { Get new node }
        t^.exp := poly^.exp + e;        { Exponent of new term is sum of exponents }
        t^.coef := c * poly^.coef;          { Coefficient is product of coefficients }
        t^.link := gencopy(poly^.link, c, e);           { Link to copy of rest of list }
        gencopy := t
      end
  end { gencopy } ;

function copy(poly : polynomial) : polynomial;
  {
    Returns a pointer to a copy of poly.
  }
  begin { copy }
    copy := gencopy(poly, 1, 0)
  end { copy } ;

function negcopy(poly : polynomial) : polynomial;
  {
    Returns a pointer to a negative copy of poly.
  }
  begin { negcopy }
    negcopy := gencopy(poly, -1, 0)
  end { negcopy } ;

function sub(poly1, poly2 : polynomial) : polynomial;
  {
    Returns a pointer to a new list that represents the difference of poly1 and poly2.
  }
  var
    t : nodeptr;
  begin { sub }
    sub := add(poly1, negcopy(poly2))                { A subtract is a negative add }
  end { sub } ;

function mul(poly1, poly2 : polynomial) : polynomial;
  {
    Returns a pointer to a new list that represents the product of poly1 and poly2. It
    does the multiplication by adding the product of poly2 and the first term of poly1
    to the product of poly2 and the rest of poly1.
  }
  begin { mul }
    if (poly1 = nil) or (poly2 = nil)
      then mul := nil
      else mul := add(gencopy(poly2, poly1^.coef, poly1^.exp),
                      mul(poly1^.link, poly2))
  end { mul } ;

function value(poly : polynomial; x : real) : real;
  {
    Returns the value of poly when evaluated at x.
  }
  var
    c : integer;
    v : real;
```

```
begin { value }
  if poly = nil then value := 0 else
    begin
      v := poly^.coef;                                    { v begins as coefficient }
      if poly^.link = nil
        then c := 0
        else c := poly^.link^.exp;
      while poly^.exp > c do     { v is multiplied by power of x up to next term }
        begin
          v := v * x;
          c := c + 1
        end;
      if poly^.link = nil then value := v else     { If no more terms, v is value }
        begin
          poly^.link^.coef := v + poly^.link^.coef;    { else add v to coefficient }
          value := value(poly^.link, x)       { of next term and evaluate rest of poly }
        end
    end
end { value } ;

procedure push(poly : polynomial; var s : stack);
  {
    Pushes the polynomial poly into stack s.
  }
  var
    t : stacknodeptr;
  begin { push }
    new(t);
    t^.item := poly;
    t^.slink := s;
    s := t
  end { push } ;

procedure pop(var poly : polynomial; var s : stack);
  {
    Pops the polynomial poly from stack s.
  }
  var
    t : stacknodeptr;
  begin { pop }
    poly := s^.item;
    t := s;
    s := s^.slink;
    dispose(t)
  end { pop } ;

procedure init(var s : stack);
  {
    Initializes stack s.
  }
  begin { init }
      s := nil
  end { init } ;

begin { main }
  init(st);                                                    { Initialization }
  poly1 := nil; poly2 := nil; poly := nil;
  ok := true;
  writeln; writeln('The Polynomial Calculator is ON.'); writeln;
  write('>');                                       { Prompt for a line of input }
  while ok and (not eof) do
    begin
      read(ch);
```

```
    if not (ch in ['e', 'E', '+', '-', '*', '"', 'v', 'V', 'w', 'W', '"'])
      then writeln('Illegal command')
      else case ch of
          'e', 'E' : begin                                  { The Enter button }
                  polyread(poly, ok);                      { Read a polynomial }
                  push(poly, st)                                 { and push it }
                end;
             '+' : begin                                      { The Add button }
                  pop(poly1, st);                                    { Pop top }
                  if ok then
                    begin
                      pop(poly2, st);                              { and next }
                      push(add(poly1, poly2), st)                  { Push sum }
                    end
                end;
             '-' : begin                                 { The Subtract button }
                  pop(poly1, st);                                    { Pop top }
                  if ok then
                    begin
                      pop(poly2, st);                              { and next }
                      push(sub(poly2, poly1), st)           { Push difference }
                    end
                end;
             '*' : begin                                 { The Multiply button }
                  pop(poly1, st);                                    { Pop top }
                  if ok then
                    begin
                      pop(poly2, st);                              { and next }
                      push(mul(poly1, poly2), st)              { Push product }
                    end
                end;
          'v', 'V' : begin                               { The Evaluate button }
                  read(x);
                  pop(poly, st);                                     { Pop top }
                  if ok then
                    begin
                      push(copy(poly), st);                     { Push it back }
                      writeln('When x = ', x : 1 : 0);
                      polywrite(poly);                { Write it and its value }
                      write(' = ', value(poly, x) : 1 : 0); writeln
                    end
                end;
             '"' : begin                                    { The Ditto button }
                  pop(poly, st);                                     { Pop top }
                  push(poly, st);                               { Push it back }
                  push(copy(poly), st)                          { and a copy }
                end;
          'w', 'W' : begin                                  { The Write button }
                  pop(poly, st);                                     { Pop top }
                  if ok then
                    begin
                      push(poly, st);                           { Push it back }
                      polywrite(poly); writeln
                    end
                end
        end { case } ;
    readln;
    if ok
      then write('>')                                    { Reissue prompt or }
      else write(chr(7))                           { beep for error on input }
  end;
  writeln;writeln('The Polynomial Calculator is OFF.')
end { polynomials } .
```

CHAPTER 14 — ANALYSIS OF ALGORITHMS

This chapter is highly mathematical, but doesn't use higher mathematics; there is a vast difference. If you know that your majors will eventually take a whole course in algorithm analysis, you could tread lightly here. But you should teach at least the fundamental idea behind the "big O" notation. To prepare your students, make sure that they are exposed to the simple summation formulas for integers and squares of integers. If they gain faith that at least these simple sums have closed-form expressions, then they will be ready to consider more complicated ones.

We will be disappointed if you decide to skip the whole chapter, because we build on at least its simpler aspects in the later and very important Chapter 17 on Searching and Sorting. When they come to it, we would like students to be ready for the surprise that binary search is not always faster than sequential search. If you thought so too, peek ahead.

SOLUTIONS TO SELECTED PROGRAMMING EXERCISES

14.6 THE SUM IS 100

```
program SumIs100(output);
  {
    Computes all ordered sequences of the digits 1..9 with +, –, or null between the digits
    that produce an expression that sums to 100. There are many improvements that can be
    made to this algorithm to reduce its running time.
  }
  const
    TheSumIs = 100;
  type
    signs = array[2..10] of –1..1; { Holds the signs between the digits (0 => null) }
  var
    count : integer;
    s : signs;                               { s[i] holds the sign just ahead of digit i }

  function sum(s : signs) : integer;
    {
      Computes the sum of the expression whose signs are in s.
    }
    var
      i, term, sign, tsum : integer;
    begin { sum }
      term := 1;                                     { Current term being evaluated }
      sign := 1;                                                 { Last sign found }
      tsum := 0;                                                     { Sum so far }
      for i := 2 to 10 do
        if s[i] = 0 then term := 10 * term + i else        { If no sign, update term }
          begin
            tsum := tsum + sign * term;                        { Add in current term }
            sign := s[i];                                            { Update sign }
            term := i                                            { Start next term }
          end;
      sum := tsum                                { Assign final sum to function value }
    end { sum } ;

  procedure PrintSum(s : signs; var ct : integer);
    {
      Prints the expression whose signs are in s prefixed by an updated count ct.
    }
    var
      i : integer;
    begin { PrintSum }
      ct := ct + 1;                                  { Update the count of sums found }
      write(ct : 2, '  : 1');                         { Start the expression with '1' }
      for i := 2 to 9 do
        begin
          if s[i] = –1 then write('–') else             { Print the sign if not null }
          if s[i] =  1 then write('+');
          write(i : 1)                                         { Write next digit }
        end;
      writeln('  =  ', TheSumIs : 1)                                 { Print the sum }
    end { PrintSum } ;

  begin { main }
    writeln('      The Sum Is ', TheSumIs : 1);
    writeln;
    count := 0;
    s[10] := 1;                                        { To exit gracefully from loop }
    s[2] := –1;                                       { Start of nested loops over all }
    while s[2] <= 1 do                                          { signs = –1, 0, and 1 }
```

```
      begin
        s[3] := -1;
        while s[3] <= 1 do
          begin
            s[4] := -1;
            while s[4] <= 1 do
              begin
                s[5] := -1;
                while s[5] <= 1 do
                  begin
                    s[6] := -1;
                    while s[6] <= 1 do
                      begin
                        s[7] := -1;
                        while s[7] <= 1 do
                          begin
                            s[8] := -1;
                            while s[8] <= 1 do
                              begin
                                s[9] := -1;
                                while s[9] <= 1 do
                                  begin
                                    if sum(s) = TheSumIs               { Compute sum }
                                      then PrintSum(s, count);  { and display if 100 }
                                    s[9] := s[9] + 1
                                  end;
                                s[8] := s[8] + 1
                              end;
                            s[7] := s[7] + 1
                          end;
                        s[6] := s[6] + 1
                      end;
                    s[5] := s[5] + 1
                  end;
                s[4] := s[4] + 1
              end;
            s[3] := s[3] + 1
          end;
        s[2] := s[2] + 1
      end;
    writeln;
    writeln('Done')
  end { SumIs100 } .
```

14.8 ZIGZAG NUMBERS

```
program zigzag(input, output);
  {
    Computes and prints zigzag numbers for any order 2..8.
  }
  const
    qsize = 1000;
    qsizem1 = 999;
    zero = false;
    one = true;
  type
    object = packed array[0..8] of char;
    digits = '1'..'8';
    queue = record
      front, rear : 0..qsizem1;
      data : array [0..qsizem1] of object
    end;
```

```
var
  q : array[Boolean] of queue;                              { Declare two queues }
  s, d : Boolean;                    { Use s(ource) and d(estination) as indices }
  i, n, digit : char;
  item, titem, unity : object;
  digitsused : set of digits;
  j : 1..8;

function length(item : object) : integer;
  {
    Returns the length of item.
  }
  begin { length }
    length := ord(item[0])
  end { length } ;

procedure append(var item : object; digit : char);
  {
    Appends digit to item.
  }
  var
    L : integer;
  begin { append }
    L := length(item) + 1;
    item[0] := chr(L);
    item[L] := digit
  end { append } ;

procedure clear(var q : queue);
  {
    Sets q to an empty queue.
  }
  begin { clear }
    q.front := 0;
    q.rear  := 0
  end { clear } ;

function empty(var q : queue) : Boolean;
  {
    Returns true if q is empty, false if q is not empty.
  }
  begin { empty }
    empty := q.rear = q.front
  end { empty } ;

function len(var q : queue) : integer;
  {
    Returns length of  q.
  }
  begin { len }
    len := (q.rear - q.front + qsize) mod qsize
  end { len } ;

procedure enter(item : object; var q : queue);
  {
    Enters item into q.
  }
  begin { enter }
    if len(q) = qsizem1 then writeln('queue overflow') else
      begin { enter }
        q.rear := (q.rear + 1) mod qsize;
        q.data[q.rear] := item
      end
  end { enter } ;
```

```
procedure remove(var item : object; var q : queue);
  {
    Removes item from q.
  }
  begin { remove }
    if empty(q) then writeln('empty queue') else
      begin
        q.front := (q.front + 1) mod qsize;
        item := q.data[q.front]
      end
  end { remove } ;

procedure PrintQ(var q : queue);
  {
      Empties and prints q.
  }
  var
    i : integer;
    item : object;
  begin { PrintQ }
    while not empty(q) do
      begin
        remove(item, q);
        for i := 1 to length(item) do write(item[i]);
        writeln
      end;
    writeln
  end { PrintQ } ;

begin { main }
  clear(q[zero]);
  clear(q[one]);
  write('Enter a value of n in [2..8]: ');
  while not eof do
    begin
      repeat readln(n) until n in ['2'..'8'];
      writeln;
      unity[0] := chr(1);
      unity[1] := '1';
      enter(unity, q[zero]);
      for i := '2' to n do
        begin
          s := odd(ord(i));         { s and d will alternate between q[zero] and q[one] }
          d := not s;
          repeat
            remove(item, q[s]);
            digitsused := [];
            for j := 1 to length(item) do
              digitsused := digitsused + [item[j]];
            if d then                                        { Append larger digits }
              for digit := succ(item[length(item)]) to n do
                if not (digit in digitsused) then
                  begin
                    titem := item;
                    append(titem, digit);
                    enter(titem, q[d])
                  end;
```

```
          if s then                                       { Append smaller digits }
            for digit := '2' to pred(item[length(item)]) do
              if not (digit in digitsused) then
                begin
                  titem := item;
                  append(titem, digit);
                  enter(titem, q[d])
                end
        until empty(q[s])
      end;
    if n < '4'
      then writeln('There is 1 zigzag number of order ', n:1, ': ')
      else writeln('There are ', len(q[d]) : 1,
                   ' zigzag numbers of order ', n, ': ');
    writeln;
    PrintQ(q[d]);
    write('Enter a value of n in [2..8]: ')
  end
end { zigzag } .
```

14.10 1001 KNIGHTS

```
program Knights1001(input, output);
  {
    Compares solutions to the Knights of the Roundtable problem that use
      (a) A linked representation of the roundtable, and
      (b) A mod formula to find the next knight to delete.
  }
  const
    max = 100;
  var
    m, k : integer;

  function SLinked(m, k : integer) : integer;
    {
      Solves the Knights of the Roundtable problem using a linked representation
      of the roundtable to find the next knight to delete.
    }
    var
      kts : array[1..max] of integer;
      i, j, p, r : integer;
    begin { SLinked }
      for i := 1 to m - 1 do kts[i] := i + 1;      { Link each entry in kts to the next }
      kts[m] := 1;                                              { and last to first }
      p := m;
      for i := 1 to m - 1 do
        begin
          for j := 1 to k - 1 do p := kts[p];                   { Skip k - 1 knights }
            kts[p] := kts[kts[p]]                                 { and delete kth }
        end;
      SLinked := kts[p]                  { Report the result through function value }
    end { SLinked } ;

  function SMod(m, k : integer) : integer;
    {
      Solves the Knights of the Roundtable problem using a mod formula to find
      the next knight to delete.
    }
    var
      kts : array[1..max] of integer;
      i, j, mp : integer;
```

```
    begin { SMod }
      for i := 1 to m do kts[i] := i;                        { Initial knights array }
      i := 1;
      mp := m;
      for mp := m downto 2 do
        begin
          i := 1 + (i + k - 2) mod mp;                      { Compute knight to delete }
          for j := i to mp - 1 do kts[j] := kts[j + 1]              { and delete it }
        end;
      SMod := kts[1]                        { Report the result through function value }
    end { SMod } ;

  begin { Knights1001 }
    writeln('The Knights of the Roundtable');
    writeln;
    write('Enter number of knights and cycle: ');
    while not eof do
      begin
        readln(m, k);
        writeln;
        writeln('S (linked)  = ', SLinked(m, k) : 1);
        writeln('S (mod)     = ', SMod(m, k) : 1);
        writeln;
        write('Enter number of knights and cycle: ')
      end
  end { Knights1001 } .
```

14.11 STROLLING PLAYERS

```
program StrollingPlayers(input, output, inf);
  {
    Computes the "shortest" trip that will visit all of the Italian cities on the itinerary of the
    Group of Strolling Players. Random paths are tested and the route for the shortest
    distance found is reported. The number of routes to check is supplied as input. The
    distance table must be in the input file ITALY.DAT. Each line of this file starts with an
    8-letter city name and is followed by the distances to each of the cities.
  }
  const
    stops = 20;
    stops1 = 19;
    StartNumber = 18;                          { City number for Venice, the home city }
  type
    CityName = packed array [1..8] of char;
  var
    i, j, temp, min, total, trial, trials : integer;
    seed : real;
    route, saveroute : array [0..stops] of integer;
    km : array [0..stops1, 0..stops1] of integer;
    cities : array [0..stops1] of CityName;
    inf : text;

  function ranfrac : real;               { Declare and initialize seed in main program }
    begin seed := 1011.0*seed; seed := seed - trunc(seed); ranfrac := seed end;
  function ran(i : integer) : integer;  begin ran := trunc((i)*ranfrac) end;

  begin { main }
    reset(inf, 'ITALY.DAT');
    for i := 0 to stops1 do                                { Read input for each city }
      begin
        for j := 1 to 8 do read(inf, cities[i][j]);                       { City name }
        for j := 0 to stops1 do read(inf, km[i, j]);          { Distances to other cities }
        readln(inf)
      end;
```

```
    seed := 0.87654321;
    write('Enter number of trips to test: ');
    readln(trials);
    writeln;
    writeln;
    min := maxint;
    for i := 0 to stops1 do route[i] := i;                  { Initialize route }
    route[0] := StartNumber;                       { Make starting city the 0th }
    route[stops] := StartNumber;                      { and last city in route }
    route[StartNumber] := 0;                   { and replace StartNo with 0 }
    writeln('Trial #  Distance');
    for trial := 1 to trials do
      begin
        i := stops1;                 { Shuffle the cities to create a random route }
        while i > 1 do
          begin
            j := ran(i) + 1;
            temp := route[j]; route[j] := route[i]; route[i] := temp;
            i := i - 1
          end;
        total := 0;                       { Compute total distance for this route }
        for i := 0 to stops1 do
          total := total + km[route[i], route[i + 1]];
        if total < min then                             { If it is a shorter route }
          begin
            writeln(trial : 7, total : 10);           { announce new shortest distance }
            min := total;                                            { and save it }
            saveroute := route                      { and the route that produced it }
          end
      end;
    writeln;                                          { Display the best route found }
    writeln('The Best Route Found In ', trials : 1, ' Trials Is: ');
    writeln;
    writeln('From ', cities[route[0]]);
    for i := 1 to stops do
      writeln('   To ', cities[saveroute[i]], km[saveroute[i],
              saveroute[i - 1]] : 10, ' kilometers');
    writeln('---------------------------------');
    writeln('Total Trip Length', min : 6, ' kilometers')
  end { StrollingPlayers } .
```

Note: Cole Porter's route is 506 kilometers which is tied with 7 (out of 59) other routes (not counting routes in the reverse direction) for the shortest closed path that visits all 6 cities of "We open in Venice."

CHAPTER 15 — STRUCTURED PROGRAMMING

Structured programming was not relegated to a high-numbered chapter because it is unimportant. To the contrary, it is so important that we used structured program design from Chapter 3 onward without feeling that we needed to say so explicitly. But there are some new things here, however. If you decided not to present Nassi-Shneiderman diagrams earlier, then at least make them assigned reading now. The section on program verification is tough going, but do at least enough of it to emphasize the importance of loop invariants. Finally, if you cover nothing else, discuss the Quicksort algorithm. We used it as a case study here, but if we hadn't, we would certainly have included it in the chapter on searching and sorting, Chapter 17. The algorithm is a little gem that should be a polished part of every computer scientist, big or little.

CHAPTER 16 — SOFTWARE ENGINEERING

At one extreme, you may feel that you do not have time to do justice to this topic and merely assign the chapter for background reading. (At least do that.) At the other, you may choose to go all out and organize a Software Hut as described in the interlude that follows the chapter. We've had lots of fun doing the latter, but it does take a chunk of time that cannot always be carved out of time available for a data structures course. Perhaps you could make the Hut the basis for a separate Software Engineering seminar.

As stated in the chapter, Pascal offers limited tools for making programs robust. You can do it, but it takes some work. The principal difficulty is with incorrect numeric input. How do you catch it before the program bombs? Ironically, the Pascal concept of subrange acts against robustness. If you declare a variable to have the range 1..10 and someone inputs a value of 0 or 11, you lose control. From the standpoint of software engineering, you might better have just declared the variable as an integer and then done your own checking to see that the integer received was really in [1..10]. But what if the "integer" received was a 'q'? Because of this concern, the only recourse with most Pascal implementations is to resolve never to read an integer or a real number; read everything as a string of characters and do your own parsing. Many implementations give you a library of routines for dealing with variable-length strings; these certainly help. If you get into this, show your students how to do some elementary parsing based on these routines. The really ambitious approach would be to base the parsing on a finite state machine as shown in Chapter 8. Show how to "build" one with nested case statements that follow the syntax chart for, say, <unsigned number>.

The chapter discusses, briefly, the concept of a "live key". If your students use a terminal connected to a mainframe, then you may not be able to implement such action. But with most microcomputers, it isn't hard to do. If you are using micros, find out how to do it and show your students.

CHAPTER 17 — PROGRAMMING TECHNIQUES AND APPLICATIONS

As promised, this is the chapter that shows that binary search is not necessarily faster than sequential search. We think it worthwhile to call that to students' attention, but of course you should also say that with most data distributions they are likely to encounter, binary search is the superior method.

By the end of this chapter, we will have said at least something about thirteen different sorting methods and shown a program for most of them. Running times for eleven are compared, with selection sort being the only one whose encoding was left for the student. If you are looking for others that could be assigned, note the exercises regarding Radix Sort at the end of this chapter, and Quadsort at the end of Chapter 14. There are also exercises that propose variations on some of the methods whose encoding was given.

Will you have time to lecture on all of these methods? Almost certainly not; there are far more than the two or three given in most elementary books. But you can assign some for reading, assign others for programming practice, and still have enough left over so as to vary the content of successive editions of your course.

Finally, apart from however many methods you cover in depth, we think that students will find the comparative running times instructive. If you accomplish nothing else all semester, and certainly you will, your students will no longer use Bubblesort by reflex action whenever they need to sort something.

SOLUTIONS TO SELECTED PROGRAMMING EXERCISES

17.13 TELENUMS

```
program TeleNums(input, output);
  {
    Uses a hash table to store and retrieve company names when given their telephone
    numbers.
  }
  const
    size = 907;                              { Size of hash table — a prime }
    size1 = 906;                             { Maximum subscript in hash table }
  type
    str = packed array [1..8] of char;
    entry = record
      name, Num : str
    end;
    table = array[0..size1] of entry;
  var
    temp, null : entry;
    i, c, h, n1, n2, n3 : integer;
    HTbl : table;
    inf : text;

  function hash(n1, n2, n3 : integer) : integer;
    {
      The hash function.
    }
    begin { hash }
      hash := (n1 + n2 + n3) mod size
    end { hash } ;

  function rehash(n1, n2, n3, h : integer) : integer;
    {
      The rehash function.  Counts calls in the glogal variable c.  Try other rehash
      functions to optimize the total number of rehashes needed.
    }
    begin { rehash }
      c := c + 1;
      rehash := (h + 1) mod size
    end { rehash } ;

  function dgt(c : char) : integer;
    {
      Returns the 1-digit integer corresponding to the character c.
    }
    begin { dgt }
      dgt := ord(c) - ord('0')
    end { dgt } ;

  begin { main }
    reset(inf, 'HASH.DAT');
    for i := 0 to size1 do HTbl[i].name[1] := ' ';          { Initialize hash table }
    c := 0;                                                 { and rehash counter }
    while not eof(inf) do
      begin
        for i := 1 to 8 do read(inf, temp.name[i]);    { Read a name from input file }
        for i := 1 to 8 do read(inf, temp.Num[i]);          { then a phone number }
        readln(inf);
        n1 :=  dgt(temp.Num[1]) * 100 + dgt(temp.Num[2]) * 10 +
               dgt(temp.Num[3]);                  { Break the number into 3 integers }
        n2 := dgt(temp.Num[5]) * 10 + dgt(temp.Num[6]);
        n3 := dgt(temp.Num[7]) * 10 + dgt(temp.Num[8]);
```

```
      h := hash(n1, n2, n3);                                  { Hash the number }
      if temp.name[1] = ' ' then                              { If name is blank }
        begin                                                 { look it up in table }
          write(temp.Num);                                    { but write it first }
          while (HTbl[h].Num <> temp.Num) and (HTbl[h].name[1] <> ' ') do
            h := rehash(n1, n2, n3, h);                       { Rehash until }
          if HTbl[h].Num = temp.Num                           { the number is either }
            then writeln(' is Number for ', HTbl[h].name)     { found }
            else writeln(' is not in directory')              { or not found }
        end
      else                                    { If name is not blank, store into table }
        begin
          while HTbl[h].name[1] <> ' ' do h := rehash(n1, n2, n3, h);
          HTbl[h] := temp
        end
    end { while not eof } ;
  writeln;
  writeln(c : 1, ' rehashes were needed.')
end { TeleNums } .
```

17.18 BIG RECORDS See Problem 10.41

CHAPTER 18 — NUMERICAL METHODS

This chapter exists because the people who made the syllabus for the Advanced Placement Test in Computer Science apparently think that we give a big dosage of numerical methodology in one or the other of our first two courses. (We don't, do you?) Now, don't mistake our thrust. Numerical analysis is a great and honorable subject; both of us cut our eye-teeth in the area, and all computer science students should learn something about it — eventually. Whether your course syllabus includes a whole module devoted to numerical methods, or whether you would just like to give an occasional assignment that involves getting a good numerical approximation, this chapter should prove more than sufficient. At the least, you might consider as assigned reading those parts of the chapter that discuss the impact of precision on accuracy. As early as Chapter 2, we stressed that, though obviously related, precision is not a synonym for accuracy despite all the books that use those terms too loosely. Have your students review the definitions for each term given in that chapter, or in the Glossary.

Chapter 18 mentions certain extended-precision enhancements that some of the Pascal dialects offer for those infrequent occasions when normal single-precision real arithmetic is not adequate. Find out if your implementation has an extended-precision enhancement and, if so, tell your students about it.

One final thought. If you chose not to emphasize Appendix F or say anything about the internal representation of real numbers earlier, you might now want to do so in this context where precision is so important.

SOLUTIONS TO SELECTED PROGRAMMING EXERCISES

18.17 CHEBYSHEV POLYNOMIALS

```
program Cheby(input, output);
  {
    Prints Chebyshev Polynomials of order 2 to n by recurrence relation and also by
    trigonometric computation of individual terms.
  }
  const
    max = 100;                                        { Maximum order possible }
    pi = 3.14159265358979;
  var
    i : integer;
    n : integer;                                      { Maximum order (input) }
    x : real;                        { The argument for all orders of T(x) (input) }
    a : real;                       { arccos(x) which does not change during loop }
    T : array[0..max] of real;                                       { The T(x) }
  begin
    writeln('Calculation of T (x)');
    writeln('                   n');
    writeln;
    write('Enter values for x (-1 to 1) and maximum  n: ');
    readln(x, n);
    writeln;
    if x = 0
      then a := pi / 2
      else a := arctan(sqrt(1 - x * x) / x);          { Calculate a = arccos(x) }
    T[0] := 1;                                                     { Initialize }
    T[1] := x;
    writeln(' n       T[n] {recursion}        T(n) {trig}');
    writeln;
    for i := 2 to n do
      begin
        T[i] := 2 * x * T[i - 1] - T[i - 2];                 { Recurrence relation }
        writeln(i : 2, T[i] : 20 : 10, cos(i * a) : 20 : 10)
      end
  end { Cheby } .
```

18.18 BESSEL FUNCTIONS

```
program Bessel(output);
  const
    max = 20;
    x = 2.0;
  var
    n : integer;
    f, sum : real;
    J : array[0..max] of real;
  begin
    writeln('Bessel Function Generator');
    writeln;
    writeln(' n          J (',x:1:2,')');
    writeln('             n');
    writeln('------------------------');
    J[max] := 0;                 { Prepare to apply recurrence relation backwards }
    J[max - 1] := 1;
    for n := max - 1 downto 1 do          { Apply recurrence relation backwards }
      J[n - 1] := (2 * n / x) * J[n] - J[n + 1];
    sum := J[0];
    n := 2;
    while n <= max do              { Calculate the weighted sum of the even terms }
      begin
        sum := sum + 2 * J[n];
        n := n + 2
      end;
    f := 1 / sum;          { Since sum should be 1, the normalization factor is 1 / sum}
    for n := 0 to max do
      writeln(n : 2, '     ', f * J[n] : 20)               { Normalize and print results }
  end { Bessel } .
```

CHAPTER 19 — ARTIFICIAL INTELLIGENCE

The presence of this chapter is in accord with our intent that the text be a true introduction to computer science. As such, it should and does address one of the most fertile and active areas of research in computer science: artificial intelligence. Make the chapter assigned reading and then hold a half-hour discussion on the question of whether machines can think or might ever be conscious in the human sense. If you have procured the diskettes for the text programs (or if you have someone that just loves to keyboard), place Eliza and G1A in your class file and tell your students to interact with them. (Give a prize for the transcript of the funniest Eliza session and read it in class?) If nothing else, assign some of the programming exercises. For this chapter, you might want to let the students pick a problem or two from all those listed rather than directing them to do particular ones.

CHAPTER 20 — NUMBER THEORY

Number theory is certainly not in itself a branch of computer science, so we cannot justify the existence of this chapter as we did the last one. But what has always been fun about number theory is that the statements of the theorems and conjectures in this field are generally more comprehensible to amateurs than those of any other branch of mathematics. This also makes number theoretic problems candidates for very satisfying computer investigations, and that is the prime (and composite?) reason for using the text of the chapter as a prelude to its programming exercises. Even if you don't lecture the material, you might want to reach forward and assign one or another of these exercises at some earlier point in your syllabus.

SOLUTIONS TO SELECTED PROGRAMMING EXERCISES

20.6 FUSARO PAIRS

```
program FusaroPairs(output);
  {
    Generates and writes all Fusaro Pairs. Each 5-digit product is split into its first 4 digits
    and its last digit so that the program will work on systems using two-byte integers.
  }
  var
    abc, s, count, abc1, abc2, abc3, de, abcd, e, a, b, k, m, n : integer;
    digits : array [1..5] of integer;
  begin
    count := 0;                                              { To count the pairs }
    writeln('      Fusaro Pairs');
    writeln;
    for a := 2 to 9 do if (a <> 4) and (a <> 7) then                    { Remainder a }
      begin
        if (a = 2) or (a = 9) then b := a else                          { Remainder b }
          if a < 6 then b := a + 3 else b := a - 3;
        abc := 99 + a;                                { First 3-digit number to check }
        while abc < 1000 do
          begin
            abc1 := abc div 100;                { Break 3-digit number into its digits }
            abc3 := abc mod 100;
            abc2 := abc3 div 10;
            abc3 := abc3 mod 10;
            de := 90 + b;                                  { Last 2-digit number to check }
            abcd := 1000;
            while (de > 9) and (abcd > 999) do     { Count de down until product }
              begin                                        { of abc and de < 10000 }
                digits[1] := de div 10;     { Separate 2-digit number into its digits }
                digits[2] := de mod 10;
                digits[3] := abc1;                      { Copy digits of 3-digit number }
                digits[4] := abc2;
                digits[5] := abc3;
                e := abc * digits[2];  { Compute product so there will be no overflow }
                abcd := abc * digits[1] + e div 10;     { when using 2-byte integers }
                e := e mod 10;             { abcd is first four digits and e is last digit }
                if abcd > 999 then
                  begin
                    n := e;                                          { First unused digit }
                    m := abcd;                                            { Other digits }
                    k := 1;
                    while k < 6 do                   { Search for all digits in digit array }
                      begin
                        s := 1;
                        while s < 6 do                              { Search for this digit }
                          if n = digits[s]
                            then
                              begin                                             { Found it }
                                digits[s] := -1;                    { Remove it from array }
                                n := m mod 10;                          { Next unused digit }
                                m := m div 10;                               { Other digits }
                                s := 7                                         { End search }
                              end
                            else s := s + 1;
                        if s = 6
                          then k := 7        { Did not find this digit so no Fusaro pair }
                          else k := k + 1              { Found it, look for next digit }
                      end;
```

```
            if k = 6 then                      { All digits found, so Fusaro pair }
              begin
                count := count + 1;                        { Count it and print it }
                writeln(count : 2, ':  ', abc : 3, '  x  ', de : 2, '  =  ',
                             abcd : 1, e : 1)
              end;
            de := de - 9                               { Get next 2-digit number }
          end
        end;
      abc := abc + 9                                   { Get next 3-digit number }
    end
  end
end { FusaroPairs } .
```

20.7 PDI

```
program PDI(output);
  {
    Computes and prints all the Perfect Digital Invariants with 2, 3, or 4 digits.
  }
  type
    nodeptr = ^node;
    node = record
      info : integer;
      link : nodeptr
    end;
  var
    i, j, k, l, ij, ijk, ijkl : integer;
    powers : array [0..9, 2..4] of integer;
    PDIList : nodeptr;

  procedure insert(item : integer; var L : nodeptr);
    {
      Inserts item into the SLLL pointed to by L, maintaining numeric order.
    }
    var
      p : nodeptr;
      firstnode : Boolean;
    begin { insert }
      if L = nil
        then firstnode := true
        else firstnode := item <= L^.info;
      if firstnode then
        begin
          new(p);
          p^.info := item;
          p^.link := L;
          L := p
        end
      else insert(item, L^.link)
    end { insert } ;

  procedure PrintList(L : nodeptr);
    {
      Prints the SLLL L.
    }
    begin { PrintList }
      while L <> nil do
        begin
          write(L^.info : 6);
          L := L^.link                                 { Find next node }
        end;
      writeln
    end { PrintList } ;
```

```
begin { main }
  writeln;
  writeln('The Perfect Digital Invariants with 2, 3, or 4 digits');
  writeln;
  PDIList := nil;                                        { Initialize SLLL of PDI's }
  for i := 0 to 9 do     { Create a table of 2nd thru 4th powers of the digits 0..9 }
    begin
      powers[i, 2] := i * i;
      powers[i, 3] := powers[i, 2] * i;
      powers[i, 4] := powers[i, 3] * i
    end;
  for i := 1 to 9 do                                 { First digit of a number to test }
  for j := 0 to 9 do                                { Second digit of a number to test }
    begin
      ij := 10 * i + j;                                          { The 2-digit number }
      if powers[i, 2] + powers[j, 2] = ij
        then insert(ij, PDIList);                              { If PDI, insert in list }
      for k := 0 to 9 do                             { Third digit of a number to test }
        begin
          ijk := ij * 10 + k;                                    { The 3-digit number }
          if powers[i, 3] + powers[j, 3] + powers[k, 3] = ijk
            then insert(ijk, PDIList);                         { If PDI, insert in list }
          for l := 0 to 9 do                         { Fourth digit of a number to test }
            begin
              ijkl := 10 * ijk + l;                              { The 4-digit number }
              if powers[i, 4] + powers[j, 4] + powers[k, 4] + powers[l, 4] = ijkl
                then insert(ijkl, PDIList)                     { If PDI, insert in list }
            end
        end
    end;
  PrintList(PDIList)                                   { Print list in numeric order }
end { PDI } .
```

20.8 LUCKY NUMBERS

```
program LuckyNumbers(input, output);
  {
    Generates the Lucky Numbers.
  }
  const
    max = 1000;            { Maximun Lucky Number this program will compute }
  type
    numbers = array [1..max] of Boolean;
  var
    n, total, sum, s1, s2 : integer;
    luckies : numbers;

  procedure GetLuckies(var luckies : numbers; n : integer; var total : integer);
    {
      Computes the Lucky Numbers in 1..n by setting the elements of luckies with
      unlucky indices to false.
    }
    var
      i, j, k : integer;
    begin { GetLuckies }
      for i := 1 to n do luckies[i] := true;                      { Initialize the array }
      i := 2;                                             { The first deletion increment }
      total := n;
      while i < n do                                                { For all deletions }
        begin
          j := 1;
          while j <= n do                          { Search for ith number still in list }
            begin
              k := i;
```

```
        while k > 0 do                               { k is counting down from i to 0 }
          begin
            if j > n
              then k := -1                           { Stop while loop if past n }
              else if luckies[j] then k := k - 1;        { Count down for each }
                                                         { undeleted number }
            if j <= n then j := j + 1             { Continue search  at next position }
          end;
        if k = 0 then
          begin
            luckies[j - 1] := false;                 { Delete last number found }
            total := total-1
          end
      end;
    repeat                                           { Find next deletion increment }
      i := i + 1
    until (i > n) or luckies[i]
  end
end { GetLuckies } ;

function CountTwins(luckies : numbers; n : integer) : integer;
  {
    Counts the number of twin luckies.
  }
  var
    i, count, last : integer;
  begin { CountTwins }
    count := 0;
    last := 1;
    for i := 2 to n do
      if luckies[i] then
        begin
          if last = i - 2 then count := count + 1;
          last := i
        end;
    CountTwins := count
  end { CountTwins };

procedure FindSum(sum : integer; var s1, s2 : integer);
  {
    Finds lucky numbers s1 and s2 such that s1 + s2 = sum.
  }
  var
    found : Boolean;
  begin { FindSum }
    found := false;
    s1 := sum div 2;                    { Start looking in the middle of the list }
    while (not found) and (s1 > 0) do
      begin                         { and work down }
        if luckies[s1] and luckies[sum - s1]
          then found := true
          else s1:=s1 - 1
      end;
    if found then s2 := sum - s1 else s2 := 0
  end { FindSum } ;

begin { main }
  writeln('The Lucky Number Generator');
  writeln;
  write('What is the largest Lucky Number you want? (',
        max : 1, ' is the maximum) ');
  readln(n);
  writeln;
```

```
  if n > max then
    begin
      writeln;
      writeln(n:1,' is greater that ',max:1,'. ',max:1,
              ' will be used.');
      n := max
    end;
  GetLuckies(luckies, n, total);
  writeln;
  writeln('There are ',total:1,' Lucky Numbers between 1 and ',
          n:1,'.');
  writeln;
  write('There are ', CountTwins(luckies, n):1,
                    ' pairs of Twin Luckies.');
  writeln('        n / ln(n) = ',round(n / ln(1.0 * n)):1,'.');
  writeln;
  write('Enter an  even integer in 2..',n:1,': ');
  while not eof do
    begin
      repeat
        readln(sum)
      until (not odd(sum)) and (sum >0) and (sum <= n);
      writeln;
      FindSum(sum, s1, s2);
      writeln(sum:1,' = ',s1:1,' + ',s2:1,'.');
      writeln;
      write('Enter an  even integer in 2..',n:1,': ')
    end
end { LuckyNumbers } .
```

CHAPTER 21 — CRYPTOGRAPHY

```
THOBF CBSBD OBSXQ SJNOG BRCDD NNDBM JLQNS SBMUS POJBJ
MBOQK JDEBP LQTUD SRDHF MDDXD INQDU GBSJM TSSTD SPQBM
ERUTE DOSTZ MHLDX HMKFM KNZQF ZEHOF BAPTU HUZOC QTAYM
HOFPU FQTNN DPEUG FDYDS BJRFR BSUGF DOCPE UGFBI ZQSFQ
```

If you cannot deduce the algorithm used to produce the above message, looking at the listing of program *crypto* will reveal it. The problem that follows is simple enough for an exam during which the student isn't asked to do lots of other things, or might be assigned in two parts. First, ask the students to think about the cryptogram for a day or so (some will see the pattern in a minute or two) and report what they find at your next class. Then give them this assignment:

Problem:

Write a program that reads a plaintext message stored in an external file whose name is specified at run time. Encipher the message in accord with the algorithm used to encipher the sample message. Ignore any incoming characters that are not letters (including blanks and end-of-line characters that need no special test). Write the enciphered text to file CIPHER.TXT in 5-letter groups of uppercase letters. The solution is on the following page.

Solution:

Here is yet another program that shows that the computer scientist's best friend is the **mod** operator. Because of the later use of "**mod** 26", the expression 26 + *k* will become either +1 or −1. We use intrinsically positive increments in order to cope with implementations like Turbo Pascal whose **mod** operator is really a remainder operator.

```
program crypto(input, output, plain, cipher);
  {
     Enciphers a textfile and writes it to CIPHER.TXT in five-letter groups.
  }
  var
    ch : char;                                   { Holds each incoming character }
    s : string[20];                              { To hold name of plaintext file }
    cc : integer;                                { Character count }
    k : -1..+1;                                  { Alternator }
    plain, cipher : text;

  function upper(c : char) : char;               { ASCII version }
    begin if c in ['a'..'z'] then upper := chr(ord(c) - 32) else upper := c end;

  begin { main }
    write('Plaintext file? ');
    readln(s);
    reset(plain, s);
    rewrite(cipher, 'CIPHER.TXT');
    cc := 0;
    k := -1;
    while not eof(plain) do
      begin
        read(plain, ch);
        ch := upper(ch);
        if ch in ['A'..'Z'] then
          begin
            cc := cc + 1;                        { Count the character }
            k := -k;                             { Reverse the alternator }
            write(cipher, chr(ord('A') + (ord(ch) - ord('A') + 26 + k) mod 26));
            if cc mod 5 = 0 then write(cipher, ' ');   { Output 5-letter groups }
            if cc = 45 then
              begin
                writeln(cipher);                 { New line after 12 groups }
                cc := 0
              end
          end
      end;
    while cc mod 5 <> 0 do
      begin
        write(cipher, chr(ord('A') + (ord('W') - ord('A') + 26 + k) mod 26));
        k := -k;
        cc := cc + 1
      end;
    if cc <> 0 then writeln(cipher);
    close(cipher)
  end { crypto }.
```

SOLUTIONS TO SELECTED PROGRAMMING EXERCISES

21.1 KEYWORDS
21.2 CIPHER ALPHABETS
21.3 WORD PATTERNS

```
program WordTransforms(input, output);
  {
    Reads words until the end-of-file and prints each word without duplicate letters,
    a cipher alphabet based on the compressed word, and the word's letter pattern.
  }
  type
    str = packed array [0..80] of char;
  var
    word, NewWord : str;

  procedure ReadWord(var word : str);
    {
      Reads a word that takes up an entire input line, omitting nonletters and converting to
      upper case.
    }
    var
      i : integer;
      ch : char;

    function upper(c : char) : char;                              { ASCII version }
      begin if c in ['a'..'z'] then upper := chr(ord(c) - 32) else upper := c end;

    begin { ReadWord }
      i := 0;
      while not eoln do
        begin
          read(ch);
          if ch in ['A'..'Z', 'a'..'z'] then
            begin
              i := i + 1;
              word[i] := upper(ch)
            end
        end;
      readln;
      word[0] := chr(i)
    end { ReadWord } ;

  procedure print(word : str);
    {
      Prints word and ends the line.
    }
    var
      i : integer;
    begin { print }
      for i := 1 to ord(word[0]) do write(word[i]);
      writeln
    end { print } ;

  function pos(c : char; w : str) : integer;
    {
      Returns the position of the character c in w. If c is not present, 1 + length of
      w is returned.
    }
    var
      p : integer;
```

```
    begin { pos }
      p := 1;
      while (c <> w[p]) and (p <= ord(w[0])) do p := p + 1;
      pos := p
    end { pos } ;

  procedure KeyWord(word : str; var NewWord : str);
    {
      Sets NewWord to word with all duplicate letters removed.
    }
    var
      i, NewWordLen : integer;
    begin { KeyWord }
      NewWordLen := 0;
      for i := 1 to ord(word[0]) do
        if pos(word[i], word) = i then              { If word[i] is first instance of that }
          begin                                                          { letter in word, }
            NewWordLen := NewWordLen + 1;                               { add it to NewWord }
            NewWord[NewWordLen] := word[i]
          end;
      NewWord[0] := chr(NewWordLen)                             { Set length of NewWord }
    end { KeyWord } ;

  procedure CipherAlphabet(word : str; var NewWord : str);
    {
      Creates NewWord as the cipher alphabet based on word.
    }
    var
      i, len : integer;
    begin { CipherAlphabet }
      len := ord(word[0]);
      word[len + 1] := 'A';                                 { Append the alphabet to word }
      for i := 2 to 26 do word[len + i] := succ(word[len + i - 1]);
      word[0] := chr(len + 26);
      KeyWord(word, NewWord)                                       { and take its KeyWord }
    end { CipherAlphabet };

  procedure WordPattern(word : str; var NewWord : str);
    {
      Sets NewWord to word pattern of word.
    }
    var
      key : str;
      i, len : integer;
    begin { WordPattern }
      NewWord[0] := word[0];
      KeyWord(word, key);                                          { Take KeyWord of word }
      for i := 1 to ord(word[0]) do                              { and substitute proper }
        NewWord[i] := chr(ord('A') - 1 + pos(word[i], key))        { letter of alphabet }
    end { WordPattern } ;

  begin { main }
    writeln('Test of three word transformation routines');
    writeln;
    write('Enter a word: ');
    while not eof do
      begin
        ReadWord(word);
        writeln;
        write('Word without duplicate letters: ');
        KeyWord(word, NewWord);                                      { Compute keyword }
        print(NewWord);                                                { Print keyword }
        writeln;
```

```
      write('Cipher alphabet: ');
      CipherAlphabet(word, NewWord);                { Compute cipher alphabet }
      print(NewWord);                                 { Print cipher alphabet }
      writeln;
      write('Word pattern: ');
      wordpattern(word, NewWord);                     { Compute word pattern }
      print(NewWord);                                   { Print word pattern }
      writeln;
      write('Enter a word: ')
    end
  end { WordTransforms }.
```

21.6 PLAYFAIR

```
program Playfair(input, output);
  {
    Enciphers and deciphers plaintexts message according to the Playfair rules based upon
    an input cipher alphabet.
  }
  type
    five = 0..4;
    str = packed array[1..80] of char;
    lattice = array[five, five] of char;
  var
    grid : lattice;
    plain, cipher : str;
    plainsize, ciphersize  : integer;

  function upper(c : char) : char;                              { ASCII version }
    begin if c in ['a'..'z'] then upper := chr(ord(c) - 32) else upper := c end;

  procedure PrepareGrid(var grid : lattice);
    {
      Reads 26 letters (skipping J) to fill the 5 x 5 grid and displays it.
    }
    var
      i, j : five;
      ch : char;

    procedure decipher(var grid : lattice);
      {
        Transforms the original grid by rotation along both horizontal and vertical axes.
        This transformation, will turn the enciphering grid into one that deciphers.
      }
      var
        i, j : five;

      procedure swap(var a, b : char);
        var
          t : char;
        begin { swap }
          t := a;
          a := b;
          b := t
        end { swap } ;

      begin { decipher }
        swap(grid[2, 0], grid[2, 4]);
        swap(grid[2, 1], grid[2, 3]);
        for i := 0 to 1 do
          for j := 0 to 4 do swap(grid[i, j], grid[4 - i, 4 - j])
      end { decipher } ;
```

```
begin { PrepareGrid }
  writeln('Enter the 26 letters of the alphabet in any order:');
  writeln;
  for i := 0 to 4 do                                          { Read grid }
    for j := 0 to 4 do
      begin
        read(ch);
        if ch in ['j', 'J'] then read(ch);                    { but omit 'J'}
        grid[i, j] := upper(ch)
      end;
  readln; writeln; writeln('Do you want to');
  writeln; writeln(' (E)ncode or');
  writeln(' (D)ecode');
  writeln; write('Enter E or D: ');
  readln(ch);
  writeln;
  for i := 0 to 4 do                                          { Write grid }
    begin
      for j := 0 to 4 do write(grid[i, j]);
      writeln
    end;
  writeln;
  if ch in ['D', 'd'] then decipher(grid)
end { PrepareGrid } ;

procedure ReadMessage(var plain : str; var plainsize : integer);
  {
  Reads a plaintext message of up to 80 characters.
  }
  var
    i : integer;
    ch : char;
  begin { ReadMessage }
    i := 0;
    while not eoln do
      begin
        read(ch); ch := upper(ch);
        if ch = 'J' then ch := 'I';               { Convert all plaintext J's to I's }
        if ch in ['A'..'Z'] then
          begin
            i := i + 1;
            plain[i] := ch
          end
      end;
    readln;
    plainsize := i
  end { ReadMessage } ;

procedure WriteMessage(cipher : str; ciphersize : integer);
  {
  Writes ciphertext in groups of 5 letters separated by a blank.
  }
  var
    i : integer;
  begin { WriteMessage }
    for i := 1 to ciphersize do
      begin
        write(cipher[i]);
        if i = 65 then writeln;              { Don't split a group at end of screen }
        if i mod 5 = 0 then write(' ')              { Output a blank every fifth char }
      end;
    writeln
  end { WriteMessage } ;
```

```
procedure encipher(plain : str; plainsize : integer; var cipher : str;
                   var ciphersize : integer; grid : lattice);
  {
    Enciphers the plaintext message according to the Playfair rules.
  }
  var
    k, m : integer;
    p1, p2, c1, c2 : char;              { Plaintext and ciphertext letter pairs }
    ip1, jp1, ip2, jp2 : integer;                 { Coordinates of p1 and p2 }

  procedure getcoords(var row, col : integer; letter : char; grid : lattice);
    {
      Searches the grid to find letter and sets coordinates i and j accordingly.
    }
    var
      r, c : integer;
    begin { getcoords }
      for r := 0 to 4 do
        for c := 0 to 4 do
          if grid[r, c] = letter then
            begin
              row := r;
              col := c
            end
    end { getcoords } ;

  begin { encipher }
    k := 1;
    m := 1;
    while k <= plainsize do
      begin
        p1 := plain[k];
        if k < plainsize then p2 := plain[k + 1] else p2 := 'X';
        if p2 = p1 then
          begin
            if p1 <> 'Q' then p2 := 'Q' else p2 := 'X';
            plain[k] := p2;
            k:=k - 2
          end;
        getcoords(ip1, jp1, p1, grid);                { Get coordinates of p1 }
        getcoords(ip2, jp2, p2, grid);                { Get coordinates of p2 }
        if ip1 = ip2 then       { Letters are on same row; take letters to the right }
                            { using mod arithmetic to produce cyclic addressing }
          begin
            c1 := grid[ip1, (jp1 + 1) mod 5];
            c2 := grid[ip2, (jp2 + 1) mod 5]
          end else
        if jp1 = jp2 then         { Letters are in same column; take letters above }
          begin
            c1 := grid[(ip1 + 1) mod 5, jp1];
            c2 := grid[(ip2 + 1) mod 5, jp2]
          end else                                { Letters delimit a rectangle }
          begin
            c1 := grid[ip1, jp2];
            c2 := grid[ip2, jp1]
          end;
        cipher[m] := c1;
        cipher[m + 1] := c2;
        k := k + 2;
        m := m + 2
      end { while };
    ciphersize := m - 1
  end { encipher } ;
```

```
begin { main }
  PrepareGrid(grid);
  writeln('Enter your message ( 80 letters or less).');
  writeln;
  while not eof do
    begin
      ReadMessage(plain, plainsize);
      encipher(plain, plainsize, cipher, ciphersize, grid);
      WriteMessage(cipher, ciphersize);
      writeln;
      writeln('Enter your message ( 80 letters or less).')
    end
end { Playfair } .
```

LIST OF PROBLEMS

† Denotes a problem whose solution is in Appendix A of Pascalgorithms.
* Denotes a problem whose solution is in this manual.

For each chapter, problems above the line are Self-Study Questions. Those below the line are Programming Problems.

†1.1 Classify Devices
†1.2 Memory Size Limits
†1.3 Babbage's Digits
1.4 Disk Characteristics
†1.5 LA Rams

---

†2.1 Task Algorithms
†2.2 Skis around Tree
†2.3 Block Calendar
2.4 Balance Checkbook
†2.5 Labyrinth
†2.6 Occupational Languages
†2.7 Ambiguous English
†2.8 Syntax Charts
†2.9 Name Syntax Chart
2.10 Personkind
†2.11 Op System Terms
2.12 File Creation

---

†3.1 McCarthy
†3.2 Shortest Program
†3.3 How to Change a Variable
†3.4 Four Primitive Types
†3.5 Legal Constants
†3.6 Legal Identifiers
†3.7 Write(Five)
†3.8 Separators
†3.9 Calculated Risk

---

†3.10 Odds
†3.11 Rank3
*3.12 Squeeze
†3.13 Squares
*3.14 Two Digits
*3.15 Dollars

†4.1 Parameters
†4.2 Actual for Formal Parameters
†4.3 Null Procedure
†4.4 Convertible

---

*4.5 Big Letters
*4.6 Rank3 Revisited
†4.7 Countoff
*4.8 Calendar Month

†5.1 Legal Reals
†5.2 Pred/Succ
†5.3 Sunday..May
†5.4 10..10
†5.5 Enumerated Types
†5.6 Set Expressions
†5.7 Largest Squareable Integer
†5.8 trunc and round
†5.9 Independence

---

†5.10 Trig Identity
*5.11 Pi and Such
†5.12 Stirling Approximation
†5.13 Hal Constants
*5.14 Hal Again
†5.15 Shapes
*5.16 Payday

†6.1 Reading eof and eoln
†6.2 write(green)
†6.3 { sic }
†6.4 Numlist1
†6.5 New Line?
†6.6 Reads and Writes

---

†6.7 Out Damned Spot
*6.8 Alphabet
†6.9 Who Knows What Evil..
*6.10 Stars
*6.11 Cubes
†6.12 $n\pi$
*6.13 Count Words

†7.1 Operator Precedence
†7.2 Unary Minus
†7.3 Square Big Numbers
†7.4 Lowercase Without if
†7.5 16 Boolean Operators

---

†7.6 True **mod** Test
†7.7 Overlapped Subranges
*7.8 DeMorgan
*7.9 Pascaline

List of Problems

†8.1 Loop
†8.2 Legal Statements
†8.3 **repeat** to **while**
†8.4 Equivalent **for**?
†8.5 Label vs Case Label

---

†8.6 Vicious Circle
*8.7 Football Scores
*8.8 Hex Table
*8.9 QPA
*8.10 Numeric Names
†8.11 E
†8.12 Wallis's Formula
†8.13 More Pi
†8.14 Ballpark Estimates
*8.15 Monthly Caseload
*8.16 What's Next
*8.17 Who Goes There? (FSM)
*8.18 FSM Baseball
*8.19 Binary Fractions
*8.20 Supercalc

†9.1 Legal Headers
†9.2 Double use of Alpha
†9.3 Doubleboth
†9.4 L-Value, R-Value
†9.5 sqr(pow(a))
†9.6 Output of Nests

---

*9.7 Pow Wow
†9.8 Ranfrac
†9.9 Backwords
*9.10 Floors and Ceilings
†9.11 Real Parts
*9.12 Common Logs
†9.13 Signum
*9.14 Raised Letters
*9.15 Real Heroes
†9.16 LCM
9.17 Relprime Test
*9.18 Sine Check
9.19 Random Gaps
*9.20 Ackermann's Function
*9.21 Negative Powers
*9.22 Leap Year
*9.23 Day Numbers
*9.24 Day to Day Operations
*9.25 Monthly Payments
*9.26 Sharper Darts
*9.27 Buffon's Needle
*9.28 Race Against Time
*9.29 Track 29
*9.30 Age of Reason
*9.31 Max Headroom
*9.32 Tower Power
*9.33 Hexrep

†10.1 Valid Arrays
†10.2 Conditions For Using Array
†10.3 Legal Strings
†10.4 Rotate
†10.5 Glass House

---

*10.6 Rotate
*10.7 Opposite Numbers
*10.8 Border Patrol
*10.9 Local Peaks
*10.10 Corkscrew
*10.11 Lissajous Figures
*10.12 Palindromes
*10.13 Smarter Bubbles
*10.14 Selection Sort
†10.15 Shrimps
*10.16 Transpose
*10.17 Saddle Point
*10.18 I-Ching
†10.19 Monotone Search
*10.20 Touring Machine
*10.21 Close Encounters
*10.22 Calendar
*10.23 Poker Hands
*10.24 Bridge Hand
*10.25 Pascal's Triangle
*10.26 Seven Come Eleven
*10.27 Wordfinder
*10.28 Dumbbells
*10.29 Lindstedt Cubes
*10.30 Bingo
*10.31 Logical Bit Addition
*10.32 Correlation Coefficients
*10.33 DNA
*10.34 Magic Squares
*10.35 Crossword Puzzle
*10.36 Gray Code
*10.37 Heads or Tails
*10.38 Multiplication
*10.39 Long Division
*10.40 The Plot Thickens
*10.41 Subvector

†11.1 Large Files
†11.2 Merge Conditions
†11.3 Rain in Spain
†11.4 Powerset of Zoo
†11.5 Dossier Record
11.6 Library Record
11.7 Elwood P. Dowd
†11.8 No L

---

*11.9 Hidden Messages
*11.10 Bowling Scores
*11.11 Vanna
*11.12 Record Merge
*11.13 Storage Packs
*11.14 Letter Sets
*11.15 Prime Sieve
*11.16 File Join
*11.17 Single Space
†11.18 File Splitter
*11.19 Real Quick
*11.20 Electoral Vote

†12.1 Printing a SLCL
†12.2 Insert into a DLLL
†12.3 Delete Node Pointed To
12.4 Knights Recurrence Relation
†12.5 Expression Tree
12.6 Generalized Postorder
12.7 Binary Tree Theorem
†12.8 Intermixed Blue & Red Beads